GREEN ORANGES

GREEN ORANGES

A JOURNEY INTO HONDURAS TO FIND
REDEMPTION, HOPE, AND TRANSFORMATION

SHIN FUJIYAMA

COPYRIGHT © 2025 SHIN FUJIYAMA
All rights reserved.

GREEN ORANGES
A Journey into Honduras to Find Redemption, Hope, and Transformation

FIRST EDITION

ISBN 978-1-5445-3285-1 *Paperback*
      978-1-5445-3286-8 *Ebook*

THIS BOOK IS FOR MOM AND DAD.

CONTENTS

INTRODUCTION 11

BOOK 1
1. FAILURE IS A SHOT AT REDEMPTION 15
2. DON'T RUSH THE COFFEE 25
3. IT TAKES MORE THAN GOOD INTENTIONS 35
4. FACE YOUR FEARS AND GO FOR THE ASK 45
5. IT TAKES A TEAM 51
6. DON'T WAIT FOR PERMISSION 61

BOOK 2
7. EVERYTHING THAT CAN GO WRONG, WILL GO WRONG 75
8. JUST FOCUS ON THE NEXT SMALL STEP 93

BOOK 3
9. INFRASTRUCTURE IS NOT ENOUGH 115
10. BE INTENTIONAL ABOUT WHO YOU SURROUND YOURSELF WITH 127
11. YOU MUST ADDRESS VIOLENCE TO ADDRESS POVERTY 137

BOOK 4
12. WHAT'S RIGHT ISN'T ALWAYS BLACK AND WHITE 165
13. FAMILY IS WHERE LIFE BEGINS AND LOVE NEVER ENDS ... 183
14. MOMENTS ARE MORE IMPORTANT THAN GOALS AND ACCOMPLISHMENTS 195

BOOK 5
15. TOUGH MOMENTS ARE OPPORTUNITIES FOR TRANSFORMATION 213
16. YOU WILL NEVER KNOW YOUR LIMITS IF YOU DON'T TEST THEM 223
17. NO STRUGGLE IS INSURMOUNTABLE IF WE FACE IT TOGETHER 241

EPILOGUE 267
TIMELINE 269
ACKNOWLEDGMENTS 271
ADDITIONAL READING 273
ABOUT THE AUTHOR 277
NOTES 279

By purchasing this book, you are making a difference in the lives of children in Honduras. A portion of the proceeds from this book will go to One Thousand Schools, formerly known as Students Helping Honduras. If you would like to learn more about the organization or find ways to get involved, please visit us at onethousandschools.com and reach out to us.

* * *

Some events, names, identifying characteristics of individuals, and chronology of occurrences in this book have been changed. Some characters have been combined. Any errors of fact likely reflect the dimming of memory due to the passage of time.

INTRODUCTION

MICHAEL AND I WERE PLAYING NINTENDO IN MY BASEMENT when two high schoolers came in. They were friends of my sister. We didn't notice at first because our backs were to them. But when one said, "I don't like how you're looking at me," we looked up.

Michael and I were in middle school then. We were kids who spent our weekends reading *Aquarium Fish* magazines and camping with the local Boy Scout troop. I'd known Michael since the first grade. He was the kind of friend who would stand up for me if I was being teased about my eczema. If someone had me cornered—which often happened, as I was always the smallest and scrawniest boy around—he would push them off. Michael wasn't the biggest kid either, but he was never afraid to confront who was troubling me.

Now we stared at the two high schoolers, Nintendo controllers still in our hands.

"I said, I don't like how you're looking at me."

They were close to us now; they were big, terrifying. They shoved Michael. I backed away, trembling, and they surrounded Michael. They shoved him again, hard. Between their bodies, I could see my friend's face transform with an emotion I'd never seen there before. Fear.

Then the bullies hit him.

They pushed his head to the ground. Kicked him in the back. Pummeled him with their fists. My heart was racing. For the first time in our friendship, it was Michael who needed my help. These bullies were larger than any middle schoolers we'd dealt with; I knew I couldn't fight them off, even if I had been good at fighting. But I should jump in there. At the very least, I could take some of the blows that Michael would have taken. It would be a small help, but it would be something.

I didn't move.

Do something, I told myself. *Anything*.

But I didn't move.

They kept kicking Michael for what felt like an eternity. With each blow, I hated myself more and more. I felt a sense of disgust at my inaction; my body shrank by the second. I was unforgivable.

For the rest of my life, I would regret what I didn't do.

BOOK 1

CHAPTER ONE

FAILURE IS A SHOT AT REDEMPTION

THIS STORY BEGINS WITH SOCCER.

It's a strange place for this story to start, considering where it goes and where it ends, but if I had to think about it honestly, soccer is where it all began.

My first brush with soccer wasn't the most inspiring. It was in elementary school, in 1988, and my family had immigrated from Japan to the US not too long before. There I am, running onto the soccer field in my green jersey. Coach tells us to warm up, but I'm in the first grade and don't understand English. So I copy what everyone else is doing. I huff and puff. I'm easily the smallest kid there, and I'm recovering from a congenital heart defect. I can barely keep up.

The game starts, but Coach wants me to keep warming up from the sidelines. I pass the ball with Mrs. Baker, my friend's mom. Coach shows me how to use the side of my foot to kick the ball, then hurries away. I can't kick the ball straight to save my life. When it rolls onto the field, Coach tells me to go further out to practice. I do. I repeat the drill over and over. It's getting dark but I'm so engrossed I don't notice. I daydream. I am running onto the field and kicking the ball. It's the best kick Coach has ever seen. *Wow*, Coach thinks. *He must have practiced that pass!*

I'm covered in sweat and dust when I hear cheering. I look up to see my teammates high fiving each other in the dark. "We won! We won!" they yell. "Great game!" the parents say. I go up to Coach to see if there is time left for me to play. I'm as warmed up as I could be. He covers his eyes with his hands—the action is overdramatic.

"Shiiiin. I'm so sorry! I forgot to put you in the game because I didn't see you! Why were you so far out on the sidelines?"

I try to answer but the broken English I'd learned in ESL class doesn't make any sense.

"Next weekend, little guy!" Coach slaps me twice on the back and walks away. "Good job, Brandon! Good job, Jonathan!" he yells. I try to kick the ball one last time into the goal; it goes way out of bounds. I see my mom park her blue minivan and walk over. She's pushing both Cosmo and Gaku, my younger sister and brother, on an old stroller over the grass. "How did it go?" she asks excitedly. Cosmo pokes her head out and waves. I close my eyes, feeling like a leftover breadcrumb.

The story gets better though, although it only gets better in high school and because of Coach Peas. All throughout my childhood in Fairfax County, Virginia, I showed signs of attention deficit hyperactivity disorder (ADHD). In elementary school, exasperated teachers reprimanded me. They told my mom to homeschool me. Mom apologized on my behalf and fought for me so I could stay in school. In middle school, I was in the detention hall more than anyone I knew. I just had too much energy, and I didn't know where to focus it. But in high school, I found competitive soccer.

The head coach of McLean High School was Ted Peas, more commonly called Coach Peas. His grey beard reminded me of an Ewok, the furry and courageous being in *Star Wars* that overpowers bigger enemies to save their forest. In my freshman year, I told him that I was interested in trying out for the JV soccer team. I was honest though. I told him I had only played rec league soccer, that I wasn't as fast or as skilled as the guys on the team. That I would probably be wasting his time.

Coach Peas looked me up and down and laughed.

"So what if you're the smallest player out there on the field?" he said. "You've probably been heckled your whole life. But you can see that as a blessing, because you have more fuel for motivation than everyone else."

Coach Peas wasn't much bigger than me, but he had been a champion wrestler in high school. He had done it through discipline and hard work. As a fifty-something-year-old, he still trained with the eighteen-year-old wrestlers who were twice his size and pinned them down like straw dummies.

"Don't waste a second worrying about things you can't control," he said. "You need to out-train, out-hustle, and get more creative than everyone else. Being small and weak means that people will have low expectations of you. That means you have the chance to surprise the crap out of 'em!"

In preseason training that year, Coach Peas pulled me aside to give me advice more than he did with everyone else. He taught me to see certain burdens as blessings. Having really bad eczema meant zero time dating girls and more time training. Being short meant more leg space on the school bus to stretch my muscles. Coach Peas squeezed out every drop of my victim mentality.

He ignited something in me. I showed up first to every pre-season workout and trailed behind the upperclassmen like a bloodhound chasing them. As they ran past me, they would ask how old I was to get on my nerves. I would just keep running and running. After the conditioning workouts, I'd walk to Lewinsville Park and play pickup soccer with other immigrant kids until the sun went down. At school, I dribbled the soccer ball going from class to class, and rolled the ball around with my feet when I played the violin in orchestra class. At nighttime, I'd walk around the house in ankle and wrist weights. Before going to bed, I'd read biographies of famous soccer players like Ronaldo, John Harkes, and Mia Hamm or watch movies like *Karate Kid*, *Rudy*, and *Rocky*.

That year, I made the JV soccer team as the twenty-third player to be picked out of twenty-three. Everyone else was better than me, but Coach Peas said I had the best work ethic. I had earned my place. I remember sprinting home as fast as I could and realizing that I was crying.

For four years, soccer kept my life from falling apart. The external structure and routine of the practice sessions focused me. The more I trained, the less disruptive I became in class. And soon, soccer became who I was. My parents encouraged me: they came to all of my games, and paid for expensive soccer camps from their savings. I was proud to wear the McLean High School team jacket. Being on the team made me feel like I was part of something bigger than me.

I mattered.

Then I graduated, enrolled at the University of Mary Washington (UMW), made the soccer team for one season, and got cut the next. My spot went to an incoming freshman. I had great work ethic, sure, but I lacked size, strength, and athleticism. Work ethic didn't make up for them.

I wish I could say I took this in stride. After all, this was just some liberal arts college team in Fredericksburg, Virginia, not the FIFA world cup. But I was crushed. I lost all motivation.

I stayed up late playing Xbox. I did the minimum amount of schoolwork. I wasn't even sure if I wanted to finish college. I had never been into partying or drinking much, but I started to go out several nights a week. I stood awkwardly against a wall, talking to people I would never see again, pretending like I was having more fun than everyone else.

All the while, a strange emptiness grew in me. I was purposeless. I felt hopeless. Growing up, I always thought I would live a meaningful life, but that belief was beginning to look more and more like a joke.

So you see, it does all start with soccer. Because that's how I found myself sitting alone in the campus cafeteria, with a long winter break stretching before me and nothing to do but watch movies in my parents' basement. And that's when I picked up a neon green flyer on the table and began to read it, not knowing it would change the trajectory of my life.

* * *

The circumstances that got me to Honduras the first time were serpentine and strange. The neon flyer I picked up was from the Campus Christian Community (CCC). They were looking for volunteers to travel to Haiti during winter break. Haiti was more appealing than just watching movies. But I was hesitant about the CCC. Was this one of those trips where foreigners try to proselytize the local people? I didn't want to be a part of that…

I went to the meeting to find out. It was more casual than I expected: people were chatting, open, friendly. There was an energetic girl at the door who said, "Welcome to the Campus Christian Community!" to every new visitor, handing out name tags, with a bright smile.

The star of the show, though, was Bob.

Bob Azzarito was a middle-aged man with an athletic build, and the first time I heard him speak, his voice reminded me of Fred Rogers from *Mister Rogers' Neighborhood*. He was the most laid-back campus minister I would ever meet. He wore jeans and T-shirts everywhere. He spoke in his soothing, Fred Rogers voice. And the trip to Haiti was definitely not about proselytizing. We would be going there to learn the local culture and work alongside the Haitians in their community projects.

The more he spoke, the more excited I became. This was the first time I had felt motivated about *anything*, in ages. It felt good. I talked to my parents, got my immunizations, and gave Bob the deposit money to buy the plane tickets.

Then, just weeks before winter break, the trip to Haiti was canceled.

"There's too much civil unrest," Bob said, and the murmurs of disappointment were loud. We had all been looking forward to this.

"But," Bob said, holding up his hands, "we're going to Honduras instead. Our Little Roses is an organization that works with families and vulnerable girls in San Pedro Sula, and they've invited us to learn about their programs."

I was not enthusiastic. Working with children didn't interest me, and I wasn't sure if I would enjoy it. Plus, I had my heart set on Haiti. But Bob assured me that we would mainly be doing carpentry work at Our Little Roses, which seemed somewhat interesting. And the airline was willing to switch our destination without any extra cost.

So I said yes. Why not? It would only be one trip.

* * *

I met Ani on the first day. She was part of the group of little girls in colorful dresses, jumping up and waving at us. When she spotted me on the bus, she yelled: "*¡Veee! ¡Hay un chinito, mira, hay un chinito!* Look, a little Chinese guy!" She waved. I waved back.

The bus parked in the courtyard with two well-kept brick buildings, and we unloaded our baggage. "Mister, I help you!" Ani yelled. She was missing two of her front teeth. "Hwa, Hwaaa!" she screamed, slicing karate chops in the air. She squinted to pretend she was Asian. "Why you say *aloz*, and not *arroz*—rice?" She giggled and continued to talk with an Asian accent. I didn't know how the week was going to go. I had been in Honduras for less than two hours, and I was already being teased by a six-year-old child.

My suitcase was three times Ani's size, but she helped carry it for a few feet. She grinned as she huffed and puffed. When we made it to the guest house (she let me take my bag from her at some point), she gave me a high five. Then she held her fist out and waited.

This, I would learn, is the Honduran high five. I would use it many times in the coming years, but the first person who showed me was Ani.

"Nice to meet you," I said, bumping her tiny fist. "My name is Shin."

"Tomorrow, we play *fútbol*!" she said.

"Fútbol?"

WACK! She kicked me in the legs. "Yes, *fútbol*, like this!" She pretended to kick me again, giggled, and dashed away.

The next day, we played soccer. Before the game started, someone poked my back, I turned and *BAM!*—Ani had slammed a soccer ball into my chest. "Time to practice!" she said, eyes sparkling. She showed me a crazy move where you do a cartwheel and then shoot the ball. "Your turn!" she said.

After our soccer practice, Ani brought out a children's book. She didn't know how to read yet, so she kept making up stories based on the pictures. She teased me for the less-than-fluent Spanish I learned in high school (which made me wish I had paid better attention in class), and I teased her right back for trying to pronounce words through the gap in her missing front teeth.

Ani and her friends tried to teach me the lyrics to their favorite songs. Like walking karaoke boxes, they knew all the words. Ani asked: "What does it mean, I'm addicted to you? Don't you know that you're TOXIC?" She flipped her hair left and right. We all laughed as she moved her eyebrows up and down like Britney Spears. She was a funny girl.

When Ani didn't want to sing anymore, she pulled at my shirt and we walked around the soccer court. She pointed out birds up in the sky, and I looked up. When I looked down, she hit me in the chin. "Gotcha!" she laughed. She collected interesting rocks, treating them like gold. She found bugs that I would have never seen and put them on her fingers. She pretended to smash them to scare me but then blew at them. They flew away. We played jacks, and then tag. Spending time with her was effortless.

Ani's exuberance hid a difficult story. Honduras was in the throes of gang wars, particularly between MS-13 (La Mara Salvatrucha) and Mara 18 (18th Street Gang), collectively known as the *Mara*. San Pedro Sula, where Our Little Roses was, was the epicenter of a turf war. The violence rippled out into everyone's lives, but it disproportionately affected women.

Sonia Nazario, a Pulitzer Prize-winning journalist and author of *Enrique's Journey: The Story of a Boy's Dangerous Odyssey to Reunite with His Mother*, would later publish an article in The New York Times called "Someone Is Always Trying To Kill You."[1] It describes what gender-based violence looks like in Honduras. Honduras is one of the deadliest places on earth to be a woman—a 2015 survey ranked it in the top five countries, with El Salvador and Syria.[2] Most women are killed by drug cartels and gangs, and 41 percent of women killed in the country showed signs of extreme mutilation and cruelty. Women have been chopped up to pieces, strangled in front of their children, or skinned alive like chickens. Nazario writes:

> It's about machismo—the culture of which goes back to colonial times, when conquering Spaniards came without wives and treated the indigenous like slaves. Today, in a world ruled by gangs and narco groups, it's about engendering maximum terror in your enemies, and you do that by showing how macabre you can be in the way you torture or kill. Honduras is locked in a war of grisly one-upmanship, and women's bodies are the battlefield.

The law offers little protection. Domestic violence laws were introduced in Honduras in 1997, but they are weak.[3] If you're caught beating up a woman for the first time, it's a "fault," not a crime. Likewise, a court may issue restraining orders, but the police rarely enforce them. According to a 2018 study conducted in San Pedro Sula, more than 96 percent of women's murders remain unsolved or go unpunished.[4]

The girls at Our Little Roses came from broken homes that nearly crushed their spirits. Our Little Roses did what it could to revive them. Its community of sisters, staff, mentors, and advisors gave the girls a sense of belonging, advocated for them, and supported them every step of the way. As a result, many of the girls rebuilt their lives and even made it to college, which was an extraordinary accomplishment in Honduras.

My week at Our Little Roses flew by. I sprung up each morning looking forward to the day, and I didn't want to leave. We spent the week helping with carpentry work, but every time I took a break, Ani would find me. It became our ritual to play jacks: she would challenge me, and she would beat me.

So that's how I found myself on the morning of my departure—playing jacks. "Three jacks! Four jacks!" I shouted, throwing the ball into the air. I was on a roll, and very determined to leave Honduras with at least one victory. But I fumbled, and Ani picked up the ball from where it had rolled away.

"My turn," she said, with a big grin.

I watched her pick up one jack after another in quick succession. When she beat me, she jumped into the air. "¡*Perdiste!*" she yelled. "You lose!" She slapped my shoulder. "You must practice in America!"

It was difficult to say goodbye. When the time came, I was so overcome, I hid my face. I came to Honduras believing I didn't want to spend time with children. I was leaving knowing that children were wonderful beings who created and gave joy wherever they went, and admiring more than ever organizations like Our Little Roses that gave them a fighting chance. I wanted to return.

* * *

"Hello, I think I've got the seat next to you," said a middle-aged man in a midwestern accent.

As the plane took off, we struck up a conversation. His name was Henry and he was from Milwaukee. He had begun volunteering in Honduras in 1998, after Hurricane Mitch devastated the country. He assisted a Honduran nun named Sister Tulia, who ran a nonprofit organization in a small city called El Progreso, by sending money and visiting every few months.

"Do you speak Spanish?" he asked.

I knew enough to get by. When Henry said he was looking for a translator and was willing to pay for their expenses and airfare, I perked up. I told him I had translated for our group at Our Little Roses—I didn't tell him that Bob had given me the role only because nobody else spoke a word of the language. The exact week Henry planned on returning to Honduras coincided with my spring break. He pulled out a piece of paper and wrote down his contact information. "Call me when you get home," he said.

I couldn't believe my luck. At the Miami airport, I told the group about Henry. "That sounds too good to be true," someone said. Others chimed in. It was dangerous to travel to Honduras with a stranger you'd just met on a plane, and they were worried. My excitement fizzled, and then died. On the final flight, I stared at the piece of paper with Henry's contact details, torn between my desire to be sensible, and my need to return.

CHAPTER TWO

DON'T RUSH THE COFFEE

I WASN'T SURE WHY, BUT I DECIDED TO TAKE MY CHANCES with Henry. I brushed up on my Spanish for two months, and then in March, I flew with him to Honduras. Three Catholic nuns met us at San Pedro Sula airport. One of them was Sister Tulia, a small, middle-aged woman with short hair. We piled our luggage into a pickup truck and set off.

It was pitch dark as we drove down pothole-ridden highways. The ride was awfully quiet. I glanced at Henry, who stared ahead with a glazed look. I realized I had no idea where they were taking me. Or what we were doing that week in El Progreso.

I panicked.

I had made a terrible mistake. Any moment now, Henry and these "nuns" would drop the pretense. They'd turn, push a gun in my face, and tell me I was being kidnapped. I kept my hand on the door handle, prepared to open it and launch myself onto the grass. I'd seen enough movies to know I would need to wrap my arms around my head to avoid lethal injuries. Eventually, Henry fell asleep in the car, and so did Sister Tulia. I stayed vigilant, convinced they were trying to catch me off guard.

"Mr. Shin, please wake up. We've arrived at the convent."

So much so for staying vigilant—I'd fallen asleep. I wandered, bleary-eyed, from the truck to my room and collapsed again.

In the morning, I felt calmer. Henry, my alleged kidnapper from the night before, visited me with shaving cream on his ears. He looked so benign, I couldn't help laughing. When he looked in the mirror, he laughed too. At breakfast, everyone was welcoming. We were going to visit Home for Children (HFC), which was run by Sister Tulia.

The HFC building had a large courtyard in the middle and was surrounded by fields and fruit trees. Fifty children were eating in the dining hall, laughing and talking loudly. I made friends with a curly-haired girl called Yapa. She was an honors student at the local high school, and knew exactly what she wanted to do with her life. Inspired by Sister Tulia, she wanted to go to college and work in a humanitarian organization.

El Progreso was so much smaller and less developed than San Pedro Sula. On our way to HFC, street children tapped on our car windows at stoplights, begging or trying to sell us gum. Families with sacks of trash on their backs walked along the highway. Yapa's certainty in the face of her odds was incredible, and I admired her. I had the world at my feet, and I wasn't sure if I had the motivation to even finish college. To distract myself from the confusing emotions her assertions brought up, I pointed at the folded tortilla on my plate.

"What's this called?" I asked.

"They're *baleadas*," Yapa said. "It's what we eat for breakfast and dinner here in Honduras."

I squinted suspiciously. I was pretty sure *baleada* meant *to be shot at*. Yapa laughed. Apparently, an old lady used to sell tortillas with bean paste and cheese at the railroad station in town. One evening, there was a shootout between gang members. The poor lady tried to duck but was hit by stray bullets. When she returned from the hospital to sell food again, people began to call her *la baleada*—the lady who got shot. That's how the dish got its name.

I chowed down, not knowing if Yapa was being serious or not.

* * *

Baleadas were my first introduction to the complexity of El Progreso, where violence and hardship were entwined into people's lives with normalcy that was shocking to me. Siete de Abril cemented that impression.

Siete de Abril was a community Sister Tulia worked with; it was named after the date it was formed (seventh of April), as is the tradition in Honduras. It was a *bordo*—a riverbed shantytown. The poor from rural areas came to bigger cities like El Progreso and San Pedro Sula, seeking work. They often created informal settlements on land that wasn't theirs, usually along a river where they had access to water. About a hundred families moved into Siete de Abril after losing their homes to Hurricane Mitch, a category five hurricane, in 1998.

No taxi wanted to take us to Siete de Abril. Drivers wagged their fingers at Sister Tulia and laughed as if our destination was ridiculous. The sense of danger in Honduras, never out of my mind, pressed in again. Was this place safe? When we finally found a taxi, I asked Sister Tulia why she worked with this community.

"Have you heard of the parable of the drowning babies?" she said.

I shook my head.

Here's how it goes. One summer, several friends are hanging out at a river, eating baleadas. Suddenly, they see a baby floating down the river. As true Samaritans, the friends jump in and rescue the drowning baby. Before they can celebrate, they notice another baby drowning. They rescue the second baby. When they look up the river, they see more babies floating their way. The friends rescue the babies as fast as they can, and divide up responsibilities to be as efficient as possible.

But more babies keep coming. They begin to tire. One of the friends, too exhausted to save another baby, starts walking along the riverbank.

The others yell at him: "Where are you going? We need your help here!"

He doesn't look back. "I'm going upstream, he says, to see who's throwing the babies into the river."

"Siete de Abril is a source," Sister Tulia said. "When I realized too many kids from this community were ending up at HFC, I decided to work with the community itself."

I understood. You don't need to save drowning babies if you can stop them from being drowned in the first place.

As we got closer to Siete de Abril, the taxi driver told me to roll down my window. I was baffled—the air conditioning was on.

"Quickly," he urged. "The *banderines* are always watching."

The *banderines* were teenage boys who hung out at the entrance of Siete de Abril. They got paid by the neighborhood gangs to keep an eye out for police cars or foes. Windows rolled down meant you were a friend. Windows rolled up meant you were a foe. Tulia assured me I didn't want to know what would happen if they thought we were foes.

And then we were in Siete de Abril. It was a maze of dirt roads between houses of cardboard and tarp, and full of life. Dogs, chickens, and pigs scurried through the streets. Children ran among them, barefoot, kicking plastic balls or carrying firewood on their heads. The church was a simple tin roof and a sign hanging off it: *Iglesia* (church). Posters of political candidates and Pepsi Cola winked at me from every corner. Women washed clothes on striated stones and hung them to dry on barbed wire. Mud stoves were lit, and the smell of cooking filled the air. A group of old men sipped *guaro*, the Honduran equivalent of moonshine. Others clustered around corner shops, downing soft drinks. Reggaeton music blasted from speakers hooked up to car batteries, the community's only source of electricity. Siete de Abril may have been built as a temporary settlement, but somewhere along the line, people had realized they were not going to leave. And so they made a home.

*　*　*

Sister Tulia, Henry, and I had left the car by the river; now, we walked along the streets, cold sweat pooling at the base of my spine. When people saw the food and medicine we were carrying, a crowd surrounded us. They grew rowdy. Anxious to get their share, they jostled closer, pressing into us, shouting. When someone shoved a grandmother, Henry pleaded with everyone to calm down. Tulia dispersed the crowd by promising we would drop off food at each person's house. Then she enlisted the help of a few children, who put the bags on their shoulders and their tricycles. Like this, we wandered slowly through Siete de Abril. When we walked along a cliff overlooking the river, a boy tugged me by my shirt to prevent me from falling. He did it with the kind of grace that only a child who has walked a donkey could.

The families of Siete de Abril welcomed us. Yamilet, a husky woman with a baby tied to her hips, swung a machete at my head and then chuckled when I cried out in horror. She was only aiming for the papaya near me. Now she showed me how to cut up the orange-yellow fruit and eat its sweet flesh. Marta, a woman wearing a pink baseball cap, invited us for coffee and her children squealed with delight as I playacted how hot the coffee was. *Débil*, they called me, weak, as we all laughed.

Of all the families, this visit to Marta's has stayed with me. Marta's three girls had orangish-blonde hair, which I later learned was a sign of malnutrition. When they first brought buckets for us to sit on, I asked what grade they were in. But I regretted the question immediately. No one in Marta's family had gone to school. They spent seven days a week collecting recyclable trash to sell to the local factory. Marta wanted her kids to be educated, but they had to work so the family could eat.

Besides, Siete de Abril didn't have a school. The closest school was several neighborhoods away—to get to it, kids had to wade through a flooded river, school bags on their heads. It was dangerous. Just that year, a little girl from the community had been found strangled on the riverbed. MS-13 controlled the south side of El Progreso, where Siete de Abril stood, and their reign was one of intimidation and murder. Their headquarters was only two hundred meters away from Siete de Abril.

It was such a different childhood from mine. Each night, Mom would gather my three siblings and me onto her bed and read books to us. Sometimes, we read books in Japanese. Other nights, we read in English. At first, none of us knew how to pronounce words like burrito and bread roll. We would say *blead loll* and *bulito*. But Mom read hundreds of books with us over the years, and our reading skills soared. I grew up thinking that every kid in the world had parents who knew how to read, a mini library in their house, and access to a school. I had no idea how lucky I was.

Marta's children were tough—nothing fazed them. When I leaned too hard against a wooden post and caused the whole house to shake, the girls teased Henry and me for covering our heads. They took everything in stride. The single mattress that the family shared. The bottles and aluminum cans on their floor (leaving them outside was not an option; they'd get stolen overnight). One of the girls had a gash on her ankle, and she simply rubbed it with saliva.

We spent a long time in Marta's home, drinking coffee and talking freely. I learned that Marta feared a *desalojamiento*, which was when the government razes an entire shantytown. There was talk of one in the coming months. To secure her lot, Marta had paid a significant sum to men in the community who had formed a group called the Land and Housing Committee. But they hadn't given her a land title. She'd signed documents, but she couldn't read them. Still, the committee promised Marta she would receive her land title once the government legalized the settlement.

This was my first introduction to the madness of Honduras's property system. I would grow more familiar with it in the years to come, but for now, I didn't understand. How could someone sell land that they didn't own? Were these families being taken for a ride or was this how things worked?

"The property system in Honduras is so unorganized," Sister Tulia said, "only God seems to know how it functions."

But Marta's worries didn't only extend to a *desalojamiento*. The fragile nature of her house meant it was vulnerable to raids. There was a hole in her cardboard wall opposite me, the wind whistling through. A gang had tried to slice the wall with their machetes and kick down the corrugated tin. Marta crouched inside, clutching a kitchen knife with her children huddled behind her. Luckily, the intruders stole what was outside the house and ran off.

Marta herself seemed unaffected by this. Such things happened daily, she told me. But the predatory nature of the violence scared me. "What did the police say?" I asked.

"The police?!"

Everyone laughed except me.

When it was time to leave, we thanked Marta and gave her a bag of food. The kids fought over who got to carry the rice and beans to the table, giggling. Marta told me that Sister Tulia was the only one willing to have coffee with her. Aid organizations and political parties would visit, take photos, make empty promises, and leave. They didn't bother to learn her name.

* * *

We saw Marta and her family once more before I left El Progreso. We were distributing food and medicine in the mountains behind Siete de Abril. These mountains were a landfill. Although Tulia had warned us of this, neither Henry nor I were prepared for what we saw. When we stepped out of the taxi, the smell was so overwhelming we could barely breathe. There was so much trash it covered two mountains. And there were people—so many people, including children—rummaging through the trash. To put food on their tables, they risked getting deadly infections, stepping on dirty needles, or falling down cliffs. Some of them lived alongside the garbage dump in makeshift houses with salvaged mattresses. I had never seen humans living like this. It took everything out of me to stay composed.

Sister Tulia got straight to work distributing supplies. I helped her, marveling at what a force of nature she was. Thank God people like her existed. Three kids were waving at us enthusiastically, their faces covered in soot. They were Marta's kids. They ran over to give us high fives, and Marta followed soon after.

"We were the first ones here this morning," she told me. Trash trucks came in at random hours. To get the best trash, you had to wait around and beat everyone else to it.

"I like getting here early," Mariana said. She was Marta's youngest daughter, and had a strange yellowish hue to her skin. She held up a plastic doll for me to examine. "We get to keep everything that the first truck brings us."

Marta leaned in. "It's Mariana's fifth birthday soon," she whispered. "We're trying to save enough money to buy a cake. We'll need eighty lempiras (four dollars), which I know is a lot. But I think we can do it."

Mariana, who was eavesdropping, giggled and danced excitedly. I thought about the plastic bottles in their house, the river water in the bucket, the candles on the table, the children's discolored hair, the hole in the cardboard wall. Families from different cultures celebrate birthdays with a cake. Some families, though, had to risk their lives to do so.

* * *

My week at El Progreso had a profound effect on me, so deep I didn't fully understand it. On our last evening, Henry and I had dinner inside a car wash. I don't know who came up with the idea of a restaurant inside a carwash, because everything smelled like soap and motor oil. But the place was packed. We ordered grilled meat and fried plantain chips, and the food arrived sizzling. It was delicious. Still, it felt strange to eat so heartily after a week in Siete de Abril, where people struggled to buy rice and beans.

Henry and I had grown incredibly close over this week. We'd spent every waking moment together and laughed during every meal. He didn't care that I was an inexperienced college student who wasn't that good at translating. I, in turn, warned him about all the diet soda he was guzzling—like a "worried grandson," he said to me, chuckling. Now he put his fork down.

"I want you to continue helping Tulia and the people of Siete de Abril without me," he said. "My back problems are worse—the doctors are telling me not to travel so much."

I told him the doctors were being ridiculous. "You still have a hundred years left in you."

"My health won't allow it. I'll support you from Milwaukee."

"But what am I supposed to do? The situation in Siete de Abril is overwhelming."

Henry shook his head. "I wish I had the answer."

The conversation shook me. The situation in Siete de Abril *was* overwhelming. The roots of their poverty were so generational, so intertwined, and so much more complex than I could have imagined. I couldn't see the difference I could make—where would I even begin? And I certainly couldn't without Henry or Sister Tulia; they were my anchors.

"We need to do this together," I said. "Who's going to remind you in the morning that you have shaving cream on your ears if you stay in Milwaukee?"

We both laughed. When we finished eating, Henry lumbered out to the bathroom, holding his lower back to ease the pain. As I watched him leave, an intense loneliness engulfed me.

─── CHAPTER THREE ───

IT TAKES MORE THAN GOOD INTENTIONS

A TRAVEL GRANT FROM UMW ALLOWED ME TO RETURN TO Honduras for the summer. I wanted to help, no matter how small a difference I could make. Henry couldn't join me because of his back pain, so I flew down on my own, planning to spend time in Siete de Abril, become fluent in Spanish, and intern at different nonprofits.

I got an internship at Defending Homeless Children (DHC), a residential rehab center for street children. It was located on the outskirts of El Progreso. Every morning, I got on my rusted bicycle and pedaled to work, past the iron statue of a plantation laborer holding a bushel of bananas. Honduras had been a banana republic for the past century—a politically unstable country with an economy dependent on banana exports. In the 1900s, in exchange for kickbacks, the Honduran oligarch gave US banana corporations tax-free concessions, large tracts of land, and political influence. The two groups operated the nation like a private commercial enterprise, and the banana trade left a legacy of widespread poverty, inequality, and government corruption throughout

Central America. It was one reason why so many families—including those in Siete de Abril—didn't have land to live on.

At DHC, I worked with Luis, the program director, and Yalena, a young woman with worn tennis shoes who was the head activities coordinator. Yalena grew up in a small community tucked into the banana plantations. When she moved to the city, she was shocked by the number of homeless children. So at nineteen, Yalena joined DHC to help change that; she quickly moved up from assistant to head activities coordinator, working alongside Luis.

My work consisted of a variety of jobs. On my first day, I played soccer with the boys, some of whom looked too young to be in grade school, and others who had mustaches and biceps. I played forward with Erik, a ten-year-old kid with scars on his shaved head, and gave him the assist for his game-winning goal. He took his shirt off, sprinted around as if he had just scored the winning goal for the FIFA World Cup, and gave me a thumbs-up. At lunch, he held my shirt as if preventing a pet goat from running away.

Sometimes, I taught. They were simple lessons, alphabets, mostly, but it was tough work. The boys kept arm wrestling each other and throwing paper airplanes. In the adjacent room, Yalena was teaching the same lesson to a much larger group—she did it effortlessly.

DCH's aim was to train the children in skills they would need to reintegrate into society, such as basic literacy, non-violent conflict resolution, and things as elementary as toothbrushing. They had limited resources, but the team worked tirelessly in the humidity and heat, pausing now and then to break up violent outbursts and fistfights.

My first experience of such violence was with Erik. I was teaching a class when I heard shouting. I ran outside and saw ten-year-old Erik fighting a teenager. It was not a tame fight: they were punching and kicking each other, using whatever they could to attack. At one point, they picked up desks and flung them. Luis dived in, grabbing the older boy and pulling him away. I grabbed Erik. The two boys wrestled out of our grips, grabbed large rocks, and started swinging at each other. Using all of our strength, Luis and I pulled the two boys into different rooms.

The fight shook me. I noticed many of the kids had scars on their bodies. Some were missing fingers.

"They're conditioned by violence," Yalena said later. "To survive the violence on the streets, they have to be violent themselves. It's the only way to mask how scared and vulnerable they feel."

Several kids had even turned to sniffing *resistol*, an industrial-strength glue that had helped them suppress hunger on the streets and deal with despair. At DHC, they quit cold turkey, and the intense withdrawal symptoms initially made them more violent.

But how did they end up on the streets in the first place? The answer was one I'd heard before—they came from broken neighborhoods where kids were left without food, abandoned, or abused. When Yalena mentioned that several kids were from Siete de Abril, I thought of Tulia's parable of the babies in the river.

According to the United Nations, there are approximately 140 million orphaned children and a minimum of thirty million street children in the world, with the average age on entering the street being nine years.[5] One study found that over 40 percent of street children in Honduras had significant nutrition problems.[6] Forty-one percent ate just one or two meals per day on average, and 29 percent belonged to a street gang. More than half sniffed glue. Four in ten drank alcohol occasionally, and one in five smoked marijuana.

For years, many governments sought to discipline street children by imprisoning them. The above-mentioned study found that 40 percent of Honduran street children were imprisoned.[7] According to Casa Alianza, the largest NGO in Central America working with homeless youth, 1,817 street children were murdered in Honduras from 1998 to 2003.[8] Many were killed with gunshots to the back of the head in summary executions that went unpunished. These murders were a form of "social cleansing," carried out by vigilante groups. The Honduran government claimed, however, that the killings were gang-related. Regardless of who was responsible for the murders, it was disheartening to learn that street children were often treated as irredeemable delinquents who represented a threat to civilized society.

An hour later, Erik apologized for hitting me with the rock. He stayed close, teaching me Honduran slang words and telling me about his favorite soccer teams. I figured out why he had gotten into the fight—the other kids bullied him. Erik was the only Garifuna at DHC, an ethnic minority group of mixed African and indigenous descent. I also figured out that behind his hardened veneer, Erik was a good kid. He only fought back against kids who were bigger than him; he left the smaller ones alone.

It was challenging and thankless to work with children who have been cast aside, but Yalena, Luis, and the team at DHC did it with patience and endless optimism. Each time a child learned a new letter in the alphabet or a social skill like raising your hand to speak, Yalena would cheer and say something to make him smile. They inspired me. The seed that had been planted when I met Ani at Our Little Roses—and grew when I visited Siete de Abril—now bloomed into certainty. I wanted to work with children who had been cast aside. It's what I wanted to do for the rest of my life.

* * *

Three things happened that summer that deepened my understanding of true service.

The first was a football match. When I arrived at Siete de Abril, I ran into Mauricio, the captain of the community soccer team. With his mullet, Musketeer beard, and his white tank top rolled up to showcase a burly stomach, Mauricio was unmistakable. We passed the ball between us for a bit, and I quickly realized Mauricio wasn't the team captain because of his soccer skills. He couldn't kick the ball straight to save his life. He kept kicking it off the cliff into the gushing river below, and then having to strip down to his boxers, and climb down a sheer cliff face to get it back. I fretted for his safety every time. He kept grumbling that the ball was no good.

When he invited me for the tournament on Sunday, I accepted with joy. He spoke about the tournament like it was the most important thing in the world. "Be here at 7:00 a.m. sharp," he told me earnestly. "Don't be late, you can't be late."

I turned up at 6:55 a.m. and then waited almost an hour before he arrived, looking like he had just gotten out of bed. "Shiiiiin!" he yelled, delighted, and then he frowned. "Why are you here so early?"

Juanita was with him—she was his *eight*-year-old daughter, as she corrected him when he called her seven years old. Now she tapped me on my shoulder and said, "You're not scared of jaguars or monkeys, are you?"

"Jaguars or monkeys?" I replied in my best-startled voice and looked up at the mountain.

"ARRGHH!!!" she suddenly yelled and pretended to bite me in my side. I yelped, pretending to be scared to hide the fact that I actually was kind of scared. "Don't worry, my dad will protect you," she said and hugged her father's arm. "I'm coming too. I'm the team assistant."

It took another hour for the team to assemble. Mauricio yelled something, and people began to howl. I wasn't sure why they were howling, but as I joined in—I liked it. It gave me a strange rush. Then we began trekking up the cloud-covered mountain, to the village at the top.

We hiked several hundred feet into the deep jungle. As we walked into clouds, the air became misty and cool. We were arms-length from the blue sky. The dirt road had narrowed into a thin, muddy trail, fringed by vines that reminded me of *The Jungle Book*. The air was full of birdcalls, monkey screeches, and mysterious noises. The teenage boys who tagged along aimed rocks at random animals using their rubber slingshots. They were determined to catch their dinner along the way. When Juanita saw me applying sunblock and bug spray, she teased me and told me I looked like a pasty clown. Every time we heard a rustle, she sensed my dread and yelled to scare me. "¡*Cagado!*" she repeated. "Scared!" I pretended to squirt bug spray in her eyes, which made her laugh and scurry away.

It was a grueling hike—certainly different from sauntering onto a soccer field back home. How was I going to withstand a ninety-minute game at the peak? I drank the last bit of water from my bottle and regretted having brought so little. One more hour of this and I was sure we would reach Guatemala.

By the time we made it to the village, my legs felt like Jell-O.

As we stretched our leg muscles, I asked Mauricio why he started the team. He chuckled and called Juanita over. He gave her a light noogie as she tried to run away. "I do it for her." There were a lot of drugs, gangs, and crime in the neighborhood. Mauricio couldn't always be there to keep his daughter safe because of the long hours he worked as a security guard. (He pretended to shoot an imaginary shotgun as he told me this. "Pa! Pa! Pa!" he yelled, as if he was a Honduran Rambo. If Mauricio shot his gun anything like he shot his soccer balls, I wouldn't want to be nearby.) If the guys on the team have something to look forward to and be proud of, they spend less time on the streets. "Maybe the neighborhood—where my Juanita lives—is a little safer because of it," he said. "That's why I do this."

My own love for soccer seemed selfish in comparison: a need for accolades, praise, recognition. Mauricio played for his community, to keep everyone alive. It was a simple refocusing from the self to the greater good. It humbled me.

Yalena had the same effect when she invited me for a hike. I usually spent my weekends sleeping in, drinking Natural Light Beers, and watching *Fresh Prince*, but this time I went with her. We took the 6:00 a.m. bus into the Mico Quemado—Burning Monkey—mountain range, then walked up one hill, and then another. She'd brought a heavy duffle bag that we took turns carrying. I had no idea where we were, but I followed Yalena happily.

As we talked, I learned that, in addition to her responsibilities at DHC, she was studying for a college degree. She left the house at six in the morning, worked all day at DHC, then took an hour-long bus ride to her university in San Pedro Sula. She arrived home late at night, did her homework, and slept for a few hours. Then she did it again the next day.

It began to pour at some point, and we walked in silence. Yalena's duffle bag was getting heavier and heavier. What was in there? I secretly hoped that it was food for a picnic. But when we finally reached our destination, it wasn't a picnic spot but a village. We were mobbed by children chanting Yalena's name. She hugged as many of them as she could, laughing.

"I brought you what I promised," she said, unzipping the bag.

It was full of notebooks, pencils, and school supplies. I had never met someone who did what Yalena did at DHC, who also studied for her college degree, *and* who spent her free time climbing mountains to deliver school supplies. Like my chat with Mauricio, watching Yalena made me question my perspective and undisciplined life. The version of service they showed me was pure, resilient, and humbling.

* * *

But it was the third incident that really drove the point home. At the end of the summer, Cosmo came to visit me.

Cosmo, the little sister who waved at me from the stroller on the fateful day I first played soccer, was now a junior at the College of William & Mary. She joined me as we planted vegetables at Siete de Abril and ran soccer practices at DHC. She spent a lot of time with Yapa, the young girl at HFC who wanted to follow in Sister Tulia's footsteps, helping her with English homework.

By the end of two weeks, Cosmo sat me down.

"Something," she said, "is missing from your efforts."

Even though I didn't want to admit it, she was right. The kids could easily play soccer without me. Yapa could learn English on her own. The families certainly didn't need me to help plant crops. Moreover, because of our limited Spanish skills, we were often a burden to the Hondurans, who had to explain things to us. Furthermore, Cosmo thought that two months—which I had believed would be more than enough time to establish relationships, learn how things worked, and make a significant impact—was far too short. The impact we made that summer was, at best, marginal. Her comments stung because they were true.

"You could do so much more," Cosmo said. "Raise money for them. Every organization we came across in Honduras lacks funds. Sister Tulia even said she was struggling to raise funds for HFC this year."

The thought was too large; it was petrifying. Volunteering was one thing, but raising money from others? I pushed back with every excuse imaginable. "I've never organized an event or done public speaking before," I said. "We're students who don't even have degrees." But Cosmo was adamant. If I wanted to offer real, long-term commitment and service to the people of El Progreso, if I wanted to offer more than just my good intentions, then funding was the way forward. I could even start a nonprofit organization eventually. "I'll help you," she said.

"I really will. And Yapa will too. She wants to run a nonprofit organization; this is her dream."

For a moment, I teetered on the edge. This was ridiculous—I didn't have the ability to do this. For a brief, startled moment, I thought of Michael and those bullies in my basement. It wasn't the same thing at all, and yet... *Do something*, I'd told myself then. *Anything.*

How often had I wished that I had acted that day. Would I feel the same about this?

"We'll do it together," Cosmo said, holding out her hand. Her eyes were shining with excitement. "If you organize a fundraising event at UMW, I'll organize one at William & Mary."

When I was in sixth grade, I was in safety patrol. I would walk Cosmo to school in my neon-orange chest strap, raise my arm to remind drivers to slow down, and keep my sister from harm's way. She would follow my lead and sometimes hold onto my shirt as we crossed intersections together.

At some point in life, our roles had reversed. Now it was Cosmo who led the way. I shook her hand, and decided to give it a go.

─────── CHAPTER FOUR ───────

FACE YOUR FEARS AND GO FOR THE ASK

BACK AT UMW, I BOUGHT A PLASTIC JAR FROM THE DOLLAR store and headed to the campus center. Representatives of student clubs were setting up tables to promote themselves; the table I had booked was in the corner. It was my first campus fundraiser, a penny drive. My aim for today was simple: raise one hundred dollars for Sister Tulia and HFC. I set down my jar and arranged a few photos of Honduras that I had printed out. *Let's do this.*

Lunchtime approached, and the foot traffic picked up. People glanced over. Friends waved. None of them stopped by. When I smiled, they walked faster. After an hour, I rearranged the photos to make sure they were straight. It didn't change a thing—nobody came. I took a deep breath and got up. I stood in front of my table, said hello to strangers, shook their hands, and introduced myself. It was scary but it worked. People donated their spare change and asked me questions. It paid to be more proactive. When the building got quiet after dinner, I decided to call it a day. The jar was half-full.

I carried the jar back to my dorm room like it was a national treasure. My hands shook with excitement as I organized the coins into piles. There were even a few dollar bills. I began counting.

I had raised less than twenty dollars.

I counted again. There were dollar bills! Surely I'd raised more. But the total came to the same: twenty dollars. I couldn't believe it—what a complete failure. Frustrated, I slid everything back into the jar, wanting to throw it into the trash can.

When I told my roommate what had happened, he told me I had turned a fifty cents jar into twenty dollars; that was a forty-fold return on my investment. He encouraged me to keep going. If I started a campus club, I could get other students involved and raise more money.

His positivity gave me courage. I didn't know the first thing about creating a campus club though, so I took another deep breath and called the President of the UMW Human Rights Club, Meghan. I didn't expect her to know who I was: I usually sat quietly in meetings, too intimidated to speak. But not only did Meghan know who I was, she remembered I had spent the summer in Honduras. After I told her about my plans, she advised me to email classmates, post flyers, and organize my first interest meeting. I needed five people to start a club.

"I've never made a flyer before," I whispered.

"You'll figure it out. Just get started and I'll help you through the process."

So I made my first flyer: designed in Microsoft Word and using Comic Sans font. I stapled them everywhere. I emailed friends with the date and time of the interest meeting—"be there early to grab the best seats," I wrote. A couple of days before the meeting, I saw some of my flyers crumpled up and on the ground. I picked them up and restapled them to the bulletin boards, telling myself that maybe the wind was strong the night before. Then I walked a mile to the grocery store and bought two boxes of cookies for my new to-be members. They smelled great. I was careful not to eat any; I wanted to make sure there were enough to go around.

There were more than enough. Two people showed up to that first meeting: Nick and Lauren. I hid my disappointment, and talked enthusiastically about Honduras. They clapped softly; we ate some cookies. It was a good meeting. The turnout may not have been as big as I hoped, but we tripled our membership that day.

* * *

For guidance, Cosmo and I reached out to Dr. Greg Stanton, one of my friends' fathers. He had worked for thirty years in the international human rights sector, and ran Genocide Watch, an organization that fought genocide around the world. He said we needed to start a 501(c)(3) nonprofit organization. We brainstormed and decided on a name: Students Helping Honduras (SHH). Then, with his help, we filed the paperwork.

That winter, I returned to El Progreso with six members from UMW, including Nick and Lauren. We spent the week getting to know the families at Siete de Abril, playing soccer at HFC, and exploring the city. On our last day, we met up with Sister Tulia. Over many cups of coffee, she told us her vision for HFC that year. She was raising $100,000 to take in kids from another group home that was closing down, make renovations at the facility, and pay off HFC's debt. I told her we were committed to helping her raise the money. As I made my brazen promise, the group cheered. "I'll be thankful even if you raise just a few hundred dollars," she said, and laughed a grandmother's laugh at our idealism.

* * *

In the fall semester, pastor Bob called me over to the CCC.

"I heard about what you're trying to do," he said. "And I'm going to get you in front of Doris Buffett, a philanthropist here in Fredericksburg."

I laughed. Doris Buffett was the sister of Warren Buffett, the richest man in the world at the time. She had started the Sunshine Lady Foundation to help the needy. I'd met her, actually—briefly, when she gave a guest lecture at my economics class. "I give hand-ups instead of handouts," she'd said; I remembered that clearly. It took me ages to work up the nerve to approach her, and when I did, all I could say was "Thank you" and give her a Christmas card from Honduras.

She was a celebrity. She didn't have time for a college student.

"What's the worst that can happen?" Bob said. "You've been going door to door, facing hundreds of rejections. What's *one more* rejection?"

Bob took my hesitation as a yes. Next thing I knew, he pulled some strings and I was standing outside Doris's ordinary-looking home, too nervous to knock.

"Go on," Bob said.

I knocked. We were led in and I quickly realized the only thing ordinary about Doris's house was its outside. We walked past hundreds of sculptures, paintings, even a piano programmed to play concertos by itself. When we stepped into an elevator disguised as a room, it hit me that we were inside one of those houses featured on *MTV Cribs*. Then the elevator doors opened, and Doris was there.

"Hello there!" She jumped up from her seat and greeted us with a purposeful spring to her steps. "Oh! Are you the young man from Mary Washington who gave me that holiday card from, where was it, Honduras?"

I couldn't believe she remembered me, but I tried to remain as calm as possible. I nodded.

"Wonderful! I loved it so much that I kept it right here!" She pointed to a shelf with the card perched on top. My jaw hit the floor.

Doris gave us a tour of the house as she talked about the people her foundation supported: victims of abuse, sick children, people struggling with mental illness, prisoners, and vulnerable women in Mexico and Afghanistan. "I'm making sure Warren's money is given away to the worthiest of causes before I die. I stay up late reading letters from people who need help. I want the final check I write to bounce, from having given it *all* away. I'm almost eighty years old, so I'd better hurry up!"

Bob poked me. It was my cue.

I cleared my throat. For the next two minutes, I told her about my efforts to raise funds for HFC. She asked about my relationship with HFC, and I said they were trustworthy. I had known them for about a year.

"Whoa! You've known them for just one year? Here's my first piece of advice, young man. *Never assume*. Never assume that people have good intentions. You gotta observe carefully and make them *earn* your trust. The world of giving has a dark side to it, mired by corruption, greed, and ego. I've seen it all. Be careful." Doris's stare was so intense I had to look out the window. "One last thing! To empower the people you work with, don't give handouts. Give them—"

"Hand-ups," I completed. "You said that at your speech."

"Very good! You were listening! What we need to promote is *self-sufficiency*. Now *that's* where the money should be going. Now, what's your fundraising goal? How much money are you trying to raise?"

"One hundred thousand dollars."

"*One hundred thousand!*" She chuckled, then thought for a while. She turned her head toward the window and stayed silent for a few seconds. "I'll tell you what!" she exclaimed. As she stared at me, I fought every urge to look away and instead kept my eyes locked. "It was quite bold of you to come here. How much have you raised so far?"

"Me?"

"Yes! You!"

"Let me get my spreadsheets and fundraising plans out to show you what I'll be doing." I dug into my backpack.

"No, no! I don't need to see any of that! Just tell me where you are!"

"I raised a little over twenty dollars during my first penny drive, and we've raised a bit more, since."

She laughed out loud. "You have a long way to go!" Doris stayed quiet and looked me up and down—from my feet all the way up to my eyes. All five feet and three inches of me.

"Aha!" she yelled. "It'd be easy for me to just give you the $100,000 right now… But of course that wouldn't prove to anyone how much you care. Now, on the other hand, if I gave you *a challenge*? You could show me how hard you're willing to work for what you believe in."

"A challenge?"

"Yes! Okay, Shin—if you go out there and raise $33,333 with your friends on campus, I'll give you the $66,666 you need to reach your goal. At our foundation, we call this a challenge grant. I have this strange feeling you can do this!"

"But school ends in about three mont—"

"Yes or no?"

I was speechless. I wasn't an activist. I had never organized a fundraising campaign, or made a real public speech. Yet somehow, Doris thought I could raise $33,333. If I failed, it would be embarrassing, the greatest public failure of my life. But it was also a once-in-a-lifetime opportunity. I said yes.

———— CHAPTER FIVE ————

IT TAKES A TEAM

AS SOON AS WE LEFT DORIS'S HOUSE, I RAN TO CLUB SOCCER practice. After a scrimmage, I told my teammates about the challenge grant. I didn't expect anyone to donate much. After all, many players on the team paid the twenty dollars yearly due in small installments. A few of them went to their cars to bring the spare change they kept in their cupholders. Steve, my co-captain, shook his soccer bag so that coins and smelly socks fell out. Vitto, my housemate, and several others gave donations. Just two hours into the campaign, my teammates helped me raise over a hundred dollars.

* * *

Ten people showed up for our meeting that week, which was a record-breaking crowd. When I told them about the challenge grant, Lauren laughed with excitement. "We're gonna wake up this sleepy campus!" yelled Nick, who was by then the club's vice president.

"Let's write down some ideas on the chalkboard," said Strider, a student bodybuilder who spoke with a gentle voice. He grabbed a piece of chalk and wrote as people shouted suggestions. Speed dating. Soccer tournaments. Benefit dinners. Pie-throwing booths. Basketball tournaments. Cookie deliveries. An hour later, every inch of space on the chalkboard was filled.

To turn our plans into action, we penciled in events on a jumbo-sized calendar. Next to each event, we wrote down how much money we thought it would raise—$100 for a bake sale, $500 for a car wash, $750 for a benefit party. When we added up the projected revenues, we groaned. The total was far below the $33,333 goal.

"We need to fill up our weekends," said Strider, "and do two or three events per day."

Like weightlifters penciling in detailed meals plans, we returned to the calendar to add more events. For an upcoming Saturday, we planned a morning car wash at a local gas station, an afternoon bake sale on campus, and an evening benefit party at my apartment. When we did the math, we found it was possible to raise more than $1,000 per day. When we thought we were out of ideas, Kristin, a freshman, raised her hand. She suggested a campus-wide *walkathon*. All we needed was a trail. It was an event with huge fund-raising potential, and we could bring the different groups on campus together.

I was hesitant at first, given the logistics of such an event. But when we talked about it, we realized the process would be simple. All we had to do was sign people up, get them to find sponsors, and collect the donations at the event. The vote was unanimous: the walkathon would be our capstone project.

At eleven at night, we called the meeting to a close and staggered home. The next morning, we went to work.

* * *

I have always hated public speaking. I blame it on an experience in sixth grade, on our final speech exam. Mrs. Rhine had each of us recite Robert Frost's poem "The Road Not Taken," as a test of our oratory and memorization skills, but I was sure she was testing us on how much torture we could withstand.

"Shin," she said. "It's your turn."

I took a deep, shaky breath and reminded myself of how far I'd come from that little boy who couldn't explain to his coach why he was practicing a pass far away from the field. I had graduated from the ESL program now; I could do this. I focused on the class giving me a standing ovation at the end, and how good it would feel. My friends gave me fist bumps as I passed them. All eyes were on me.

"Two roads diverged in a yellow wood..."

I paused. My voice sounded strange. It was so shaky I sounded like I was standing on top of a washing machine. In fact, my body was trembling as if I were inside one. I tried to recite a few more lines, but Mrs. Rhine was laughing. She was covering her face, but it was clear she was laughing. When my classmates noticed Mrs. Rhine, they started laughing too. Soon, the entire class was laughing so hard they were crying. It was my worst nightmare.

Never again would I put myself through that.

Yet here I was, writing to every student club in UMW to set up presentations for the walkathon. I wrote my speech out; I practiced it endlessly in front of my bathroom mirror. My first speech was with the Anime Club, and they came wearing cute anime shirts and Pokémon paraphernalia. It didn't matter. They terrified me. I mumbled a few words, handed out flyers, and ran straight to the bathroom in case I needed to vomit. It got better after my twentieth or thirtieth speech. My legs finally stopped shaking at my fiftieth speech. The key, I learned, was just lots of practice.

I didn't just present at student clubs. I would show up early to my classes or slip into random lecture halls to pitch the walkathon before the professor showed up. After meetings, we would pick a dorm and go door to door to talk about the organization. If nobody answered, we slipped a flyer under the door. When I ran out of groups to speak to on campus, I spoke at different civic organizations and high schools in the Fredericksburg area. Bob set up speeches for me in various churches.

But there were pitches that I couldn't have prepared for. I once spoke to a crowd of fifty people, all in suits, trying to fit everything I had into the five minutes they'd allotted me on the schedule. When I finished, a middle-aged man raised his hand.

"Young man!" he boomed. "How can you guarantee that this children's home none of us has heard of is going to use the money wisely? I'm not sure what your qualifications are, but it seems overly ambitious for people so young to be dealing with something of this magnitude in a foreign country."

He kept going—a stream of questions and reprimands I didn't know how to respond to. After all, they were questions I had been struggling with myself.

"Do you have a 501(c)(3) nonprofit status?"

I explained we were waiting for the IRS to send the approval letter. But he kept grilling me, occasionally glancing at his colleagues as if to pull them in on the joke. I could see Nick in the back of the room, his face in his hands.

"This whole endeavor," the man announced, "worries me greatly."

Then he sat down triumphantly.

I felt so small. Nick whispered, "Good job," when I reached him, but it made me feel worse because I knew it wasn't true. A few people donated before we left, but I was demoralized.

On the ride home in Nick's old sedan, I replayed the man's comments and beat myself up for my jumbled answers. The comments hurt because they were true on so many levels. There was no way to guarantee that what we were trying to do would work. I felt terrible that Nick had skipped his philosophy class to give me a ride, but felt even worse that he worked with a leader who choked when the stakes were high. As we got onto the highway, he broke the silence. "None of us could have expected those questions," he said. "We can't always control what happens to us." He reminded me that we had raised a little over a hundred dollars at the event, which was all that mattered. As Nick talked about how much SHH mattered to him and how badly he wanted to help Tulia and the kids at HFC, I began to feel a surge of energy. When the two of us walked over to our weekly meeting that evening, I realized how much SHH had grown. More than fifteen people filled the room.

* * *

We had our last team dinner at Seacobeck Dining Hall. It was the end of the year. The walkathon was less than twenty-four hours away.

Lauren teared up—she couldn't believe what we'd managed to accomplish together. We had organized more than fifty events and sent out hundreds, if not thousands, of donation appeal letters. That semester, Lauren hadn't missed a single meeting or event. Neither had Strider, who was downing his fifth glass of milk this dinner. I didn't know what I had done to deserve such loyal and committed friends.

We had raised more than $10,000. Nick believed it was a campus record for a group our size. But while we were proud, none of us were celebrating—we were only one-third of the way towards our $33,333 goal. Tomorrow would be our final effort. It was exciting and petrifying.

I woke up at the crack of dawn to a cloudy sky, and a campus that was still asleep. I arrived early at the walkathon's starting point, thinking I'd be the first one there. I wasn't. Several members were already setting up.

"Good mornin'," said Nick, holding a handful of posters and markers.

"This is it!" said Lauren, trying to contain her excitement through deep breaths. Strider arrived, carrying a water jug filled with ice. We took tables and chairs from a nearby building. Lauren scribbled "Register Here" with a Sharpie on a poster paper and taped it to a table. After we set up an area for a local rock band we had invited, we ran out of things to do. Our walkathon was so barebones and unadorned, it certainly didn't look like the kind of event that was supposed to raise $20,000.

After we got into a huddle to pump ourselves up, the sky began to rumble and a dark cloud appeared. It began to storm. "The posters!" yelled Nick. We ran to take the posters down, but it was too late. They were drenched, and the words had already bled away. "Run for cover!" someone yelled. The group dispersed as rain poured down. Nick and I ran over to the dining hall where we shivered and ate breakfast. As I looked out the window, I knew all of our hard work had gone down the drain.

By the time I got out of the shower back in my apartment, the rain had stopped, and the grey sky was turning blue. With less than an hour left, I bolted out the door. Given that it was the weekend before final exams, the campus was still quiet and empty. I arrived at the starting point to see Nick and Lauren already sitting at the registration table. Not a single soul was there except for the three of us. It was so quiet, I could hear the trees rustling in the wind. My worries rose up to choke me. Maybe we had written the wrong date on our flyers. Maybe nobody would show up. What if we failed to meet Doris's once-in-a-lifetime challenge?

I heard a voice behind me say, "Shin."

When I turned, I couldn't believe it. Mom was here. She had pasty sunblock all over her face and a washed-out baseball cap over her head. "We made it," she said. Dad appeared from behind her, wearing his performance sunglasses and nodding stoically. My brother Gaku and my sister Koko followed. My family had driven from Falls Church, over an hour away, to attend the event. I gave each of them a hug and introduced them to the team.

Shortly after, the entire Anime Club showed up. I was so amazed I didn't know how to thank them. I never thought anyone would come to an event hosted by an organizer who lost his words at his pitch. Nick and Lauren began registering them as more people trickled in. Suddenly, we heard a commotion from the parking lot.

"There's a big mob in green coming towards us," Strider said in a worried voice. A rowdy group of young people wearing green and yellow got out of their vehicles and began marching towards us. As I took a closer look, I realized it was Cosmo and her crew from the College of William & Mary. They had driven two hours from Williamsburg to make it to the walkathon.

Cosmo gave me a bear hug and handed me a manila envelope filled with donations. "We've been workin' our butts off," she said, "just in case y'all were slackin' at Mary Wash!"

When Cosmo asked me where the registration table was, I could barely find it. Hundreds of people were in line, blocking my view. People kept pouring in, forcing us to delay the start. As Nick directed the crowd, he would catch my eye and point to his watch. I kept nodding. Dr. William Crawley, a professor of history, found me in the crowd and shook my hand. "I've been writing a history book about our university," he said. "Of all the student-organized events the school has seen in its one-hundred-year history, I think this is the biggest one *ever*. Way to go!" I just kept shaking his hand, lost for words.

When we registered almost everyone, the team and I got up on the wooden stage. There were so many people on the lawn, I could barely see the grass. Student clubs, sports teams, fraternities, churches, synagogues, Buddhist temples, mosques, civic organizations, high schools, representatives from an organization in Missouri that raised money for the campaign, and even Ghanaian marathon runners—all of them were there, chanting. The energy that filled the air was unlike anything I'd ever experienced.

I wanted to soak in the excitement a bit longer, but it was time to say something. I held the microphone, took a deep breath, and stuttered a few words. When I ran out of things to say, I handed the microphone to Cosmo.

"What's up, Mary Washington?" said Cosmo. "Are y'all ready to get this started?" The crowd erupted. "*Cosmo! Cosmo! Cosmo!*" The mob in green and yellow began to yell and blow whistles. For the next five minutes, she electrified the crowd. Cosmo was an Asian Oprah.

"When I count down from five, we're gonna start this thing...*ARE YOU READY?*"

"Yeaaaaah!!" the crowd screamed. The entire campus reverberated as the mass counted down in unison: "Five...! Four...! Three...! Two...! One...! LET'S START!!!!!!!!!"

The rock band, on cue, blasted their instruments and the walk began. The mile-long loop through the campus was so jammed, people crowd surfed to make it to the front. I shook hands and thanked participants as they walked by. The team worked nonstop, ensuring that people had enough water, latecomers knew where to register, and everyone had a good time. As the evening breeze began to cool the humid air, people wished us luck and started to leave. My family stuck around to take some photos and eventually left. Cosmo told me to call her when we got the total count and drove off with her friends.

After we cleaned up under the waning sun, I called the team over. "Thank you," I said. "No matter the outcome, I'm proud of what we accomplished. You've been incredible." Lauren, sweaty and exhausted, started crying. Nick closed his eyes and nodded his head. Before we dispersed, Strider hugged each person.

Nick and I stayed back to count the money. At the time, we didn't have a website or an online donation processor. We had a pile of manila folders, cash, jars full of coins, and checks that covered the plastic table in front of us. We began to count under a dimly lit lamp. As the evening turned dark, I told Nick we needed to hurry. People were giving us strange looks when they saw all of the cash on the table. After about two hours, I got up to pace around.

"We're almost done," said Nick.

I thought of all the people who had supported us, all the classes I had skipped to make it to our meetings, and the first penny drive. It felt like a decade ago.

"I have the total," said Nick.

His hands were trembling as he wrote down a number on a piece of paper with a blue Sharpie. I covered my face with both hands and squeezed my eyes shut. It felt like my heart was going to explode.

"Are you ready?" he asked.

"No."

Nick laughed and flipped over the paper. I removed my hands and looked. "EIGHTY THOUSAND DOLLARS," it read. I closed my eyes and reopened them to make sure I was reading the number correctly. It still said EIGHTY THOUSAND DOLLARS. Speechless, I stumbled over to a wooden bench and lay down. I exhaled slowly. It felt like a million butterflies were being released from my stomach. Tears trickled down my cheeks. Then Nick grabbed me, pulled me to my feet and we were screaming, howling, wild with the elation of it. "Aaaaaaaa!" We ran around as if we were out of our minds. We screamed and screamed. I jumped up and punched the sky with my fists like Rocky Balboa. "We did it!" yelled Nick. "We did it!" We had nearly tripled Doris's challenge.

When I met Doris later that week, she grinned and shook my hand. "I had a feeling you were going to do this," she said. "Let me go get your check!" I secretly hoped that Doris would give me one of those surfboard-sized checks you see on TV, but it was a regular-sized check.

When I lifted it into the air, I didn't complain. The flimsy piece of paper in my hands was worth more money than anything I had held. It was worth $66,666.

Doris told me what Margaret Mead had once said: "Never doubt that a small group of thoughtful, committed citizens can change the world; indeed, it's the only thing that ever has." The quote rang true. A small group of students had raised more than $140,000 in a few short months. I couldn't wait to tell Sister Tulia the good news.

———— CHAPTER SIX ————

DON'T WAIT FOR PERMISSION

I DIDN'T KNOW IF OUR WALKATHON WAS A FLUKE, BEGINner's luck, or if we were on to something. But being able to make a difference was invigorating, and I knew there was only one way to find out.

So when I went back to Siete de Abril that summer and Mauricio told me that they needed a building for their school, I got to work. For now, his little Juanita was learning under a Ceiba tree with the other students, a whiteboard leaning against its ancient trunk. I called Immanuel Presbyterian, a church in Virginia that had begun to support us, to see if they could help. They pulled through. We built the one-classroom school with wood so that it could be disassembled if the land dispute escalated. Siete de Abril was, of course, still a temporary settlement.

What next? "Roofs," Mauricio said. He pointed to the rotting tin roofs, patched together with tarp. "One bad storm"—he slapped his hands together—"and we're beans in a baleada."

So we replaced the roofs, with funding from the CCC and Rotary

International. I helped with the labor. I bought food. And I would have gone on like this—identifying one problem, then stepping in to help—if I had not met Camila.

The first time I talked to Camila, I was carrying lumber and she was tugging at my T-shirt. She was only nine or ten, dressed in a Clifford the Big Red Dog tank top. I was pretty sure she had no idea who Clifford was; I had yet to see a single book—except for the Bible—in the community. She was so small, with dark brown eyes that reminded me of Corduroy the bear, yet her brassy demeanor reminded me of the grandmas who worked at the street markets in town.

"Chinito," she said in a scratchy voice, "You should buy my *naranjas*—oranges. They're the best in town."

She placed an orange in my hand. It was nothing like the perfect, genetically modified oranges you find in the US.

"How much do the naranjas cost?"

"They're usually two lempiras [about ten cents]. But for you, one lempira each."

It was an irresistible offer, but I had a question for her: "Why are your naranjas green?"

"The best naranjas in Honduras are always green." She rolled her eyes, as if it was obvious. "So how many will you buy?"

I wasn't sure if I was contributing to child labor, but her family could probably use the money. I gave her a twenty-lempira bill and bought the entire basket. She held the bill up to the sky, squeezed her eyes, and folded it carefully into her pocket. She then peeled two oranges with a dull knife. I gave her one, and we ate together in the shade. As I had suspected, the oranges tasted like oversized lemons. They were so sour I had no idea how I would eat so many of them. I pursed my lips, and Camila giggled.

"Here," she said. She pulled out a plastic bag with sugar in it and dumped a pinch of it onto my orange. As soon as I took a bite, I yelped violently. The white powder wasn't sugar. *It was salt.* Camila laughed and poured a black powder onto my orange. When I bit into it again, I almost spat it out. *Pepper.* Why was this little girl pranking me? But she wasn't—Camila was pouring salt and pepper on her own orange and eating it joyfully as if it were the best in town.

Each morning, Camila waited for me at the entrance of the community, and I would buy a basket of bruised oranges from her. We would sit on a tree stump and eat together, Camila sprinkling salt and pepper with great care as she talked about her family, friends, something she found in the river the day before. With each orange, I got to know Camila a little better. I even grew to like green oranges with salt and pepper. Camila had the demeanor of a grandma because she had been carrying the weight of providing for her younger siblings.

Joking around with Camila kept me entertained during the backbreaking work. She tried to help me with the construction work, but the supplies were too heavy for her to carry. So I gave her my backpack instead. She carried it faithfully, following me everywhere. Not that long ago, I didn't know she existed. She was one of millions of kids who lived in a shantytown and sold fruit out of a basket. Now I knew about her life and how she liked her oranges, and I cared about her deeply. I wished her a good life. It no longer mattered that we had grown up thousands of miles apart.

One morning, Camila was waiting for me as usual. She didn't have her basket of oranges. It had stormed the night before, and the rain had turned her mud floor into a puddle of muck. Her roof had leaked, and she spent the night with her family huddled under a plastic tarp.

Now, puffy-eyed and small, she handed me a paper wrapped in plastic.

As she paced and stared at her feet, her eyes began to water. I wasn't prepared for that. I looked at the paper. It was a drawing of a house with a door, two windows, and orange trees growing on both sides. Above it, in barely legible handwriting, it read: *Chin and [C]osmo, help us. We are poor and low on resources.*

To Camila, I was, without a doubt, the richest person she knew. After all, I was the only person who could afford her entire basket of naranjas every day. My vision began to blur, and my chest ached. She deserved to be speaking with Bono or Bill Gates, not a college student who made minimum wage mopping floors on campus. Things around me began to swirl in circles, so I excused myself and sat under a mango tree, staring at the river. I thought about everything I'd learned about Siete de Abril. The girl who was murdered in this river. Marta's biggest fear: a *desalojamiento*. Juanita learning under a tree instead of a school. Kids picking up trash at a landfill, breathing in toxic fumes. In the decade that Siete de Abril had existed, conditions hadn't improved. They still had to rebuild their houses every time it rained.

The letter forced me to admit a brutal truth I had been pretending didn't exist—distributing food or fixing a couple of roofs was like putting a Band-Aid on a deep, infected wound. This was generational poverty, deep-rooted and complex. I had been shamefully patting myself on the back and then going home, while Camila and everyone else would continue to lack every other basic need.

Camila tugged at my soccer jersey. By then, it was I who had swollen eyes. She punched me in the ribs and asked me if I was okay. We sat together for a while. When it was time for her to go, she left me some oranges in the dirt.

I flew back to the US with a promise to myself: I would do everything to return, this time with a real answer to Camila's letter.

* * *

I asked Doris for a meeting, and went to her house to explain the situation at Siete de Abril. What they needed most were proper houses, with plumbing and running water.

"How much would it cost?"

"To build one for every family," I said, "a total of $200,000."

"Two hundred thousand! That's double your goal from last year!"

We discussed specifics. Parents in the community would be willing to provide the manual labor, so it would be the cost of the materials, the land, tools, and expertise. Doris began to pace.

"I'll tell you what," she said, snapping her fingers. "If you can raise $100,000, I'll match it so you can reach your goal." Without hesitation, I shook her hand. Another challenge grant was exactly what we needed. It gave us a reason to stretch ourselves, approach people who scared us, talk to the press, and grow the organization. As I ran back to campus, I felt like my veins were going to burst from all of the adrenaline.

More than twenty SHH members showed up to the first meeting of the spring semester. "The math tells us one thing," I said. "We need to hold a fundraising event every twelve hours, starting tomorrow." The intensity of the meeting made me feel like I was in a half-time huddle inside the locker room.

"That's insanity!" someone yelled. They weren't wrong.

Strider raised his hand timidly and pointed out that people had said the same thing when we announced the previous year's goal. We could do this.

"Let's begin strong by writing *one thousand* fundraising appeal letters," said Nick.

Lauren nodded, adding: "I'll order the pizza."

After the meeting, we baked cookies and brownies late into the night. Our bake sale the following day was a success. We sold out quickly and made several hundred dollars. Success brought with it unintended consequences. Other student clubs noticed what we were doing and began to sell their own baked goods right next to us. Soon, we were competing with a half dozen clubs that had free-standing posters and custom-made tablecloths. We didn't have any of the fancy stuff they had, but by the time the other tables sold three cookies, we had sold three trays. The difference was, they sat behind their tables and stayed quiet. We, on the other hand, stood in front of our tables and sold cookies as if our lives depended on it. As the team grew, we began to organize multiple bake sales simultaneously in different corners of campus.

Each weekend was a great fundraising opportunity. We would host events until late into the night and then get up at 6 a.m. to sell pancakes at the local Applebee's or wash cars at a gas station in the freezing cold.

When we had two months left in the semester, we entered an online voting contest sponsored by Dodge Motor Company. To win the cash prize, we needed to get the most people to click a "vote" button on their website. We entered the contest late and started in last place, behind countless nonprofit organizations. We worried that if we spent too much time on a competition we may not win, we'd lose time for other events. After a long meeting, our team decided to take the risk and go all in with the contest. During the contest's final days, we knocked on every door in every dorm and set up signup tables throughout campus. I must have hit the refresh button on the page a hundred times each day to see how many votes we had. We won the competition and the twenty-five-thousand-dollar prize. We were on fire.

I accumulated so many posters, supplies, and jars full of coins from all the events, I eventually needed office space. When I found out how expensive it was to rent a building in Fredericksburg, I decided to convert my closet into the organization's first headquarters. I moved all of my clothes to the side and shifted my desk, chair, and penny jars into the free space. When my roommate, who was unaware of the change, reached into the closet to get something that night, he yelped with fright. What he grabbed wasn't a jacket—it was the head of an Asian man staring at a computer screen.

After we had gone door to door in every dorm, we decided to do the same in Fredericksburg. On the first day, Nick and I started on College Avenue, right along the campus. We were scared, but we knocked on the first door with great enthusiasm.

A woman wearing slippers opened it.

"Hello! I'm Shin, and this is Nick." I shook her hand. "We're students from Mary Washington, and we're raising money for our nonprofit in Honduras."

"Honduras?" The lady scowled. "Why should we be helping people in Honduras when we have enough homeless people right in our city?"

It was a fair, philosophical question that I didn't know how to answer.

"If you keep soliciting like this in our neighborhood, you might get yourselves in trouble with the police." *BOOM!* She slammed the door in our faces.

Was it possible to get arrested for what we were doing? We debated whether to continue or not. We were rattled, but after our heart rate steadied, we decided to knock on a couple more houses to see how it would go. As we walked up to the next home, I secretly hoped nobody would answer. But I knocked, and a grandma in her pajamas answered.

"Hello, I'm Shin, and this is Nick," I said with a voice shakier than before. "We're students from Mary Washington. We're raising money for—"

"Oh, come on inside." She cracked open the door. "Let me get you something to drink. You look thirsty."

The lady gave us lemonade and cookies. She asked us about our fundraising campaign and refilled our glasses as we drank. She listened. Then she gave us a twenty-dollar bill and wished us luck. The two of us thanked the grandma and stepped back onto the street. We wanted to jump around and celebrate, but a cop car approached. The officer drove past us as I hid my clipboard behind my back. I wondered if the first lady had called the cops on us, but there was no way of knowing. The possibility of getting arrested felt real. As we faced rejection after rejection, I thought people didn't donate because they didn't like how I looked or stuttered. But I realized that people had all kinds of legitimate reasons why they didn't donate. They didn't have the money. They were having a bad day. They only donated to certain organizations. As I began to understand that getting a yes was more about probability and less about me, each rejection affected me less. Nick and I raised a couple of hundred dollars that afternoon.

At our weekly meeting, Nick printed out maps of different neighborhoods and got everyone organized. Over twenty of us went door to door the following day and raised several thousand dollars. The effort paid off so much that we decided to hit the pavement each week from then on. The campaigning didn't end in the afternoons. After going door to door, I would spend my evenings pitching our second annual walkathon. I gave the pitch so many times that when I entered a campus-wide speech contest just to make an announcement about the event, I ended up winning the audience award. I couldn't make it to the award ceremony because I was giving a speech somewhere else. I would wake up at four in the morning, get my premed homework done before the sun came up, and spend the rest of the day going to classes or working on the campaign. I went to the bathroom thinking about the campaign and went to bed thinking about it. I felt like a machine that was programmed to pursue my one goal and nothing else. It was strange to remember that just a few years prior, I walked around campus in a haze and without a sense of purpose.

During one of the final meetings of the year, I got emotional as I thanked everyone for their unconditional dedication. By then, there were so many members in the club, we had to bring in chairs from another classroom. "I don't think there's one more thing we could have done," I said. I truly believed it, given our grueling schedule. We had organized speed-dating nights, bingos, yard sales, thrift sales, pizza sales, spaghetti dinners, auctions, raffles, countless bake sales, raked leaves, and cleaned garages. Before I finished, Anna, a new member of the club, raised her hand.

"There's one thing we haven't tried yet," she said. "A couple of us are planning to go door to door on campus to clean bathrooms and toilets."

"I'm in," said Strider. "I don't wanna look back on college and regret not having given my all." I choked up for the second time that evening. I had never been part of such a united, determined effort. That weekend, as I spoke at churches throughout the city, the team back on campus cleaned dirty bathrooms. Anna was proud that the cleaning effort got us a few hundred dollars closer to our goal. When your team is willing to clean toilet bowls to accomplish a mission, it feels like nothing can stop you.

* * *

On the morning of the walkathon, thirty volunteers set up stages, barbecue stands, space for dance performances, T-shirt sales, and numerous registration tables throughout the campus walkway. As we approached the start time and as the temperature rose into the nineties, my family and thousands of students from UMW, William & Mary, Virginia Tech, Georgetown University, and the University of Virginia poured into the sunny campus. With a far greater number of participants that year, the walkathon took over the entire campus.

When I was readying myself to get on stage, I felt a tap on my shoulder. "Well, hello there!" said a woman wearing sunglasses and an elegant, double-breasted blue coat. When she took off her sunglasses, I realized it was Doris Buffett. "Doris, you look like you're about to run a marathon!" I joked, giving her a sweaty hug. I wanted to ask her why she was wearing a coat in the sweltering heat, but instead, I told her she looked like Princess Diana. It made her laugh. To this day, I don't know what Doris saw in me to be so supportive. She was the first person who made a financial bet on SHH's potential, and it made all the difference.

But it wasn't only the big donations that mattered. I once received a letter from a girl named Mimi. Two pieces of paper slid out: one of them was a drawing of aliens, or so I thought. When I looked closer, I realized they were drawings of small children holding hands. Above the picture, the sender had scribbled a message in crayon: "Hi I'm Mimi and I'm six years old. I go to first grade at Hugh Mercer Elementary School." The rest was barely legible. The second letter read: "Dear Shin, My daughter Mimi heard about your efforts in Honduras. After we showed her where the country was on a map, she decided to donate her savings. We've been praying every night so that you can reach your fundraising goal. See you at the Walkathon!"

Mimi's donation was only a few dollars, but it meant an incredible amount. It was the life savings of a first grader who had earned every penny of it doing chores. I taped Mimi's letter to the wall next to my computer to remind me to keep moving forward, even on the rainy days. Mimi showed up to the walkathon with her mom and a water bottle.

None of us, including Doris, could believe how much we ended up raising that semester: $188,000. After the walkathon, Doris gave us a check for $100,000, bumping our total to $288,000. I graduated from UMW that summer, knowing that what we had accomplished wasn't beginner's luck or a fluke. We had discovered a campus fundraising blueprint.

This blueprint would later spread to more than fifty cities. It was so simple, it only had two steps. Step one was to get a group of students to visit Honduras so they could connect emotionally with its people and our cause. Step two happens as soon as the students return home: we help them organize fundraising events on their campuses.

*　*　*

Cosmo and I broke our post-graduation plan to our parents at dinner.

I felt bad for them. All their lives, they worked hard for us and invested their savings in science camps, math tutors, SAT prep courses. Mom and Dad rarely bought new clothes or spent much money on themselves. One time, Koko, my older sister, asked her second-grade teacher what the word "pearl" meant. The teacher gave Koko the task to look inside Mom's jewelry box to find out. But she found out that Mom didn't have any pearls. As a matter of fact, Mom didn't own *any* jewelry. Even after our family stopped qualifying for food stamps and entered the middle class, my parents never upgraded their lifestyle. They simply continued to invest their savings into our education. They watched me get rejected by the University of Virginia (UVA), my top choice. Where I grew up, many Asian parents defined their self-worth on their kid's acceptance into UVA. Although my parents were not one of them, I still felt like I had disappointed them. Now that I'd finished my premed course and done well on the MCAT, they assumed I'd have the nice, secure life of a doctor. That evening, I was disappointing them again.

We were moving to Honduras.

We needed to, in order to oversee the funds we had raised. We hoped to stay there for a few years, maybe longer, to grow SHH. Doris Buffett had given us two years' worth of seed funding so we could get things started. There was no financial security in our plan beyond that. There were no guarantees for our physical safety.

Mom kept looking at the wall clock that made a bird noise each hour. It had ticked faithfully for years. Mom and Dad weren't surprised. Or disappointed. They drank their green tea, and talked happily about visiting El Progreso. They were proud of us, and it meant the world to me.

When Cosmo and I packed up our belongings and said goodbye to Falls Church, we were two, idealistic twenty-something-year-olds "following our hearts" to go "make a difference" in one of the poorest, most dangerous countries in the hemisphere. Unknowingly, we became a part of what Nicholas Kristof calls the Do-It-Yourself (DIY) Foreign Aid Revolution, which starts with the proposition that it's not only presidents, United Nations officials, or those working for large aid organizations like UNICEF who can chip away at global challenges.[9] The DIY foreign aid movement has its fair share of critics, given that some projects do more harm than good. Even Kristof himself warns that young idealists are often unsophisticated about what it takes to change the world. "At first, they don't always appreciate the importance of listening to local people and bringing them into the management of projects, and they usually overestimate the odds of success," he says. "They also sometimes think it will be romantic to tackle social problems, a view that may fade when they've caught malaria."

Cosmo and I were no exceptions when we graduated from college in 2007 and moved down to Honduras. We didn't have a clue about what awaited us.

BOOK 2

CHAPTER SEVEN

EVERYTHING THAT CAN GO WRONG, WILL GO WRONG

COSMO AND I WERE WAITING IN THE WOODEN SCHOOLhouse for our first meeting to start. *When* it would start was debatable: "sometime after lunch but before dinner" apparently. I swatted away mosquitos and reread *Mountains Beyond Mountains*.

We had landed in Honduras that morning. Our taxi driver frowned when we told him about SHH and our housing project—he knew of a housing project near Siete de Abril that had failed just recently. It had started with great promise, but then M-13 moved in, took over the neighborhood, and many of the project's original beneficiaries fled. It was now the most dangerous place in the city. Then there was another housing project that collapsed: they'd built all these beautiful homes, but didn't sort out the land titles. Ten years later, those houses are still empty.

He had many more stories.

So I was here, rereading *Mountains Beyond Mountains*, and trying to forget his messages of doom. The book is a biography about Dr. Paul Farmer, a doctor who took on diseases in Haiti that were said to be "impossible" to fight, like multi-drug resistant tuberculosis. It gave me hope. Dr. Farmer confronted critics, doubters, and corruption along the way, but ultimately succeeded. It also made me feel utterly inadequate. Dr. Farmer had superhuman intelligence, courage, resourcefulness, and drive. He ran a clinic in Haiti *while* he went to medical school at Harvard and worked concurrently on his PhD.

The school was filling up—mothers rocking babies, fathers wearing straw hats, children chasing each other between people's legs. Camila gave me a Honduran high five and ran off to play with her friends. The adults instructed the kids to go outside, and the meeting began.

I updated everyone on our successful fundraising campaign: $288,000. Many cheered, but some stared at us blankly. They didn't trust us and I didn't blame them; Cosmo and I had yet to prove ourselves. The discussion circled around where we would build the houses. On Siete de Abril or somewhere else? Building somewhere else would seriously cut into our budget and timeline. But we couldn't build on Siete de Abril if the community didn't have land titles.

Eyes turned to an older man with a cowboy hat, from the Land and Housing Committee.

"We'll have the land titles in a few months," he said, fixing his shirt collar. "There's no need to worry; we can build the houses here."

Someone scoffed. "But that's what you've been saying for years. 'Just a few more months!'"

The room erupted. Arguments crisscrossed around us, building to a crescendo. A burly man with a fierce mustache—Dago—was pointing at us. "How do we know," he said, loudly, over the noise, "that you guys aren't going to claim the houses for yourselves after we build them? Hmm? We've had too many politicians and NGOs come into our village with empty promises, trying to deceive us."

We tried to reassure Dago, but our voices were lost. Men continued arguing with each other on tangents that had little to do with land titles. The women stayed quiet; I wondered what they were thinking. The community council tried its best to regain control of the meeting. They had almost succeeded—men were taking their seats, quietening down—when Dago stood up again. He pointed to the far side of the room.

"That kid and his family shouldn't be allowed to join the program. He stole my bicycle last month."

The room erupted again. The teenager denied it, and men left their seats to join the fray. As the yelling built, the taxi driver flashed through my mind. He was smiling knowingly. Cosmo and I were in over our heads.

* * *

The first thing to figure out was the land titles. After the meeting, I sought advice from as many people as possible. "Don't worry, you can build the houses right there in the community," one attorney told me. "I wouldn't build the homes there if I were you," said another. The mayor of El Progreso, Alexander Lopez, wrote us a letter granting permission to build homes at Siete de Abril. He promised to personally step in if anyone tried to take the land away. A few days later, one of the head attorneys from the mayor's office told me in confidence not to build the houses there, despite the letter. I was so confused I took a four-hour bus ride to Tegucigalpa to visit Honduras's land registry headquarters. Even there, we received contradictory information. Nobody seemed to know who owned the land at Siete de Abril, or where the law stood.

Siete de Abril was a living example of what Peruvian economist Hernando de Soto wrote about in his book, *The Mystery of Capital*. The lack of standardized property laws in low-income countries, combined with the proliferation of people who are forced to live in informal or illegal settlements, prevent the poor from breaking out of poverty. Not only are people who lack access to secure land titles unwilling to invest in better housing, more importantly, they are unable to use their houses as collateral to borrow money to start businesses. The inability to turn their "dead" assets into "liquid" capital, a practice largely taken for granted in the West, keeps the poor from accessing a major gateway to success.[10]

In the end, we held a vote on whether to build on Siete de Abril or somewhere else. It was a long and heated meeting. Members of the Housing Committee spoke about the hours they'd dedicated to getting the land titles, about the sweat and toil. "We're inches away," they promised. But it was a thin, elderly woman who never spoke in meetings that turned the tide. She was furious and overcome. Every year, the committee took a fee and promised that *this* year they'd get the titles. She was done believing it. Could you imagine working in the hot sun for months, replacing cardboard houses with fine homes, only to watch it get taken away? Was it worth the risk?

Everyone decided it wasn't. They voted in favor of new land.

I was assigned the task of finding the land, negotiating for it, and buying it. I had never bought land, let alone in a foreign country where the laws were unclear. As for negotiating...I couldn't even haggle with the grandmas who sold me vegetables. My protests were waved away. "Just look for plots with signs that say *Se Vende* [for sale]," people said. "It's easy." And so the hunt began.

Sometime during my search for this land, I came down with dengue. "Came down" is a docile phrase. I thought I was going to die. I woke up at three in the morning with the sheets soaked with my sweat, and just about made it to the bathroom—tiptoeing past Cosmo not to wake her—when I tasted acid in my mouth. I sat on the toilet and grabbed the trash can, not a moment too soon. Green liquid ejected out of my mouth and nose in rhythmic bursts. I spent the night on the toilet, alternating between diarrhea and vomiting.

I woke up in a hospital. Dengue was confirmed: a mosquito-borne, tropical disease known as the breakbone fever. The doctors were worried it might be hemorrhagic dengue, a deadly strain. I drifted in and out. Cosmo stayed, sleeping nights in a plastic chair. I don't remember much. I only remember waking up once to go to the bathroom, and being in so much pain, I was certain I was dying. When I sat on the toilet, it felt strange—too cold and too low. I looked down and realized the plastic seat was missing. In the many toilets I'd been in Honduras, this was often the case. Pain pulsed at the back of my eyes as I tried to figure out where all the toilet seats had gone. Was someone collecting them? Were they being stored in a facility? Then I put my face in my hands and cried. I was dying, and my last thought was going to be about toilet seats.

* * *

I didn't die. We began searching for land again, as I slowly recovered. We had more than one hundred options soon, and community members began visiting the best plots. They voted on a thirteen-acre land in northern El Progreso that was flat, beautiful, and just a few blocks away from the main road that led to the city. If the price was fair, it was the land to buy.

A large, imposing man walked into the coffee shop. He wore a brown cowboy hat, his dress shirt tucked into a thick leather belt. His mustache made him look like a cross between a WWF wrestler and a Mariachi singer. When he spotted me, he saluted. I took a deep breath and smiled as confidently as I could. It was time for my first negotiation.

"Are you Señor Shin?" he asked.

"Yes, and you're Señor Angelo?"

He smiled, flashing a couple of gold teeth. As we shook hands, I tried not to stare at his bulging biceps. Angelo took a seat. He pulled an object from his waistband and placed it on the table—*clunk*. A revolver. "In a Honduran business meeting," he said, "we don't conceal things." I nodded and pretended to laugh as if I already knew that. As soon as I saw the gun, I knew that practicing my negotiation skills at the vegetable markets hadn't prepared me for this. The grandmas at the market didn't pull out weapons. They pulled out potatoes.

Angelo looked at my waist. I guessed it was my turn. I cleared my throat and pulled out what was concealed in my pocket: a number two pencil.

"I want $100,000 for the land," he said. "It's thirteen acres of good land without any *hipotecas*—liens."

I chuckled as dramatically as I could to show him that his initial offer was ridiculous. I could buy two million oranges from Camila for that price. If we paid anything like that, we wouldn't have enough money left to build the houses. My market research told me that the land was worth $70,000–80,000. I asked him if he was sure about the lien (a claim against assets typically used as collateral to satisfy a debt) to cover the fact that I didn't know what a lien was.

"I'm currently talking with a doctor who wants to buy the land *next week*," he said, looking me in the eyes. "I'm giving the land to whoever pays me first."

Next week? He was bluffing. Wasn't he? I couldn't tell. I felt pressured, but the last thing I needed to do was look desperate. "I can give you $40,000."

Angelo contorted his eyebrows as if I'd just spat in his face.

"I'm not here to waste my time. I need a serious offer."

"Listen, I have a list of over a hundred plots on sale. If you don't give me a realistic price, I'll give our money to someone else." *Don't think about how disappointed the community will be if you don't get this land. Don't think about it.* Had Angelo noticed my nose was beginning to sweat?

"$90,000 if you give it to me in one lump sum."

It was not a terrible offer, but we would likely run out of money in the middle of construction if we paid that much. My heart began to beat faster as I kicked around the price in my head.

"Give me a break," I said, with force behind my voice that surprised me. "The plot doesn't even have road access. I'll give you $45,000."

"I'm here to *make* money," he said. "Not *lose* money."

"But the land isn't even connected to an electricity grid or water system. We'd have to do that ourselves, out of our own pockets." I stared him down.

"Haven't you seen the textile factory nearby? Or the shopping mall and university that they're building? The land is going to be worth double by next year."

For several hours, Angelo and I negotiated. We bluffed, bantered, and got to know each other. It was exhausting to put up a performance for that long. After my third cup of coffee, I gave him my final offer: $66,000. Angelo stayed quiet for a few moments. The community had scheduled the groundbreaking ceremony for the project for December, which was just a few weeks away. Bob and a group of supporters from Virginia had already booked their flights to join us. If the negotiation failed, I would be in a scramble to find another plot of land. It would be disastrous if I couldn't find something on time.

Angelo grinned and extended his right hand. "Deal."

I took it gratefully. I noticed his palm was sweatier than mine.

After our attorney filed the paperwork, Cosmo and I met Angelo at a street corner. "It's yours now," he said, handing us the land title. I gave Angelo the bank-certified check, and he tipped his cowboy hat in gratitude, then sauntered off. Cosmo and I held the document up, into the sky. The housing project was no longer just an idea. We had made our first concrete step.

Shortly after, Angelo was gunned down. City-dwellers suspected it was because the wrong people found out he had made all that money. I was shaken. Someone I had coffee with only weeks ago was now dead; I couldn't wrap my head around it.

I was also scared. Cosmo and I were about to embark on a project that would cost hundreds of thousands of dollars; it was essential to keep a low profile as we moved forward. But El Progreso was a small place. Word got around quickly.

* * *

The property we'd bought was beautiful, full of mango and coconut trees, with wild grass that reached our chests. There was a dry creek bed. Here and there, we glimpsed wildlife that petrified Cosmo and me. We saw a python once, and Mauricio took great pride in showing us a massive tarantula with two fangs and beady eyes. "They flick their venomous hairs like tiny needles," he said, moving his fingers like antennas. "They jump, and you'll be dead in twenty minutes if you get bitten." Mauricio laughed as I shuddered and backed away.

We'd chosen the name of the community by vote: *Villa Soleada*, Sunshine Village. It was in honor of Doris Buffett's Sunshine Lady Foundation. Some of our happiest memories were after we'd bought the land and before we began construction. Everybody gathered in the school, and we handed out sheets of paper. "Let's draw what we want the village and homes to look like," I said. We spent the afternoon like this, sketching our dreams. We laughed at soccer fields as large as the property itself, or houses too small to fit the giant humans drawn next to them. But it was exciting. We knew what we were working for. Towards.

We went over the project's memorandum with the community. SHH agreed to provide all the tools and construction supplies for the construction of the village. The community members agreed to provide all of the manual labor. Everyone would work in shifts during certain days of the week. A group of fathers who had worked in the industry agreed to lead the construction. We gave the drawings to them so they could combine the ideas to create a mockup. Though the memorandum was extensive, it was a work in progress. We still didn't know how to organize shifts for people in the community who were elderly or sick. We didn't know how we would decide which family would get which house. We didn't know where we would safely store all of the supplies.

Several families decided to opt out of the project. One family decided to stay in Siete de Abril to remain close to their church. Another family sold vegetables from the back of a rickshaw, and didn't want to lose their customers in the area. Others decided to stay because they were involved in the business of selling the disputed plots of land. The head of the land and housing committee decided to stay. It turned out to be a deadly decision for him—shortly after, a group of men assassinated him. It was a fate not uncommon in Honduras for those involved in land disputes. Marta and her family also decided to stay. She wanted to remain close to the garbage dump, the only place of employment she'd ever known.

Sixty of the seventy-two families in Siete de Abril chose to move. Many of the decisions to stay surprised me, but I also understood that each family had the right to decide their own fate. The truth was, nobody, including me, knew which set of families would end up better off in the long run. As the taxi driver said, numerous things could go wrong with the project. The families who planned to move to Villa

Soleada took on a significant amount of risk for a chance—but not a guarantee—at a better life.

The first thing we needed to do was cut down the brush and wilderness that covered the land. We didn't have lawnmowers or chainsaws, so we picked up machetes. I was getting to know the community better now. You had jokesters like Mauricio, with his football and bravado. You had people who claimed to be community leaders, and who no one respected much. You had a few mothers and young men who said little, but whom the community always listened to.

Wilfredo was one of those. In the many years I would know him, Wilfredo was a man of rare temperament and almost no despair. He bore everything graciously, with a stoic nod. We shared a love of football, and he would become one of my closest friends. Now he was showing me how to sharpen my machete on a gritty rectangular block. "There's no reason to rush through the sharpening process," he said, as he placed the machete on his knees and dragged the stone over it. "The more time you spend preparing your machete, the less time you spend cutting."

Behind us, a commotion was breaking out. Dago was refusing to let the women cut grass. "That's a man's job here in Honduras," he said, snatching away their machetes. Cosmo and I looked at each other, taken aback.

The women, sweaty and discouraged, congregated. Among them was Yamilet, the same woman in Siete de Abril who swung a machete at my head and fed me a papaya. Yamilet's story was similar to so many in Siete de Abril. She was born in El Progreso as the eldest of six children. Schooling wasn't an option: she spent her childhood caring for her siblings while her mother worked. When her mom moved to Guatemala to find a better job, Yamilet became the head of the household at thirteen. Eventually, she took her siblings to Guatemala and reunited with their mother. They stayed in a crammed, concrete room. Yamilet worked as a line cook at a cafeteria and then at a small watch factory. When her mother got sick two years later, they moved back to El Progreso. But everything they had remembered was gone. Hurricane Mitch had torn through the country. They ended up at a refugee camp with 250 other families, and eventually at Siete de Abril. Yamilet had to quit her job at the *maquila* (textile factory) when she gave birth to her first daughter. Her husband abandoned them.

Now she was here, looking to make a better life for her children. Dina, the baby strapped to her hip when I met her at Siete de Abril, was no bigger than the papaya we shared, happy and full of life. Yamilet walked up to Cosmo. "We might not be able to cut the grass as fast as the men," she said in a soft but firm voice. "But we're part of the project just as much as they are. We had agreed that both men and women would work."

She walked over to the pile of machetes and grabbed a handful, glancing at Dago. His thick arms were crossed. She hesitated, but then handed the machetes to the women, and they began cutting. The men argued amongst themselves. Cosmo and I didn't know what to do. As Westerners, we had come into the project embracing the idea of gender equality. Now our ideas of right and wrong were put into question. Were we imposing a concept that was insensitive to the culture, social norms, and traditional gender roles in Honduras? We didn't know how to proceed.

In the end, Wilfredo resolved it. Dago grumbled, but he folded his sleeves and got to work. "I hope you can forgive the old man," Wilfredo said. Dago was his uncle. "His old-fashioned ways can sometimes cause trouble, but he means well."

Mango and coconut trees swayed with the breeze as colorful birds flew out of the canopy, and a long row of people wearing straw hats hacked in unison. I swung my machete awkwardly. *Phhhhttt!* The two-feet-long blade made a high-pitched sound as grass flew into the air. "It's all in your wrist," Wilfredo said as he crouched down and showed me the proper technique. I swung the machete with my wrist, but I lost my grip. It launched into the air, barely missing Wilfredo's head. He laughed nervously and stayed further away from then on.

It was back-breaking work, but it felt good. The brush was so high, we swung away not knowing where the end was.

***

We spent two weeks clearing the land. Wilfredo and his brother Adriano then began to hammer wooden footing stakes into the ground and run strings between them. During this process, we got caught in a storm. Rain poured in sheets; lightning cracked the sky. The grassland turned into a swamp. I saw moving objects in the murky water, and scenes from the movie *Anaconda* flashed through my mind.

We began wading out, Wilfredo and Adriano ahead of me. It was so loud I couldn't hear them. The water was at our knees. For me, it was at my hips. I tried to follow Wilfredo, but the current kept pulling me back. I kept going. I don't know how we made it to the truck.

The next morning, we couldn't drive into Villa Soleada. The area before it had turned into a swamp. If we tried to walk through it, we got stuck in the deep mud. The truck would definitely not make it. Our groundbreaking ceremony was just days away—how were we going to get all of the visitors or supplies into Villa Soleada?

"We need to create a road here," said Wilfredo. "We need *piedras*. Rocks."

We ordered a dump truck of stones from a local quarry. The pile they created was so high, it looked like the Great Pyramid of Giza. The stones were sharp as well—they cut my soft hands. How were we going to move all of those stones with our bare hands? It was madness. But the community members were already forming a long human line, passing stones between them and placing them in the mud. Doña Nibia, the oldest woman in the community, was there working. I stopped fussing and joined the line.

The whole endeavor reminded me of the legend of Sisyphus, a mortal condemned to move rocks up a mountain in Hell, only to watch them roll back down, repeatedly, for all eternity. I wanted to stop, take a break, never return, but everyone was working so hard I kept going. It took hours to move the entirety of Giza. By then, even the roughest, most-calloused hands were raw and bleeding.

The swamp remained as deep as ever.

"This is where God tests us," said Wilfredo, smiling and draping a towel to hide his tired eyes. "We must now order another dump truck full of piedras."

Dump truck after dump truck delivered stones, and we continued our punishment. The community worked tirelessly and without complaint. Eventually, one stone turned into ten thousand stones and ten thousand stones turned into a road. We could drive into Villa Soleada.

Hundreds showed up for the groundbreaking ceremony. Sister Tulia, teenagers from HFC, Bob, supporters from the US, the mayor of the city, politicians, local journalists—all of them drove down the stone road we had built. A pastor from the community gave a prayer to bless the project. People said a few words. Mauricio told everyone in the community to set their differences aside and work in unity. Yapa spoke, and I imagined her speaking as the head of an international NGO one day. I nudged Wilfredo to say something, but he just smiled and lit a cigarette. He was a man of few words.

"*Viva Villa Soleada!* Long live Villa Soleada!" yelled Alexander Lopez, the mayor of El Progreso. As rain beat down on the blue tarps, Roberto Micheletti, the Head of the Honduran Congress, took the microphone. In his raspy voice, he urged everyone to work hard to turn Villa Soleada into a model community for El Progreso. We cheered.

Then we began to dig. Mud splashed everywhere, but we were so jubilant nobody cared. "Dig as deep as you can," Wilfredo said. "The foundation hidden underneath the building is like what family is to a community. It's what sustains everything." We swung our pickaxes harder.

* * *

When I told Wilfredo we needed to order enough supplies to last us the month, he shook his head and gave me a grave look.

"That's a risky move. We should buy just enough to last the week."

I disagreed. Since the beginning of the project, community members had instructed me to order weekly supplies. I had done so because I trusted their guidance, but over the months, I had grown tired of the protocol. We would frequently run out of materials and lose time. We had to constantly be on the phone with small family-owned hardware stores to negotiate prices for every nail purchased. We had to correct so many delivery mistakes, I wondered if the "errors" were part of a scam. It was a draining process.

Now we were ready to put roofs on the homes, and it would be easiest to buy the roof panels and beams at once. "It's about efficiency," I told Wilfredo.

"I don't recommend it, but it is your decision."

I ordered truckloads of supplies. They filled the storage shed to the ceiling, the galvanized metal so shiny I felt like I was inside a treasure chest. I was strangely proud as I looked at them—you could tell how sturdy the beams were when you tapped them. These homes were going to withstand the strongest of storms.

A couple of days later, I was woken up in the middle of the night by a phone call. It was Mauricio.

"Shin, the Mara raided us. They took everything."

What? I sat bolt upright.

"They knew where we had our supplies stored. They took all the roofing supplies, tools, and welding machines. Dago and Siprian were roughed up, but they're alive."

Dago and Siprian were the two fathers guarding the shed. I nearly wept with relief. When I got to Villa Soleada, the men looked shaken.

"They tied us up. They shoved our faces into the ground—I thought they were going to shoot us in the back of our heads."

I should have listened to Wilfredo. It was important to be efficient, but even more essential to listen to the community's guidance. We called the police. They took notes disinterestedly. "We had to use the last bit of our fuel to get here," an officer said, rubbing his thumb with his index finger. We gave him money. Nothing would happen from the police report.

We tried to eat lunch. Wilfredo and the other men discussed the possibility of another raid. Madesto, a father with a penchant for violence, pulled out a gun. "We must fight back!" he yelled. "We'll protect the supplies at night. Who's with me!?" Men and women raised their hands. They began sharpening their chipped machetes.

My cell phone rang, and everyone went quiet. It was Canaleta, our roof contractor. "Señor Shin, I was notified that the welding tools I had left behind in your storage shed were stolen. This is a big problem. I can't work without my equipment. I won't be able to feed my daughters."

Not knowing how else to respond, I apologized.

"You'll need to pay me back for what was lost," he said. "You said you would keep my tools safe."

I felt bad for him. He had just started the job with us and had worked hard on the roofs of the first homes. Reimbursing him for the loss seemed like the sensible thing to do.

Wilfredo got up from the dirt. "Something smells fishy," he said. "From what I know, the roofer is an MS-13 gang member."

"That can't be possible," I said, forcing a laugh. "He has a roofing business and two daughters."

"A lot of people who you would never expect are in the Mara. We've been living in this town long enough to know who they are."

"Think about it," added Mauricio as he paced. "Everything was going smoothly for months. And then a few days after we hire this guy, we get raided. They knew exactly where to go in the pitch dark for the supplies!"

"Are you saying that Canaleta took his *own* equipment during the raid and is now asking us to give him money for it?"

The idea of someone masterminding such a gambit was beyond me. The community was divided: some thought we should pay Canaleta, others didn't. Some believed he needed to "pay" for what happened to Dago and Siprian.

Canaleta arrived with three men. The community stared him down. I didn't like the tension in the muggy air, so I shook Canaleta's hand as confidently as I could and smiled. Here I was, wearing a purple fanny pack, shaking hands with an alleged MS-13 gang member.

I gave him the cash. He grinned, flashing his gold teeth. "So when do you want me to come back to finish the roofs?" he asked.

I lied and said we couldn't continue due to financial difficulties. I needed to cut ties with Canaleta; the community clearly didn't trust him. I couldn't look him in the eye—what if he had nothing to do with this?

Before he drove away, Canaleta leaned out of his truck window. "*Hermano*, brother. Have you considered the possibility that the raid never happened? This may have been an elaborate ruse invented by the community you're working with. Don't trust a single soul here for your own good!"

Canaleta's words played on my mind all day. He was either out of his mind or warning me of what was to come. I shouldn't let one man's opinion of an entire community erode my trust in them, but I couldn't help but wonder if the families truly wanted the project to succeed or if they had other intentions. The more I thought about it, the more confused I got. It took years to build up trust, and only seconds to put cracks in it.

———————— CHAPTER EIGHT ————————

JUST FOCUS ON THE NEXT SMALL STEP

AFTER A LONG DAY OF WORK, WE GOT ONTO THE BUS TO GO back to Siete de Abril. A year and a half had passed since we broke ground at Villa Soleada, and we were on our final stretch of the construction. We were building the concrete floors for the nearly-finished homes. It was an arduous process that required everyone to mix concrete by hand eight hours a day for months on end. Though we had planned to build sixty houses, we ended up with only forty-four. More than a dozen families had dropped out of the project. They claimed the labor was too much, or changed their minds about leaving Siete de Abril.

I looked at the families left. They were exhausted. Their hands were covered in blisters and calluses; their foreheads were coated with dust. I wondered if more of them would drop out of the program, given how backbreaking the work was. Did they regret signing up? What would happen to the project if everyone decided to quit? What would happen to *them* if the construction turned out to be one giant disappointment?

Don't think about it, I told myself. The driver turned on the ignition and reggaeton music blared from old speakers.

Before we could move, a woman and her daughter climbed into the bus, frantic. "I saw something," said the mother in a trembling voice. "A group of armed men wearing all black is hiding out in the bushes." She pointed her shaking finger at the end of the dirt road.

"Back!" Wilfredo said urgently. "We gotta retreat back into the property!"

The driver reversed immediately, parking on a patch of dirt. When he turned off the ignition, the music died as well, and now it was so quiet, I got the chills. I called the police. They would try to be there as soon as possible, but right now they didn't have a vehicle or fuel.

We waited.

"It may be the Donkey Killer," Wilfredo said, taking the seat beside me.

"The who?"

"He's the most feared assassin in the area. They call him the Donkey Killer because he kills his victims as if they were animals."

"Why would he be out there behind the bushes?"

"We all have wallets, cell phones, and watches." Wilfredo looked at the woman who gave us the tipoff. "Were they armed?" he asked. "The men?"

"I didn't get a close look, but I think so," she answered. "Yes, they must have been."

The Donkey Killer. I felt sick. What if we drove out real fast down the road—surely they wouldn't be able to do anything to a bus? Wilfredo believed they'd shoot at us; it wasn't worth the risk. Maybe the woman was mistaken... Wilfredo shook his head again. The Donkey Killer had raided several neighborhoods in the area this month—we shouldn't take this lightly.

The sun began to set. The men paced outside the bus, discussing the situation.

"If we remain here past nightfall," said Wilfredo, "we're no different than cattle waiting inside a slaughterhouse."

One of the pastors from the community pulled out a Bible and began to pray. Her voice grew louder and louder, and then she began to scream as if possessed. Others followed, kneeling and clasping hands. I tried to stay calm, but their panic was freaking me out. Dago was sharpening a knife, his hands trembling. Yamilet was telling the children a story to distract them, clearing her throat every now and then to steady her voice. Wilfredo discussed the situation with his brother. The two usually joked around, but that evening, neither was laughing.

It would be pitch black in a matter of minutes. I called the police again. Same answer. The men got into a huddle, then headed to the storage shed. They came back with machetes and pickaxes.

"We have a plan," said Wilfredo. "The men will get into a formation in front of the bus and sprint out. The bus, with women and children inside, will follow right behind us."

Wilfredo was a father. His children, his wife, even his elderly parents depended on him. He was one of the best, most genuine people I knew, and I wasn't keen on seeing him hurt. I wasn't keen on anyone being hurt.

"This sounds like a terrible idea."

"If we let them get us now, they'll sense weakness and come back for more. But if we put up a fight, they'll think twice about coming back."

I didn't know how to respond to something like that.

"Listen." Wilfredo grabbed my shoulder. "Most of us here have been displaced from one place to the next throughout our lives. Soon, for the first time, my family will have a home that we can call ours. I'm not about to let a group of criminals take that away!"

My throat closed. I knew Wilfredo's story. His parents met at a birthday party in Yoro; it was love at first sight. They got married and built a mud house that would become home for Wilfredo and their five other children. It had been a hard life, focused on subsistence farming, but they were happy. Wilfredo's father made one lempira (fifty cents) per day selling crops; when he discovered that he could make ten lempiras (five dollars) per day working in El Progreso, the family moved.

The four brothers spent their teenage years in the new city, working as construction laborers. Though the family earned more in El Progreso, rent was much more expensive, and they went from house to house, unable to make ends meet. The family ended up in Siete de Abril, where someone promised to "give" them a plot of land for twenty lempiras (about one dollar). They lived under a plastic tarp. After Wilfredo found his first formal job on a cleaning staff, he used his savings to buy wood and tin roof panels, then built a basic shelter. Mud, tarp, tin, and cardboard walls—those had been their houses. Villa Soleada was their chance for something better.

Unable to speak, I nodded.

Wilfredo gestured to the men, and they started to march. Hours before, I wondered how many more of them would quit the project. Now they were here, clutching construction tools to fight against firearms. "Give me a machete," I said desperately, trying to join them, but Wilfredo pushed me back into the bus. I didn't know if this would be the last time I saw him.

The bus rolled forward. Blue and red lights flashed at the other end of the road—the police. Officers jumped out and, with the men, they charged into the bushy area where the bandits were hiding. There was no one there. Either the bandits had fled, or they had never been there in the first place.

When we pulled onto the highway, we cheered and howled, grateful to be alive. I think of that moment often when I remember that night. I think of the truth I was offered in those dark hours: Everyone here was willing to die so that their families could have homes.

* * *

The incident of the Donkey Killer made it even harder to look the facts in the eye—we were running out of money.

It was 2009, and the world was in the throes of a Great Recession. I flew back to the US to go on a series of fundraising tours to meet our increasing budgetary needs. We needed $75,000 to build a well, water tower, and sewage system to turn Villa Soleada into a livable community. We needed money to run our operations. Over the months, we had hired friends from the US to help us with things like technology, budgeting, receipts, and communications. That meant we had to spend money on payroll, insurance, travel reimbursements, and office equipment. I hadn't planned for any of that, and Doris's seed funding was running out. That year, Doris decided to stop funding all international causes to focus her philanthropic efforts domestically.

Despite the global recession, I was determined to rescue our finances. After spending a couple of days with family, I took my rickety, 1994 Toyota Tercel on the road. With a sleeping bag and cooler full of lunch meats and bread, I visited our chapters at UMW, William & Mary, University of Virginia, Georgetown, and Virginia Tech to teach them the campus fundraising blueprint and help with events. The chapter members coordinated speaking engagements, sleeping arrangements, and hot meals for me, making my trips pleasant and comfortable. It was much more complicated to visit universities where we didn't have chapters. I rarely got responses to my cold calls and emails, which meant that I would show up unannounced, post flyers, slide letters under doors, strike up conversations with random students, and set up coffee meetings with anyone interested. On more than one occasion, campus security guards caught me and escorted me out.

In each city, I gave myself a ten-dollar-per-day budget to figure out what to eat and where to sleep. During my first night in Greensboro, North Carolina, I couldn't find a couch to crash on. Friends and staff had been joining me during certain weeks of the road tour, but that night, I was alone. I parked the Tercel in a grocery store parking lot and crawled into the backseat. I bundled up inside my sleeping bag, made sure all the doors were locked, and stayed as quiet as possible. Every time a car drove by, I held my breath. I knew that if the cops caught me, they would ask me to leave. As I pulled a dusty blanket over my face, I wondered how the families back in Siete de Abril felt when they went to bed each night. For them, the fear of getting kicked out was permanent.

When I woke up, I found a gym and convinced the guy at the counter to give me a free trial pass. It was rejuvenating to work out, take a hot shower, and brush my teeth. After I thanked the guy at the counter, I walked back to the car and opened the hood. Oil had been leaking all week, but I didn't have the money to fix the motor. As I watched oil drip down onto the asphalt, I quivered at the thought of someone flicking a lit cigarette under the car.

I drove to a shopping center where I grabbed a free coffee refill, a handful of complimentary condiments packets, and free ice from a soda machine to fill my cooler. As I sat on the concrete sidewalk, sipped my coffee, and made myself a turkey sandwich, I wondered if I was the most frugal nonprofit CEO in the country. Our bank accounts were running out. We needed nothing short of a miracle to survive.

* * *

That miracle came shortly after. I was on yet another campus posting flyers, when my phone rang. "Hi!" said the caller. "This is Lisa from CNN calling. Am I speaking with Shin Fujiyama?"

CNN?

"I'd like to know more about your work in Honduras," said Lisa. She explained that each year, CNN chooses a few ordinary people worldwide doing good. The network highlights their work on *CNN Heroes* and *Larry King Live*, their most-watched and longest-running show. "Someone you gave a ride to from the gym nominated you to be a CNN Hero," she said. I often gave rides to people, so I had no idea who nominated me.

After I answered some questions, Lisa told me that CNN planned to do an extensive background check. Over the weeks, Lisa frequently called while I visited different campuses. I looked up past awardees and their incredible accomplishments, and I couldn't believe they thought I was worthy enough to be on that list.

One day, Lisa asked me a question that put a screeching halt to the vetting process. She wanted to know if I knew of anyone who would accuse the organization or me of wrongdoing. I thought of saying no, but my conscience didn't allow it. I had to be fully transparent and tell her about—let's make up a name here—Pamela, one of HFC's main donors from the US.

My relationship with Pamela started when she contacted me to talk about how we had marketed our fundraising campaigns for HFC. Our messaging had focused on HFC's struggles, which created the sense of urgency that an effective campaign needed. However, Pamela pointed out that we had failed to highlight enough the good work that HFC was doing. She also said that we made HFC's fundraising team (that she was part of) look bad by revealing their funding shortfalls. Pamela was right in many ways. In the tricky business of nonprofit marketing, a message needs to be compelling yet respectful. Our campaign had lacked the latter.

Things got complicated when we started to negotiate with HFC over how we would spend the money we had raised from the first walk-athon. After we financed the building renovations that Sister Tulia had asked for, HFC's Board—which I had never seen or worked with—had asked us to hand over the rest of the money. They wanted HFC to have power to spend the funds at their discretion and pay off various debts we were unaware of. We had planned to spend the money mostly on their children's education; following Doris Buffett's advice, we wanted them to start initiatives that would help them become self-sufficient and leave the debt cycle for good. Due to our differences, we had to go into an exhausting negotiation process. The worst part about it was seeing Sister Tulia, who stayed neutral, stressed out by all of the tension.

We could have avoided the painful situation had I done things differently. I should have been more sensitive with our marketing. I should have been intentional about identifying and developing relationships with different stakeholders involved with HFC. I should have known how difficult it was for HFC to raise funds for their overhead budget and been more accepting of their request. Most importantly, I should have had the foresight to write a memorandum of understanding with HFC before embarking on the fundraising campaign. Cosmo and I recognized our mistakes, and apologized countless times to Pamela and HFC's Board members. We wanted to move forward together, but it was too late.

During the negotiation process, Pamela surprised us by filing a report in the Virginia Department of Consumer Affairs, accusing our organization of misappropriating funds designated for HFC. I had never experienced anything like it. I was confused and scared. We spent countless hours locating and sending records of expenditures and wire transfers to prove that the money had been sent to HFC, despite Pamela's claims. It was a stressful situation that took an emotional toll on everyone in our organization. Some supporters urged us to take the situation to court, but the last thing we wanted was to take an organization we cared deeply about to court or spend months of our lives in expensive hearings. Once the Department examined our records and confirmed that we had not misappropriated funds, they acted as an intermediary to help SHH and HFC decide what to do with the remaining funds. Ultimately, we decided to send HFC the remaining funds and end the partnership. When we went to HFC for the last time to say goodbye, I felt like a part of me died.

After I told CNN about Pamela and gave them her contact information, a massive investigation began. Pamela went further than I had imagined and told CNN that our projects in Honduras didn't actually exist. CNN called Sister Tulia and countless others in El Progreso to see if her allegations were valid. They called our Board members. They called Doris Buffett. They called each of the four girls, including Yapa, who had aged out of HFC and were attending local universities through a scholarship program we had started. I knew the truth was on our side, but I had no idea which side CNN would take. Just like the Virginia Department of Consumer Affairs, CNN examined our financial records to ensure we hadn't misappropriated any funds. In the end, CNN ruled out all of Pamela's allegations. Every single one of them. When Lisa called to congratulate me, I knew that we had done the right thing by confronting the stressful situation head-on.

I was called into the CNN Headquarters in DC for my interview on *Larry King Live*. I was nervous, and couldn't help thinking of others who deserved to be in my place: Sister Tulia, who had been helping the poor for decades. Yalena, who spent her weekends distributing school supplies. Yapa, who was overcoming seemingly insurmountable challenges. They were real heroes.

The CNN headquarters was a giant glass building painted blue and red. When I walked in, the doorman already had a plastic badge with the CNN logo and my name printed on it. I pinned the badge to my chest and told myself to save it to show my parents. A makeup artist led me into a room that looked like a barbershop. After I sat down, she patted a brown powder onto my face, which made me cough. I tried to practice my smile in front of the mirror, but my face muscles were too tense.

Then I was being led out into the interview stage. "Ready?" asked the woman in charge. "We're going live. In three, two, one..."

Larry asked me a series of questions as I glanced at his suspenders. As I answered him, I kept getting distracted by how bright the lights were. I couldn't remember any of the lines I practiced, but I noticed Larry nodding his head to my impromptu answers as if telling me to keep going. So I did. Before I realized it, he was asking me his final question.

"You still want to become a doctor, right?" asked Larry. I was so flattered that he knew a random fact about me, I had to take a deep breath to prevent myself from hyperventilating.

"For now," I replied, "I'm trying to help these other kids become doctors. I think that's my challenge." Larry thanked me for joining him and began to talk to the camera about the evening's next news topic. For Larry, I was just one of the thirty thousand people he had interviewed in his career. For me, it was an unforgettable experience. I couldn't wait to show my parents the badge with the CNN logo on it and tell them about the powder they put all over my face. I had no idea what would happen as a result of the publicity, but I hoped that we would garner enough support to fix the oil leak in the car.

It turned out, *Larry King Live* wasn't a live show. They recorded my episode and told me they would air it sometime soon. My parents and I watched CNN each night that week to see if the episode would air, but after a few days, I had to leave for Honduras. When I arrived at my terminal at Miami International Airport, I couldn't believe it. My *CNN Heroes* episode was airing on TV. I scanned the TVs in the vicinity and saw my powdered-up face on all of them.

I glanced around, wondering if anyone had noticed that the handsome Asian guy on TV was right there next to them. Nobody noticed. They had phone calls to make and magazines to read. Over the weeks, people from all over the country who saw the segment donated. They contacted us to ask how they could get involved or start a chapter of SHH. As school children and even the Japanese Embassy in Honduras offered their help, I started to wonder if divine luck was on our side.

* * *

Divine luck wasn't. We found the money, but Villa Soleada was hit with a series of complications and challenges, so much so that I began to despair we'd ever complete construction.

The first calamity was an act of nature. I was sleeping in our staff house in El Progreso when I heard a strange rumble. Suddenly, the bed began to bounce, as if I were inside an old dryer machine. That night, a 7.3 magnitude earthquake—the strongest ever recorded in the country's history—hit northern Honduras. Plates and glass shattered onto the floor as car alarms went off and people began screaming. When the shaking stopped, I turned on my cell phone's flashlight and bolted out of the building. The staff gathered on the lawn, shaking. We tried to sleep on pieces of cardboard, but the mosquitos and aftershocks kept us awake all night.

When the sun came up, we learned the earthquake had caused seven fatalities and destroyed 130 buildings across northern Honduras. The bridge that connected El Progreso to the rest of the country had collapsed into the river, disrupting the city's economy. And among the victims was a little girl from Siete de Abril. A makeshift wall had collapsed onto her. If the earthquake had happened a couple of months later, she would have been living in Villa Soleada—and would still be with us. We'd invested in steel rebars to increase the tensile strength of Villa Soleada's homes. Every house we had built withstood the earthquake.

We tried to plow forward with the construction, but a few weeks later, the Honduran supreme court and military overthrew President Manuel "Mel" Zelaya and sent him into exile. The government appointed Roberto Micheletti, the politician who had shown up to Villa Soleada's groundbreaking ceremony, as the interim President. As thousands organized protests throughout the country, the government declared Martial Law. Soldiers patrolled the streets and enforced a strict curfew. We stocked up on canned food and tried to figure out how to move forward with the project in the midst of civil unrest.

Things eased up after a while, allowing us to continue work. Our next challenge was bringing running water to Villa Soleada. Too many children at Siete de Abril had gotten sick from drinking cloudy river water. *Houses with running water and plumbing*—that was my promise to Camila.

We consulted with the Building Goodness Foundation (BGF), an organization that specialized in engineering projects, and they identified where we could find an underground aquifer on the property. We brought in a drill to dig a well, and it tunneled through stone—a powerful gush of water rose in its wake. To store the well water, we started building a water tower BGF had designed for us. As the structure grew in height, it got more difficult to carry concrete to the top. After some brainstorming, the men created a pulley system that hoisted buckets of concrete. I didn't like looking up at the top when the fathers were up there; I worried someone would fall.

When we finished the concrete legs and platform, we ran out of money to build the tank. Cosmo used her networking skills and convinced a local farm to donate an old water tank the size of a house.

We rented a crane truck to hoist it onto the tower. The kids crowded together on the sidelines, watching with awe. The crane was the coolest thing they'd ever seen—they talked about it for days.

When the tower was finished, we jumped right into digging trenches for the underground PVC pipes that would connect each building to the water system. The trenches were so sprawling, the village looked like the inside of an ant colony. We dug until our pickaxes snapped, then we fixed them and went back to digging. When they couldn't be fixed, we bought more, and then kept digging. We dug and dug, for months, until we finished the trenches and installed the pipes.

The last step was the electric pump. We installed it over the well, and then Wilfredo excitedly flipped the on button.

"Now!" he yelled.

One by one, people turned on the faucets in homes throughout Villa Soleada. Water sprayed from the faucet in the first home, then the second, and then every single home had running water. People popped out of the houses and thrust their thumbs up high into the air, laughing. The kids yelled in a joyful chorus: *"Tenemos agua! Agua! Agua! Agua!* We have water! Water! Water! Water!"

We moved on to the bathrooms. Without a system that would chain together a water, hygiene, and wastewater management system, the community would be unlivable. After all, 80 percent of diseases in low-income countries were related to poor water and sanitation conditions. Worldwide, one out of every five deaths under the age of five is due to a preventable, water-related disease, such as diarrhea, dysentery, typhoid, and cholera.[11] Some of the community members suggested installing pit latrines at each house, just like in Siete de Abril. It was low cost, and therefore tempting. But we knew such toilets would discharge waste straight into a pit, and the sludge could leach out and contaminate the well water. We also knew that, during heavy flooding, the pits could fill up and overflow, which would be a public health disaster.

BGF worked with engineers from El Progreso to come up with a plan for us. They proposed installing waste stabilization ponds, which were large basins in which raw sewage could be treated entirely by natural processes involving algae and bacteria. They required only sunlight and minimum supervision for daily operation. According to the engineers, we needed two ponds with clay lining that would connect to each other. One would be "anaerobic" and the other "facultative." I didn't fully understand what those words meant or the science behind the system, but I understood enough to know that the ponds would treat and destroy pathogens in the water. Essentially, we needed to build two poop ponds.

To create the poop ponds, we laid sewage pipes at specific angles in the trenches and built several manholes with underground utility vaults. We thought of digging the two ponds with shovels, but when the engineers explained how deep the ponds needed to be, we decided to rent excavators. After a couple of phone calls, heavy construction equipment drove into Villa Soleada to begin digging.

When the kids played in the dirt piles that the machines created, they found earth-colored objects that looked like trash from a clandestine landfill. It turned out, the objects were pieces of clay pottery, arrowheads, and ancient artifacts. They must have been from some indigenous tribe, perhaps the Mayans, that inhabited the area hundreds of years before us. We were picking up pieces of the past; once upon a time, this was someone's ancient home.

The constructors didn't leave the dirt as is. When they completed the two ponds, they moved the excavated dirt to the middle of the community and flattened it. That elevated surface became a source of pride and joy: a soccer field.

* * *

The challenges of building Villa Soleada were not only political or practical in nature. Socioeconomic and cultural issues ran deep, often across generations, and they complicated straightforward progress.

Like Tenaza.

Tenaza was a quiet father from the community who spent his days as a car mechanic. When he got high on drugs, he became violent and unpredictable. He would cut up water pipes, burn down whatever bothered him, and sabotage community projects. Today he was standing in the middle of the soccer field, screaming incoherently. "The apocalypse is arriving!" he yelled. He stumbled towards the organization's truck and pulled what looked like an ice pick out of his back pocket. He stared at the vehicle, yelled unintelligibly about devils, and stabbed the truck tires. Then his eyes rolled back, his mouth foamed, and he passed out. His wife pulled him into the shade, crying softly. The community members, used to Tenaza's outbursts, shook their heads and continued with the construction.

The following day, Tenaza hung his head and cried. He didn't have the money to replace the tires, but he promised to fix the car if it came across mechanical problems. His long-term struggle with addiction started when he was teenager, when he experimented with all kinds of drugs to dull the pain and shame that accompanied poverty. Now he was hooked, and couldn't stop. I had heard similar stories in the community. Many people at Siete de Abril struggled with substance abuse, which seemed to pass down from one generation to the next. His wife trembled: "Please don't kick us out of the program. Have mercy on us."

Not everyone was keen to give him another chance. "His outbursts are costing the organization too much money!" "We can't have him on the project." "He's slowin' us all down!" But eventually, we let him stay. It was kind Wilfredo who put it best: "If we kick people out because they're flawed or have problems with addiction, none of us would be here."

Substance abuse wasn't as pervasive a problem as violence. In Honduras, people carried machetes and guns, often as protection but sometimes as a form of intimidation. Madesto, a father with a toothbrush mustache, was the most striking example of this. He was hardworking and rarely took breaks, but if he disagreed with you—well, he was more likely to pull out his gun than talk things through.

And it wasn't just empty bravado. There was an element of bullying there. When the community voted to ban machetes and guns at the meetings because they were tired of being threatened into making certain decisions, Madesto wouldn't yield. "I'm not getting pushed around," he said, pulling out his .38 revolver and pointing it at our heads. "We should be able to bring whatever we want to these meetings." The more people avoided his gaze, the wider he grinned. We voted for a no-weapons policy, but there was no way to enforce it on guys like Madesto.

That evening, Madesto drank a bottle of Honduran moonshine and punched one of the teenage boys much smaller than him. When the boy hit back, Madesto pulled out his .38 and grabbed the boy by the throat. He clobbered him in the face repeatedly with the back of his loaded gun. Bones broke. Blood spurted everywhere. People had to jump in to stop Madesto from killing the boy.

We asked Madesto to leave the project. Even though we felt bad that his wife and daughter would have to leave with him, he was a direct threat to everyone's safety. But Madesto barricaded himself inside one of the half-constructed homes. "This is going to be my house," he yelled, "and anyone who tries to take this away will see a bullet between their eyes!" He continued to show up at the construction site to show us that he was still a part of the project. It was surreal to shovel concrete next to someone who had repeatedly pointed a gun at my head.

We contacted the police. They agreed to arrest Madesto for what he had done to the boy, but they didn't have a vehicle that week—we would need to drive the officers in our truck. It was a terrible request, given that we didn't want Madesto to find out who had reported him. If officers arrested him in *our* vehicle, it would be more than obvious we had contacted the authorities. But we had no choice. Alex Escobar, our CFO, picked up four officers who arrested Madesto.

"He won't see the light of day for a long time," a senior officer said as he escorted Madesto into jail. Somehow, not even twenty-four hours later, Madesto strolled back into Villa Soleada. "Whoever called the police is a dead man!" he yelled. We told Alex to stay away from Madesto for his own safety.

To celebrate his return, Madesto went to Barrio de Amistad, the community adjacent to Villa Soleada. He got drunk at the neighborhood bar and picked a fight with some gang members. In El Progreso, causing trouble in someone else's turf is a death sentence. Madesto was shot a few days later as he rode out of the community on his bicycle.

Madesto lives because Alex, the very Alex that Madesto threatened to kill, happened to drive by. He rushed Madesto to the hospital. Madesto's wife began preparing for a funeral, but he survived.

When Madesto called a month later and asked me to meet him, his voice was weaker than I remembered. I was hesitant at first, as I was almost certain he believed I hired the assassins, but I agreed to meet him at a coffee shop. When he arrived, he walked with a limp and had a cast on his arm. He trembled as he told me about the shooting, his eyes tearing up. Even though he had bullied everyone in the community, I felt bad for him. Madesto used his macho demeanor to hide whatever chip he had on his shoulder; now, even that had been taken from him. "If you buy a house for my family elsewhere," he said, "we'll leave peacefully."

There were concerns about the precedent we would set if we agreed to Madesto's proposition. But in the end, I agreed to his request so he could go somewhere far, far away. We bought a house worth a few thousand dollars for him, and he never returned to Villa Soleada.

* * *

The homes were built and the water system completed. All we needed to figure out now was how to connect Villa Soleada to the city's electrical grid. When I discovered that communities had to buy and install their own utility poles in Honduras, I knew we were in trouble. We had run out of money. Everything about the construction process cost us more than we had projected. Then somehow, President Micheletti—who grew up in El Progreso and had joined us for the groundbreaking ceremony on that rainy day—learned that we were on the last stretch of the project. He surprised us by sending a donation to pay for our electric supplies. We couldn't believe it. As soon as the check arrived, we ordered truckloads of utility poles, wires, transformers, and streetlamps. We dug holes throughout the community and cemented the poles into them.

Weeks later, we finished the installation. Technicians wearing yellow helmets connected the system to the city's grid. *Bzz. Bzzzz. Bzzzzzzzzzz!* Every lamp in the village lit up in unison. *"Ya tenemos luz! Luz! Luz! Luz!"* yelled the children. "We now have light. Light! Light! Light!"

I found Camila, now twelve years old. I told her that the lamps gave the village a yellowish-orange glow, like the color inside her green oranges. She laughed; she felt like we were on top of a giant Christmas cake, with candles lit all around us. "We can now play *fútbol* all night!" yelled Wilfredo. "My daughter can finally study under a lamp!" said Mauricio. As we hugged each other, I knew we only had one thing left to do. Celebrate.

In December 2009, two years after the groundbreaking ceremony, we gathered on a patch of grass to celebrate Villa Soleada's inauguration. Families, staff, and supporters had worked tirelessly despite countless obstacles to build this haven. As I looked at the setting sun, green palm trees turning black against a dimming sky, my eyes began to water. Together, we had crossed the finish line.

Dago brought out a giant pig the size of a boar. "Don't look," he said as he hit the pig in the head with a hammer and slit its throat. The women put the pig on to roast, handing out pork chops and pork belly soup. Cosmo brought out a portable radio and started a dance party. Doña Nibia, the oldest grandma of the community, grabbed me by the hands to dance with me. As the radio blasted bachata music, women sang along, men drank Salva Vida beers, and everyone danced.

After the party, we gathered around a straw hat. Each family picked a number from the hat to determine which house was theirs. Wilfredo clapped his hands with joy when he learned his new house was right in front of the soccer field. Juanita was happy that her house was in a quiet corner at the back, away from any noise that could distract her from her studies. Camila was ecstatic. Her house was right in the middle of the community.

Camila and her family walked me to their house. Like all the other homes, it had a wooden door in the middle and two windows to the sides. "*Como mi dibujo.* Just like my drawing," said Camila as she peeked through the door. We went inside, and she kept flushing the toilet to see how it worked. Then we all lay down on the smooth, concrete floor. Camila and her siblings poked each other, rolling around and laughing. I looked up at the steel roof and thought back on how, for years, Camila and her friends lived in makeshift houses without access to running water, sewage, land titles, or electricity. I knew that they would have all their basic needs met at Villa Soleada, and knew even more that we had proven that the cycle of generational poverty in Honduras was breakable. Camila would now be walking around with textbooks in her arms, instead of baskets of oranges. I grinned from ear to ear.

BOOK 3

---- CHAPTER NINE ----

INFRASTRUCTURE IS NOT ENOUGH

AN OLD TRUCK FOR A POTATO CHIP COMPANY WOVE INTO Villa Soleada to drop off boxes at a corner shop. It drove past children playing with dogs and cats, women rolling dough to make breakfast tortillas, and men drinking Cafe Oro with hefty scoops of sugar. Suddenly, an armed assailant jumped in front of the truck and pointed a 9mm in the air. "Get outta the truck! Now!" A second assailant pointed a pistol at the delivery guy in the passenger seat. A third pointed a revolver at the driver. All three of them had ski masks on, but they were wearing shoes and shirts the residents recognized.

Just like that, the heist began.

Mothers dropped their tortillas and men stopped sipping their coffee. Kids ran inside their homes and closed the doors. A grandmother and her two grandkids remained in their plastic chairs just a few feet away from the heist, too petrified to move. They closed their eyes and covered their mouths.

Two delivery men wearing potato chip hats hurried out of the truck, their hands up.

"Here! Take it!" the driver yelled in a trembling voice, holding out a wad of cash. The shortest of the thugs grabbed the cash and began sifting through their captors' pockets. He took their cell phones and slid them into his back pocket.

"On the ground and on your stomachs! Where's the rest of the money? Where is it?" he yelled, kicking the driver.

Another gangster shoved his hands under the driver's seat.

"Look! It's right here!" he yelled, pulling out a wad of cash. "You thought you could hide the money from us!?" He, too, kicked the driver.

"Now get outta here!" screamed the short one. The driver and his delivery man jumped into their truck and sped away.

"¡*Vamos!* Let's go!" yelled the short thug as he stuck his revolver in his leather belt. The three men dashed into the thick palm field that hugged the east side of the village. By the time the grandmother and her granddaughters opened their eyes, the three assailants were gone.

* * *

I hadn't seen Camila or her siblings on the soccer field for a few weeks now, and I was worried. When Camila's mom invited me over, I accepted gratefully. As I walked through the community to her house, I noticed a group of teenage boys smoking marijuana and laughing near the field. Nearly all of them had dropped out of school by the time they moved into Villa Soleada. They waved. I waved back, wondering how we could get them back into school.

Camila was waiting for me at the door. Her mom, Alvera, brought over a steaming cup of coffee and her stepfather, Orlando, shook my hand solemnly. We drank coffee, ate *semitas*—Honduran sweet bread that looks like half a hot dog bun with sugar on top of it—and talked about the weather. Then Alvera broke the news.

"We're leaving."

"Leaving?" I replied, spilling a bit of coffee. "For how long?"

I looked over at Camila and her brothers playing jacks on the concrete floor.

"*Para siempre.* Forever," Alvera said.

"The *LMDVS* want us out," Orlando whispered. "They said they were going to kill us if we don't leave."

The families who moved into Villa Soleada brought with them old mattresses, iron pots, sewing machines, memories of Hurricane Mitch, sofas rehabilitated multiple times, a mighty work ethic, punctured soccer balls patched up with glue and tape, Bibles passed down from grandparents—and gang affiliations. The LMDVS was a gang of young men who used to hold people up, deal drugs, and break into houses back at Siete de Abril. When they moved into their new homes at Villa Soleada, they brought their guns and criminal activities with them. They spent their afternoons doing drugs and hanging out on the dirt road that separated Villa Soleada from Barrio de Amistad, the neighboring community. People referred to this area as the Alley and avoided it. The bushes and weeds grew so tall there, the lights from the streetlamps couldn't penetrate the area.

"They've been holding people up at the Alley," said Orlando. "This month, they mugged a pizza delivery guy, a church pastor, and several people visiting Villa Soleada." The leader of all this was Equis, an eighteen-year-old who controlled the drug trade in the neighborhood. According to Orlando, Equis held people up at gunpoint for a living.

Now the LMDVS had allied with the LMB, a bigger gang in Barrio de Amistad. They worked together to organize muggings, burglaries, and hijack buses. "Things are going to get worse," Orlando said. The

LMDVS had sent death threats to several families in Villa Soleada, not just his. Camila, who was quietly listening, stopped her game of jacks and began to sob. "Once a Mara takes over a neighborhood, you have to abide by their rules," said Orlando. I couldn't believe it. The family had just moved into the house.

"The situation will calm down," I said. "It has to."

It did not. The gunshots, drug deals, and holdups in Villa Soleada escalated. Taxi drivers stopped entering the community.

The parents of Villa Soleada asked us to build a school to give their children an alternative to violence. Our student chapters in the US raised funds, and the parents built a small school with round pillars and a beautiful porch. As I expected, running the school was more challenging than building it. Students often missed classes, came to school hungry, or fell ill. Many behaved defiantly or were unable to focus because of something that happened back home. Our long-term vision and curriculum were ill-defined, and the monthly costs to run the school were higher than we anticipated. The budget shortfall meant we lacked teachers, supplies, and extracurricular activities.

While I struggled to figure out how to run the school, Camila's family quietly left. Their empty house was broken into by burglars, who stole the light bulbs, interior doors, and window frames. They even ripped the ceramic toilet off the concrete floor. When I walked through the ransacked house, I wanted to throw up. The whole thing reminded me of *City of God*, a movie about a government housing project in Brazil that turned into the most violent and drug-riddled slum in the country. Villa Soleada was turning into a Honduran City of God.

Hopeless, I sat down in Camila's empty room. It seemed so long ago that she'd come to me with that drawing: a house with two windows, a door in the middle, orange trees on the side. I thought I'd given it to her. I thought we'd done it. But the plan was always naive. I had believed that by providing housing and basic infrastructure, families could lift themselves out of generational poverty. They couldn't. We had done nothing about the challenges further upstream, like substance abuse, school desertion, unemployment, illiteracy, family breakdown, and gang violence. All of these now threatened the community's future. My head ached when I thought of all the fundraising events our volunteers had organized and the months of grueling work the families had put into the project. Enthusiasm wasn't enough. Working in solidarity with the community wasn't enough. And now our work in Villa Soleada was about to be laid to waste.

* * *

During the dark and difficult time that followed, I often thought of my meeting with Christina.

It was at the Millennium Campus Conference in the US, an annual gathering where youth leaders and organizations from around the world discussed poverty and climate change. My team and I were at the last activity, an interest fair, when a woman approached our table. I recognized her from our workshops as Christina. She wanted to grab a quick coffee to talk about SHH.

Anyone we could convert to our cause was a win as far as I was concerned, so I put on a jacket over my faded polo shirt and joined her. I couldn't stay long because I needed to help man the table, but I was excited to answer her questions about Honduras. I sipped my coffee, but was clumsy due to lack of sleep, and a splash of hot liquid spilled onto my hands. I wanted to shout in pain, but I clenched my teeth and remained as composed as possible. Christina put her coffee cup down.

"How do you know you're not doing more harm than good?" she asked.

"I'm sorry?" I shook my burning hand in the air and tried to hide my panic.

"Here's the thing." Her face turned serious. "I hear of so many foreign organizations taking away jobs in developing countries like Honduras, constructing shoddy buildings, and imposing projects that the local people don't need or want."

She looked right at me and waited for a response.

"I've read about those organizations too," I said, trying to find the right words. I wanted to explain to her that we've made it a priority to create jobs, our buildings withstood a magnitude 7.2 earthquake, and community members are involved in the planning process. But I was nervous, sleep-deprived, and my hand hurt.

As I fumbled with my thoughts and she continued like an investigative journalist, I remembered an argumentation technique called attacking the straw man. I wondered if that was what she was doing. It's when someone oversimplifies an idea and then attacks that oversimplified version. As the conversation carried on, Christina's energy began to rise. The opposite happened to me, and my shoulders started to slump. "I'm jaded by the entire development aid industry," she said. "I'm starting to think that it's all about Westerners patting themselves on the back when all they're doing is perpetuating imperialism. Paternalism. Dependency." She stared at me for what felt like an eternity.

"It's hard not to feel that way." I thought of Villa Soleada's ongoing poverty, illiteracy, and violence. I thought about our lackluster, directionless school in the community. The building was beautiful, but the results inside were mediocre at best. "I often wonder the same."

"Even if your project succeeds, don't you think it will be too small of a dent?"

Her comment hurt. I didn't know what to say. She smiled triumphantly, said goodbye, and left. I felt like I'd just been pummeled for twelve rounds inside a boxing ring. I'd gone into this meeting hoping to convince Christina of our organization's worthiness, and the opposite happened. How?

The conversation left me with a feeling I knew all too well. It was how I felt when my classmates in sixth grade laughed at my attempt at reciting "The Road Not Taken," when the hecklers in the stands made fun of my soccer jersey being too big, when I showed up to a homecoming dance and sat quietly in the corner. I couldn't put a word to it, but it was all consuming. It's how I felt in the weeks and months after Camila's family left Villa Soleada, and SHH began to fall apart.

Our team at SHH was now nearly ten employees. Most were idealistically motivated young people from the US who joined us in Honduras. In the beginning, we enjoyed a positive work culture and everyone got along. However, as the months went by, negativity and petty office politics began to overshadow the team's optimism. I even hired people from the for-profit world who were much smarter than me to fix the situation, but that didn't work. Now almost everyone was planning on quitting. Things had gotten so bad, I even heard rumors about an employee who wanted to oust me and another who wanted to start an organization nearly identical to ours—and take our donors with them. I felt like I was on a ship with countless holes at the bottom. Water was gushing in, and I didn't know if I should be scooping the water out or fixing the holes—or jumping out. The boat was sinking.

I can tell you in hindsight that the root of our problems came down to one thing: leadership. A team working under pressure needs a strong leader who gives out clear job descriptions, creates systems and structures, and inspires the team with a long-term vision. A competent leader makes their people feel heard, appreciated, and supported. As an inexperienced Executive Director, I didn't know how to do any of those things. I did my best and worked hard, but leadership isn't one of those things that you can attain by simply working harder.

I made the mistake of asking staff members to burn their candles on both ends, which smoldered their energy and commitment. We all worked seven days a week and faced chronic stressors like random violence, disease, civil unrest, culture shock, separation from friends and family, and constant blackouts. The low salary, which at first felt like a rite of passage, quickly became a source of hardship. After working at Villa Soleada for months and years, the results were disillusioning. The upstream factors that kept people poor nullified our efforts; we were losing the battle. To add to everyone's frustrated idealism and stress level, Pamela had made another round of complaints to the Virginia Department of Consumer Affairs. Our team had to spend hours on the phone to clear her accusations. We went to bed each night worried that the government would shut us down over one lost receipt. Our team was experiencing widespread burnout.

Burnout is a state of emotional exhaustion caused by long-term exposure to overly demanding work pressures and chronic stressors. It causes people to become cynical about their occupation and the people they work with, as well as doubtful of their own competency. The heartbreaking irony is that the intensity of an employee's burnout mirrors the intensity of their original commitment and idealism.

Burnout is a serious problem in the humanitarian aid industry. A cross-sectional study in Uganda found that 68 percent of humanitarian aid workers serving in Uganda reported symptom levels associated with high risk for depression; 53 percent suffered from anxiety disorders; and 26 percent from posttraumatic stress disorder (PTSD).[12] Another study from Geneva found that aid workers faced disturbingly high levels of emotional exhaustion, depersonalization, alcohol consumption, psychological distress, and a low sense of personal achievement.[13] According to the study done in Uganda, higher levels of social support, stronger team cohesion, and reduced exposure to chronic stressors were associated with improved mental health.

At the time, I had no idea what burnout was, nor had I put in the effort to address it as a reality for our team. Over the coming weeks, our staff members left one by one. We were left without anyone running our programs, maintaining our website, inputting receipts, or answering incoming messages. As I tried to figure out how to keep the organization afloat, Cosmo dropped a bombshell.

She was leaving. She was too depleted to continue—she was taking an indefinite break and moving to New York. I didn't say much when she told me. I just sat there, thinking of all the meals shared, the nights out, the milestones we had reached together. I remembered how we celebrated when we made payroll and rent during our hardest months. I thought of all we had experienced in Villa Soleada together and all that was left to do. I was confused, and I was disillusioned.

I should have shown empathy. Cosmo had worked twelve-hour days. She worked weekends. She had supported others emotionally when she herself was running on an empty tank. I should have accepted her departure as I did everyone else's. I should have understood—even celebrated her contribution. But I was young back then, and my fear of having to do everything alone brought out the worst version of myself. I did something I'd never imagined I'd do to a sister. I stopped speaking to Cosmo.

Cosmo flew out, and I realized everything was coming to an end. I spent days walking around town aimlessly and waking up to recurring nightmares of a samurai committing *seppuku*—a form of Japanese ritual suicide by disembowelment. To distract myself, I spent hours at the gym. I hid in my room and watched YouTube videos.

Bob called. He was planning to come down in the winter with a group of supporters who wanted to learn about Villa Soleada and invest in us. He had found someone who could help with our website and others who could help with fundraising. "There's a way to fix this all," he said. "I know there is."

I listened quietly, a sob lodged at the back of my throat. Bob was trying hard to encourage me and keep the organization afloat. I knew that. He was optimistic, relentless. But we would not make it to the winter.

I hung up and then called the last three employees of SHH: Aricela, Ingrid, and Gonzalo. All of them were Honduran. I asked them to meet me at the office in an hour. It was time to tell them to look for new jobs.

* * *

Aricela and Ingrid arrived first. Gonzalo, our driver, came soon after, slipping off his sunglasses and taking a seat. Everyone was quiet as I finished brewing the coffee and poured it into cups. How I would miss Honduran coffee.

I didn't sugarcoat it; I just told them everything. The dire state of our organization. How all our staff members had left. The lack of funds, the impossibility of continuing. If they were shocked, they didn't show it. They sipped their coffee, and stared at the floor.

"So," I joked, "how did everyone else's weekend go?"

They ignored my poor attempt at humor. Ingrid, who worked as an assistant at SHH, raised her hand. "Now that all the Americans have left," she said, "why don't we build a team of local Hondurans?"

I paused. I had genuinely not thought of it. In fact, I hadn't put much thought into our hiring process at all. Over the years, I had basically hired American friends who asked for a job. They were hardworking but they struggled with the language, culture shock, homesickness, and stressors that came with living in Honduras. Few of them lasted more than a year, which meant that we spent a lot of time finding replacements and training new staff members. What would our organization look like if it was run by local Hondurans who understood the language, culture, and communities better than any foreigner? We would be creating jobs in a city with a high unemployment rate. I couldn't see any downsides.

"Give us Hondurans a chance," Ingrid continued. "What's there to lose? We can run SHH's on-the-ground operations so that you can focus on fundraising. Sometimes life calls upon us to rebuild, Shin. Let us help you rebuild."

Rebuild. It was a concept the Hondurans were very familiar with; so much in their lives crumbled quickly and had to be made again. Ingrid herself had to rebuild her life when she left the orphanage she grew up in, when Hurricane Mitch destroyed the city, when she lost her job at the textile factory. And she did it with the same resilience all Hondurans possessed—I wish I had a quarter of it.

Gonzalo, a soft-hearted father who looked like a gangster because of his shaved head and red-rimmed eyes, was speaking now. He reminded me of how far we had come—we had overcome civil unrest, earthquakes, and construction issues to build an entire community on what was once a patch of dirt. "People said it couldn't be done, and we proved them wrong! If we give up now, all that work could go to waste!"

Aricela was nodding vigorously, her braids shaking. "How can we turn our backs on the families at Villa Soleada? We spent two years setting the groundwork for them to break out of the cycle of poverty—and now we leave?"

I had never considered our work at Villa Soleada as groundwork. I'd seen it as the endpoint, and either it succeeded or it failed. But if you looked at it like this...then it was okay that there was more to do. It was *expected* that there was more to do.

In that office, for the first time in weeks, I felt a warm glow in my chest. While I was wasting time wallowing in my failure, Ingrid, Aricela, and Gonzalo had been trying to scoop water out of the boat. We could do this. With local Hondurans, there was a chance to rebuild the organization afresh, to correct mistakes, and move forward properly.

I downed my coffee—it seemed like I would be drinking a lot more of it after all. It was time to try for a comeback.

CHAPTER TEN

BE INTENTIONAL ABOUT WHO YOU SURROUND YOURSELF WITH

WITH THE HELP OF INGRID, ARICELA, AND GONZALO, I began rebuilding the organization. Aricela's words kept ringing in my head. *We spent two years setting the groundwork...* If what we had created so far in Villa Soleada was the groundwork, then what came next? How did we build on this to truly tackle generational poverty?

It was difficult to find the answer—the whole thing was a Gordian knot. But I got a glimpse of the possible vision for SHH in an unlikely place: a movie theater. I was back in the US, visiting my parents in Virginia. My mom and I went on a movie date to see *Waiting for Superman*, a documentary about the broken state of education in the US. Mom rarely watched movies but she was a teacher, and I thought she might enjoy this one.

We both loved it, but it's safe to say I was the one more transformed. The movie introduced me to Geoffrey Canada, the founder of the

Harlem Children's Zone (HCZ). He grew up in a low-income neighborhood in Harlem that was torn apart by crime, drugs, and decades of poverty—the kind of neighborhood that countless kids in Honduras grow up in. After becoming an educator, Canada wanted to find out if the challenges he faced were solvable. He began experimenting, and spent his life developing a program that he called the cradle-to-college pipeline.

Canada's idea was simple: address not just one challenge but *every challenge* in the community simultaneously—education, parenting practices, and even the nutrition content of what kids ate at home. It was about providing comprehensive interventions at each stage of a child's life, starting at age zero and then connecting those interventions into an "unbroken chain of support." The program worked. HCZ was sending kids to college, helping them—and the entire neighborhood—break the cycle of generational poverty. It was powerful to hear Canada speak. HCZ was unlike anything I had ever seen.

Mom and I talked about the documentary the entire car ride home. A question had been bouncing around in my head since Canada appeared on the screen, so I just came out and asked it.

"Do you think we could do it? Create a cradle-to-college pipeline in Villa Soleada?"

We didn't have the support HCZ had, nor was SHH led by someone as smart and capable as Geoffrey Canada. But if we could…

"I like it," my mom said slowly. She saw my face and said, "I mean it, I do. All organizations start out small, HCZ included. Reach for it. Take it one step at a time."

We talked about all the mentors who had influenced me as I was growing up—Coach Peas, for instance. I wouldn't have any belief in myself if it hadn't been for Coach Peas. And Our Little Roses…look at everything that organization was doing for children like Ani simply through mentorship and care. That first visit to Honduras had such an impact on me because I saw what a difference they were making. Our Little Roses had started small too: Diane Frade had visited Honduras with her husband, met kids who had been abandoned, orphaned, or abused, and decided to help. She began by renting a small apartment to provide housing and education for ten girls who had nowhere to turn. Over the years, she built a home for seventy-five girls, hired local Hondurans to run the organization, opened a school, and ran family strengthening programs in the area.

What if we could give the children in Villa Soleada that kind of support—coaching, guidance, a set trajectory and pipeline out of poverty? Talking to Mom about it filled me with hope and excitement. Maybe it *was* possible to replicate the HCZ methodology in Honduras. Maybe Villa Soleada, which had a 0 percent high school graduation rate, could reach a 100 percent graduation rate one day.

There was only one way to find out.

* * *

Back in Honduras, I went for a run. As I hit the pavement, I shuffled through all the leadership podcasts I had on my iPod. I found one with John Maxwell, the world's leading expert on leadership, and pressed the play button. "Change is inevitable," said Maxwell into my ears. "Growth is optional." I hid the iPod in my sweaty boxers and sprinted past the central park in El Progreso. The street vendors looked at me funny— back then, you didn't see too many people going for jogs in Honduras.

As I ran through the city, I thought about something that Dad and I used to do back in high school. After each of my soccer games, Dad would sit me down and make me go through a *hanseikai*, a Japanese ritual where immediately after a game or project, you acknowledge your mistakes publicly and pledge improvement. The hanseikais were hard on my ego. I remembered scoring a goal against Robert E. Lee High

School during my senior year and hoping that Dad would want to talk at the dinner table about how incredible my goal was. I should have known better. No mistake I made escaped Dad. That night, he wanted to talk about the shots I had missed in the second half that could have given us a victory. He reminded me that I had choked when it most counted. I knew Dad was right, but as a kid, I resented him for not giving me a word of praise or one nod of approval. Because I had a big ego at the time, I didn't like to examine, confront, and take ownership of my deficiencies. I didn't like to talk about the things I was scared to do or hated about myself. Dad's words were so hard on my self-esteem that that night and many other nights during a hanseikai, I cried. It took me years to realize how valuable the hanseikais were. By the time I went on the run through El Progreso, I was ready to go through the biggest hanseikai of my life.

When I got home, I took a shower and began to reread passages I had highlighted in Paul Tough's *Whatever It Takes: Geoffrey Canada's Quest to Change Harlem and America*. I had bought the book soon after watching *Waiting for Superman*; it was a biography of Geoffrey Canada and a history book on urban poverty. It was also a three-hundred-page antipoverty blueprint. According to Canada, poverty is a disease that infected entire communities through unemployment, violence, failing schools, poor health, and broken homes. To cure the disease, his organization couldn't just treat the symptoms in isolation. They had to heal the entire community. Canada believed that effective schools were important, but not enough; these neighborhoods also needed community services, like community centers, free legal services, financial counseling, and family strengthening programs. HCZ's continuum of programs was comprehensive. They gave parents in the community intensive parenting training before children were even born. They got infants into their preschools at an early age. They had kids go through a series of schools with extended class hours, high standards, and layers of support. The organization went to great lengths for their children and families—and asked them to do the same. Barack Obama was so impressed with the HCZ model, he campaigned to replicate it throughout the US. For me, the book was a treasure chest of wisdom.

After I put the book down, I brewed a giant pot of coffee and began to call friends in El Progreso to let them know that SHH was hiring. We were looking for a chief financial officer, logistics coordinator, and various program directors. I looked at my to-do list with all of the administrative tasks I had put on the back burner for months. I needed to create systems, protocols, checklists, and structure in the organization. These were all things that were so dry they made me want to throw up, but because I didn't have a big team to manage anymore, I had the time to knock them out.

The hiring process went well. As Ingrid, Aricela, and Gonzalo suggested, we hired several young people from the city who started as local volunteers. One of them, Faustina, eventually became our CFO. Another, Hector, helped us run our volunteer program. We had also hired Marco, a local foreman who supervised all of our construction projects. Together, we began rebuilding SHH.

Meanwhile, I pondered Canada's cradle-to-college system and how we could implement it in Villa Soleada. The first step seemed to be improving the school so that we could put as many children as possible on a path towards becoming first-generation high school graduates and passing the college entrance exam. While at a conference on sustainable development, I met representatives from Bilingual Education for Central America (BECA), a renowned organization that runs bilingual schools throughout Honduras. I exchanged a series of e-mails with their executive director and visited their school in Cofradia. The curriculum, teacher training program, and methodology they'd created were impressive. As I did more research, I began to understand the value of a bilingual education in Honduras. According to a 2008 paper published in Princeton's *Journal of Public & International Affairs*, students in Honduras mostly attended public school.[14] A small portion of students (4.1 percent) who could afford monthly tuition attended private schools. These institutions were generally better equipped, better staffed, and offered a higher quality of education than the public schools. Families in Honduras that were even wealthier sent their children to an even more expensive and prestigious kind of school: the private bilingual school. These institutions taught intensive English in addition to the required core courses. In Honduras, it was common knowledge that those fluent in English had access to significantly better-paying jobs. Yet in a country with widespread poverty, private bilingual schools were out of reach for most. Monthly tuition for such schools was so high (generally hundreds of dollars per month), only 2.1 percent of the country's students attended them.

I ran the numbers: a typical family in Honduras may survive on one minimum wage (about $380 per month in 2020). They may spend fifty dollars on rent, thirty dollars on utilities, twenty dollars on cell phone bills, and two hundred dollars on food each month. That leaves just eighty dollars for school supplies, transportation, medical bills, clothes, birthday celebrations, and other extemporary items. For the poor, sending their children to a private bilingual school is practically impossible.

But we could change that.

After a series of long phone calls and site visits, we formed a partnership with BECA. In exchange for an annual fee, they agreed to run the school for us whenever we were ready. Together, we started to envision a cradle-to-college bilingual school that would eventually go from preschool through high school. I wanted to create a school that would offer extracurricular activities, tutoring services, computer classes, health services, mentorships, and free lunches to students who needed them. The plan was to support the kids from Villa Soleada through college. It would take a massive amount of funding to make it happen, but we were fired up to take on the challenge. After we signed a Memorandum of Agreement, BECA brought some of their students to visit Villa Soleada. Their students sang a few songs and showcased their English skills in front of our families. Parents were impressed and excited at the idea of their children becoming bilingual. We wanted to move forward quickly, but the amount of legal work we needed to file to open a bilingual school in Honduras was discouraging. It took countless documents and hundreds of signatures from different officials. We filed paperwork, created a building design, and got cost estimates. The process was painfully slow.

SHH was thriving though. For the first time, we had operations checklists, clear job descriptions, HR policies, a team calendar, and a sense of direction. Our growth in the US was even better. By then, SHH had chapters in approximately fifty schools and colleges across the nation. As we let supporters know about our plans to transition our school into a bilingual school, they began to organize fundraising events. Funds poured in, the families at Villa Soleada started building new classrooms, and BECA began to hire teachers for our soon-to-be bilingual school.

But nothing in Honduras is ever simple. I had to make a crucial decision: what grades did we want to open the school with? I wanted as many kids as possible to benefit from the school, but BECA warned me of the dangers of opening the school with more grades than our young team could handle. Growing the school slowly, I was told, would allow us to build up our experience and ensure a higher-quality program in the long run.

I didn't know what to do. I'd seen so many kids in the community grow up. I'd been to their birthday parties, played soccer with them, played marbles with them. Many of them used to walk around with slingshots in their pockets. Now, some of them walked around with .32-caliber revolvers. We were watching them go down the wrong path.

A high-quality, bilingual school could help change their lives. But push the school too far too quickly, and it could crumble. I'd made that mistake with the SHH team, and I didn't want to make it again.

So I decided to restrict the grade levels. That first year, our bilingual school would have only kindergarten, first, and second grades. Kids who were already in third grade or beyond would not be going to our school. It was one of the hardest and most uncertain decisions of my life. Many children who had watched the foundation for the school being set with joy and excitement were now excluded; they loitered outside the gates, hurt and resentful. So many needed our help, and no matter what I did, there was always more I could do.

* * *

We celebrated the grand opening of the Villa Soleada Bilingual School on a bright, sunny morning. Nearly fifty students in blue school uniforms with roaring tigers embroidered onto their chest pockets looked up at me, the sun shining on their faces.

"Our goal," I said to the crowd, "is to turn the 0 percent high school graduation rate here in the community into a 100 percent graduation rate within one generation. Each student who graduates will be college-ready and fully bilingual. I hope that, one day, Villa Soleada might become the village with the highest education level per capita in the city."

The crowd cheered. It was scary to make such statements in front of the families, but I had read somewhere that making a public promise about a goal gave you more resolve to achieve it. I had no idea if I was shooting myself in the foot, but I did it anyway. I told them that tuition would be free for those who helped build Villa Soleada. In exchange, I asked the parents to commit themselves to their children's education and help maintain the grounds.

"I'll be the first to cut the grass with my machete!" someone shouted.

Everyone laughed. More voices joined the chorus, as parents promised to protect the school from break-ins and dedicate their children to their education. I glanced at Wilfredo, who was standing with his wife and young daughter. He nodded his stoic nod, and cracked a rare smile.

These were jubilant times.

CHAPTER ELEVEN

YOU MUST ADDRESS VIOLENCE TO ADDRESS POVERTY

CRIME IN THE AREA WAS STEADILY GROWING. WHILE I WAS working out at a gym in El Progreso, armed gang members broke in. They told everyone to put their hands up and get on their knees. One of them kept his gun pointed right at my head as another took everyone's belongings. Violence in Villa Soleada mutated into different shapes. Gecko, a teenager from the LMDVS, held up a bill collector with a makeshift gun made of welded pipes. Later, the bill collector's boss sent men to handle Gecko—they pulled into Villa Soleada in cars with tinted windows. But Gecko was long gone, escaped into the palm jungle with a backpack filled with clothes, a toothbrush, and matches. He was used to surviving on the run.

It wasn't just outsiders who were threatened. Residents of Villa Soleada were getting held up in the Alley, that shadowy dirt road between Villa Soleada and Barrio de Amistad. When assailants mugged a mother from the community, common sense meant she should just hand the money over, but something in her snapped that day—she'd been saving for a refrigerator, and she recognized her assailants: she'd known them since they were kids playing marbles. She ran. She got away, but it was close. She could have been shot, and then her five-year-old child would have been motherless.

It's difficult to describe how all-pervasive the violence was, how it was both shocking and ordinary. Mired by poverty and corruption, Honduras could not withstand the destabilizing effects of the 2009 coup. In the years that followed, street gangs began to take over entire neighborhoods. They got into turf wars. In 2012, the year we opened the bilingual school, over seven thousand people were murdered in the small nation. At a rate of 85.5 homicides per one hundred thousand inhabitants—which was eighteen times higher than in the US—Honduras that year (and for the years that followed) recorded the highest murder rate in the world.[15] Given the overpowered police force and weak judicial system, less than 5 percent of murders in Honduras ended with a conviction.[16] Foreign drug cartels took advantage of the weakened government and moved in. They paid off corrupt officials, assassinated those who got in the way, and formed alliances with desperate locals and gang members who needed easy money. Seemingly overnight, Honduras had turned into the global drop-off center for cocaine.[17] Gradually, aid organizations began to leave. Even the Peace Corps, after serving in the country for nearly fifty years, pulled out all 158 of its volunteers.

But living there, the numbers could feel like statistics. It could feel ordinary to hear about Gecko holding up someone near the soccer field, especially when he fumbled with the bullets and his pants dropped down accidentally. For me, it was Hector who drove the reality of the situation home.

Our principal at the bilingual school, Sidonio, was leaving. He was moving to Guatemala with his family. His announcement was sudden, and I scrambled to find a replacement. Who would do a good job? Then one afternoon, while jogging through the city, I thought of Hector.

Hector was a local university student we hired in our restructuring of SHH to run our volunteer program. He worked for us part-time, on his summer breaks, but he was looking to join full-time after graduation. I called him right away. He was still studying—he was getting up at 4:30 a.m. every morning to work as a second-grade teacher at a school in a neighboring city, after which he took a two-hour bus ride to San Pedro Sula's state university. But he was only a few months away from graduation.

As we caught up on life, Hector told me how he was robbed at gunpoint outside his house. He had gathered the courage to report the crime to the police, even though gang members killed people for snitching on them. He wanted to stop the thugs from terrorizing his neighborhood, and the only way to do so was to act.

We talked about it casually, easily. I didn't think much of it.

We moved on to other topics. I asked him how he planned to celebrate his graduation. He said he'd play a few hours of FIFA. We both laughed. I wanted Hector to become our principal. Was he free to hang out at a local coffee shop at the end of the week? I wanted to meet to offer him the job. He said yes, and that he looked forward to seeing me. We hung up.

I never imagined that that would be the last time I would speak to him. Two days before our scheduled meeting, gang members showed up at the school where Hector taught and gunned him down. I learned that he tried to crawl away to hide behind a wall, leaving a blood trail. The gang members showed no mercy. They shot him several more times in front of his students. Death didn't spare good people in Honduras. It seemed to hunt them down.

The next evening, I put on a black shirt and went to Hector's funeral. I had never cried at the fact that forty thousand people had been murdered in Honduras since my first trip there. I often found it hard to contextualize numbers. But as I stared at Hector's dead body, my lungs constricted with grief. What I was looking at wasn't a statistic. Hector was someone who had shared his hopes and dreams with me. As I looked at his blue face one last time, I broke down in tears. I used to think that people turned to crime out of need or desperation. I left the funeral knowing that that was not always the case.

* * *

Six months after our inauguration, the Executive Director of BECA called me. He told me that the crime level around Villa Soleada had grown too much for their organization. BECA was going to cease their operations in El Progreso. Their decision was understandable. Gang members were holding up residents at gunpoint; breaking into homes at night; tying families up and robbing them; ransacking schools in the area; and carrying out kidnappings and murders. Just weeks before, the body of a decapitated man was found outside Villa Soleada. We had started to hear rumors that gang members in the area planned on kidnapping our staff members and ransacking the bilingual school. The gang members denied the allegations. Given the lack of information, I didn't know who to believe.

Within the week, BECA left, taking with them their teachers, curriculum, and educational supplies. As I walked through the empty campus, my head began to spin. I was convinced that there was no way we could run a school without BECA. "I'm going to help you figure this out," Bob told me over the phone. "There must be a way out." Maybe there was, and I was always thankful for Bob's encouragement. But no matter how much I paced, I couldn't think of a solution.

If our bilingual school shut down permanently, our kids would lose a year of schooling. Worse, they'd end up at an overcrowded public school in the area. We had already seen what that would look like for them. Before we had a school in Villa Soleada, we helped enroll children from the community at a nearby public school. Many of them struggled there, complaining that they were discriminated against because they were "the kids from the shanty." That worried me. The *National Longitudinal Study of Adolescent Health* brought to light the harmful effects of such treatment.[18] From 1995–97, the study examined ninety thousand students attending 145 different schools around the US. They wanted to find out what factors most protected children from negative outcomes. Researchers, through questionnaires and interviews, looked at more than a hundred variables in the students' lives. They found that the second most protective factor was a feeling of connectedness at school, where the students felt the teachers treated them fairly, they were close to peers, and they got along with everyone. Without a sense of connectedness, students were more likely to face negative outcomes such as violent behavior, emotional distress, suicide attempts, drug abuse, and teenage pregnancies.

As I walked through the empty hallways, I noticed all the small, telltale signs of violence that I had missed. The wiring for our security system was destroyed. The walls had gang symbols written onto them. At the back of the school's property, the chain-link perimeter fence had strange, gaping holes—it was clear someone was planning to break in. Just days before, the campus was filled with laughter and singing. Now, it felt so eerie that the warm, humid breeze gave me the chills. What Gary A. Haugen wrote in *The Locust Effect: Why the End of Poverty Requires the End of Violence* held true:

> The data is now emerging to confirm the common-sense understanding that violence has a devastating impact on a poor person's struggle out of poverty, seriously undermines economic development in poor countries, and directly

reduces the effectiveness of poverty alleviation efforts. It turns out that you can provide all manner of goods and services to the poor, as good people have been doing for decades, but if you are not restraining the bullies in the community from violence and theft—as we have been failing to do for decades—then we are going to find the outcomes of our efforts quite disappointing.[19]

I stood at the entrance gate, thinking of what I had said at inauguration day. *"Our promise to you is that every single child who graduates from our school will be college-ready and fluent in English!"* I shook my head. So many people had worked hard to make this school happen. Our volunteers in the US who had worked day and night to raise money for the school. The parents in the community who had worked long hours to build the classrooms. I had filled them with such hope for the future. How would I face them?

As soon as I put the steel lock on the gate and sealed it closed, a sense of hopelessness overtook me. I sat on the bench outside the gate, my hat tipped down. Yamilet, whose house was located right next to the school, saw me and walked over. She took a seat next to me and sat quietly for some time. She'd been with this project from the start, ever since she handed me that papaya in Siete de Abril.

"You're not going to let the neighborhood bullies win, are you?" she said softly. "It's just a few of them trying to sabotage the school."

"They have guns," I replied. "All we have are shovels and pickaxes."

"It's not always a matter of brute strength. We need to outsmart them."

Yamilet didn't say anything else, but she didn't leave. Other parents came over. Wilfredo took a seat on the bench, stoic as usual. Wilfredo was always unwavering, fearless, confident. I admired him. He put a hand on my shoulder, firm and reassuring.

"What we have is strength in numbers," he said, as if we were continuing a conversation.

I looked at the other parents' faces. They looked determined. They wanted to reopen the school and face the gang members head-on.

The bullying I'd experienced in school as a young kid was nothing compared to what people experienced in Honduras, the deadliest country in the world outside of war zones. I was working with families who were enduring bullying in its worst form—the violence here was systemic, ruthless, and seemingly never-ending. Given the debilitated state of the Honduran police and judicial systems, people here were practically left to fend for themselves. My blood began to boil. As Wilfredo, Yamilet, and the rest of the parents told me how they thought we could stand up to the local gangs and reopen the school, I decided to join them.

During the following days, the fathers in the community patched up the holes in the fence. The mothers scrubbed the walls with soap to erase the gang symbols. Marco, our foreman, figured out a way to better hide the wires for the security system. BECA, having laid the groundwork for a functioning bilingual school, supported us over the phone by explaining what we needed to do to keep things going. We reopened the school, and the Honduran teachers stepped up by teaching multiple grades instead of one. I taught English to two grades and made phone calls in the evenings to recruit help. Over the weeks, more staff joined to teach at the school.

We survived the fall semester, which bought us time to regroup over the summer. In June, Maxie Gluckman, a dynamic education consultant who had worked with Teach for America, flew down to Honduras. During the weeks that followed, she helped us create a new curriculum, teacher training program, and data tracking system. She breathed air into our school. Thanks to the systems Maxie put into place, we no longer had to pay another organization to run our school; we could now do it ourselves and save money.

As Maxie continued her work, and as the community members

made plans to take on the violence, I focused my attention on another pressing need: we needed to figure out a way to finance the upcoming school year. The school's startup funding had already run out.

* * *

I held a stack of flyers above my head as I waded through a shallow river. "Watch out for alligators!" joked Yapa, looking back at me and grinning. I hurried, splashing through the water in panic.

Yapa—the same Yapa I knew from HFC and who worked on her English homework with Cosmo—had started to work for us as an office assistant after she had graduated from UNITEC university through a scholarship we had offered her. By that summer, she was our country director and was in charge of our entire on-the-ground operations. It was surreal to be working with her—when she was a high school student back at HFC, we had joked about running a nonprofit together one day.

Yapa and I were crossing the river to find out if families outside of Villa Soleada would be interested in enrolling their children at our bilingual school for a monthly tuition. At first, I resisted the idea of charging tuition. I believed that not enough people would be willing to pay. My opinion changed when I read *The Beautiful Tree: A Personal Journey into How the World's Poorest People Are Educating Themselves*. The book, written by James Tooley, explained that ultra-low-cost private schools in low-income countries were using the free market to thrive. Tooley, through rigorous research, showed that families, even from slums and shantytowns, often found the money so their children could receive a superior education.[20] The book changed my mind. Not only would paid spots at our bilingual school allow us to benefit more children, collecting tuition from families who could afford it would give us the funding we needed to operate the school and build up our cradle-to-college pipeline.

Canvassing in El Progreso was different from canvassing in Virginia; instead of walking on sidewalks, we had to traverse jungles, climb mountains, and avoid wild animals. Our first stop was a cinder block house at the top of a steep hill, obscured by mist. A shirtless man was chopping wood in front of the home. Near him, a woman was hand-washing clothes.

"Hello there!" said the woman, drying her hands off with a towel. Before I could open my mouth, Yapa shook the woman's hand and began her pitch. She talked about the bilingual school, mentioned the monthly tuition (four hundred lempiras or about twenty dollars), and asked if the family had children. The woman said they had a young daughter. She glanced at the man.

"We'll think about it," said the man as he lit a cigarette with a matchstick. "Where's the school located?"

"It's in Villa Soleada, about a mile north from here."

The man stopped everything he was doing and stared at me as if I had said something scandalous.

"I would love for my daughter to attend a school like yours," he said, shaking his head, "but that area is full of gang members from *el bordo*—the river shanty. They say it's the land of the Maras there."

The woman chimed in: "I heard that when you walk out of that village—if you make it out alive, that is—you'll have nothing left but your underwear!" She went back to scrubbing her clothes, as if trying to wash away the stain of what she had just said.

I didn't know what to say. Villa Soleada's notoriety had spread. I often tried to explain that the gang members made up a small proportion of the community, but people would just shake their heads. After all, someone who was visiting Villa Soleada was hacked to death at the Alley after trying to resist a holdup. Another person's fingers were cut off and left on the dirt for everyone to see. I couldn't blame people for being scared.

That summer, a few families decided to enroll their children at our bilingual school and pay tuition. Many others were too afraid. We could have a great school and provide a cradle-to-college pipeline of services, but if we didn't stop the neighborhood gang members from terrorizing and pillaging the community—then we were not going to reach any of our goals.

* * *

A group of LMDVS guys strolled toward the soccer field. It was practice time for the new community soccer team. Fonzo, a right fullback for the village team who loved soccer as much as he loved his narcotics, stumbled onto the grass, high as a kite. He yelled obscenities, knocked over someone's water bottle, and stared dully at everyone warming up. He walked up to the one team ball we had, kicked it as hard as he could, and watched it disappear into the nearby banana farm. He and his cousin Egnacio began to laugh hysterically, like hyenas. Two of the younger players on the team glanced at me and began to make their way to retrieve the ball.

"Wait," said Jairo, one of the coaches. "We all know our team policy. He who kicks the ball out"—he looked at Fonzo—"goes and gets the ball."

"Whoa!" yelled Fonzo. "You think you're the boss here?"

"I'm just one of the coaches, nothing more. If you're high on drugs, you should probably go home."

Fonzo laughed again. "Nobody calls the shots in the neighborhood except for us. You tell the rest of 'the coaches' that we're in charge of the neighborhood now. Everyone from now on does what *we* say. You got that?"

The parents from Villa Soleada had started a soccer team to address Villa Soleada's crime problem. Wilfredo and a new guy who had arrived in the community, Jairo, had volunteered to lead the initiative. I had joined their efforts and collected cleats, uniforms, and balls from our supporters. I learned a lot about Jairo as we started the program together. He grew up in a neighboring community but had to drop out of middle school when he couldn't afford the twenty-five-cent bus fare. Bored and without money, he began running errands for a local gang. Soon, he was being initiated into a life of crime and hard drugs. But it wasn't in his nature to mug old ladies. He was sensitive and thoughtful; he adored his grandma, who had effectively raised him.

He wanted to leave the gang, but in Honduras, leaving usually meant death. He was stuck until a shootout killed most of the gang members and the rest disbanded. Jairo's life came back on track: he married his childhood crush, Lanita, and they started a family. Jairo began selling Lanita's fruit juices and homemade pastries from his bicycle. He couldn't believe how successful the business became. But once, while carrying his day's earnings in his back pocket, he was accused by a jealous neighbor of selling drugs from his bicycle. The cops threw him in jail. He was released when he was nineteen. A few months later, his wife got a phone call from her mom in Villa Soleada. "We're now living in a concrete house with running water, plumbing, and electricity," said Lanita's mom, who was giddy with excitement. "Come live with us."

So Jairo and his family moved to Villa Soleada to live with Lanita's parents. He joined the community's church and rediscovered his faith. He began studying to become a pastor. No longer a victim of his past, Jairo looked eagerly toward the future. Nobody was surprised when Jairo offered to help as a soccer coach. Like Wilfredo, he was good-natured and kind, always looking to help the community.

Fonzo ignored Jairo's instruction to retrieve the ball from the banana field. Instead, Wilfredo crossed the dirty creek to fetch it. It was heartbreaking—the most conscientious, responsible, and forward-thinking of the residents were often the ones who paid the highest price for doing the right things. I calmed Jairo down as we set things up. I followed his lead as he organized the players for a scrimmage. Egnacio, Fonzo, and the starters from the men's team went to the far side of the field. I was on the other side with Jairo, Wilfredo, and the younger boys who were usually the water boys. A few fathers finished smoking their cigarettes and joined our side.

Fonzo had spent his childhood carefree—swimming in creeks and hunting animals with his slingshot. He did everything to avoid his mom, who beat him with a broom. The physical and emotional violence in his household explained, but did not justify, why Fonzo was so conflictive and short-tempered. People in the community feared his family because they often used violence to get their way.

Despite his thin build, Fonzo could carry firewood on his shoulders like an elephant. Those shoulders, however, had a massive chip on them: Fonzo hadn't spent a single day inside a school and didn't know how to read or write. His parents didn't value education. So he tried to make up for the chip in the worst way possible. In Honduras, there was one thing that a kid at the bottom of the dominance hierarchy could do to gain respect quickly: become a feared criminal. For some, respect and admiration were like heroin and cocaine. People were willing to risk their lives to get them.

Fonzo's thirst for admiration explained his liking for soccer. He wanted to become the neighborhood star. But there was a problem: he was slow, lazy, and rarely passed the ball. He satisfied his ego by dribbling past the younger players and taunting them. Nearly the same could be said of Egnacio, his taller cousin, who was just as violent. When he wasn't obsessed with his habit of trimming his eyebrows, Egnacio spent his days sitting at the corner shop in his aviator sunglasses and telling jokes. He blasted the radio on his cheap cell phone at full volume wherever he walked. Egnacio passed the ball even less than his cousin. Despite their horrible shooting skills, the two cousins made sure to take every penalty kick on behalf of the team. On the field and off, they were the biggest bullies in the village.

That day, the game got off to a good start. Twelve-year-old Chipmunks, our youth team star, made crisp passes from the midfield. The dads, wearing cargo shorts and Crocs, defended well and passed unselfishly. By half-time, our superior teamwork had given us a 2–1 advantage. Upset and confused, Egnacio and Fonzo began to foul our players. Egnacio threw one of our youngest players to the ground and pretended it was an accident. It enraged me. I passed the ball to Chipmunks, who was as agile as a real chipmunk. He dribbled past three opponents twice his size. Onlookers cheered him on from the sidelines.

Fonzo violently slide-tackled Chipmunks from behind. Chipmunks fell, screaming. Tears filled his eyes, but he hid his face in the grass and lay silent. He knew he'd be taunted by the other boys if they saw him sobbing. The fans cried out for a red card.

Jairo and I ran up to Fonzo, who stumbled back a few steps and puffed his chest out. "That's a yellow card," I said.

"So now you're the referee?" Fonzo pointed his finger in my face. "Since when did we start playing with referees here in the hood? Nobody calls the shots in the neighborhood except for us. You got that?" He spat on the ground, and walked away.

"Yeah, you got that?" Egnacio parroted from behind Fonzo. I turned my attention to Chipmunks and helped him up. He was still hiding his face. Wilfredo ran over and told everyone to calm down.

I looked at the goal, forty yards away, and then at Wilfredo. Having played together for several years, the two of us could communicate a hundred words with the blink of an eye or a small hand gesture. Fonzo was still yelling obscenities when Wilfredo tapped the ball to me as I cranked my leg back and took a shot. I took the goalie by surprise and scored. We were up 3–1. Jairo carried Chipmunks back to our side of the field.

Fonzo yelled obscenities into the air. With just a few minutes remaining in the game, Claudio, the oldest father on the team, trapped the ball. He juked Egnacio and passed the ball to Jairo for a give-and-go. *Wack!* Egnacio came from behind and nailed Claudio in the back of his knees. Claudio fell hard. But it didn't stop there. Egnacio laughed and kicked Claudio. When Claudio tried to get up, Egnacio threw him back down. "You belong on the ground, old man!" he yelled.

I knew what was happening. Egnacio and Fonzo often looked for someone to beat up when they were about to lose a game. Claudio's eight-year-old son was on the sidelines, watching horrified from behind a banana tree.

Claudio tried to push Egnacio off him. "Nobody touches me!" yelled Egnacio, enraged. He punched Claudio and then kept punching him.

"*¡Ayúdalo!* Help him!" yelled one of the women from the sidelines.

At that moment, I forgot Egnacio was a gang member who was bigger than I was. I jumped between him and Claudio. "If you get in my way," growled Egnacio, "I'll kill you first!" He swung a right hook. I ducked. I stayed in place with my arms up as he unleashed a storm of punches until he was gassed out. Then I took a quick step forward. He stumbled back. I took another step, right at him. I kept going. As he backed up, his punches became meeker. I didn't return any blows—the last time someone beat him in a fight, Egnacio pulled out a machete, got his relatives to join him, chased his victim into his house, and hacked at the doors and windows. Some fights could not be won.

At some point, everyone on the field stormed between us. "The two of you are dead! Dead!" yelled Egnacio as his cousin pulled him back. Jairo ran in front of me and glared at Egnacio. The two cousins walked away, spitting on the ground.

"Thanks," said Claudio, hobbling with the help of his son who had run over. "I owe you my life. But it's time for me to leave the village for a while. Or else, Egnacio and his family are going to kill me."

"Nobody's goin' to touch you, Claudio," said Jairo. But he didn't sound convinced. It was as if he, too, agreed that it was best for Claudio to leave for a few weeks. Claudio told me that I needed to think about leaving too. I had challenged Egnacio, and that was dangerous.

The sun began to set as people went home. Cooking stoves lit up throughout the community, and the smell of *baleadas* and smoke slowly filled the air. Later, I learned that a group of mothers had met up in secret that evening. Under the shade of a banana tree, they decided it was time to stand up to LMDVS. They understood fully what often happened to people who snitched to the police. But the women had had enough. That evening, one of them agreed to call the cops on behalf of the community. They prayed together and dispersed.

The next day, as Claudio left the community, a convoy of cop cars drove into Villa. They arrested those allegedly in LMDVS and took them to jail. People in the community celebrated. But the families of those arrested were infuriated. I began to hear rumors that they believed *I* was the one who had called the police. Knowing how the justice system worked in Honduras, I knew that everyone who had been arrested would be released in a few days. Maybe it *was* time I left the community. But Jairo had a plan.

The two of us drove to the police station. Fonzo and the rest of the guys, handcuffed, were standing in a line in a dark room. "Which one of these guys do you want in jail?" asked a police officer. "Just give us the word, and we'll throw 'em all in there!"

Egnacio looked away when he saw me. He was trembling and his eyes were red. "There has been a misunderstanding," I said. "I'm one of their soccer coaches. And I'd like these boys back in the community so they can continue to train."

Egnacio looked up in surprise. Jairo's plan was simple: If the LMDVS gang members were going to come back to Villa Soleada anyway, why not help get them out? The police reluctantly let them go. As we returned to the community, the gang members thanked us and vowed to take soccer practices more seriously. Egnacio apologized and promised never to disrespect the coaches again.

This was the first step in a long list of measures we took to try and decrease violence in Villa Soleada. Jairo's plan worked—to an extent. Reports of muggings and holdups began to decrease, and we hoped it was the beginning of a turnaround in Villa Soleada. But systemic violence is a complicated beast, not so easily solved, and the drop in crime was only temporary. Still, it was "groundwork," as Aricela would say. We now had to build on it.

* * *

It's difficult to pinpoint when a situation like this turns around—memory always picks a moment and gives it more significance than it may have. I remember the football match with Fonzo like it was yesterday, and I can still feel Egnacio's blows on my body. But the most visceral incident I remember of violence in Villa Soleada and how we changed the trajectory of our community didn't happen to me. It happened to León.

León was a resident of Colina de Uvas, a community that shared a similar history with the residents of Villa Soleada. They too had lived in a riverbed shantytown and later relocated to a plot of land behind the bilingual school. They too came from crushing poverty in search of a better life. León was large, with bulging biceps built from hauling fruit crates all day, but he was a good man. Quiet and respectful to all. His four-year-old daughter meant everything to him. In one of our conversations, he told me how horrified he was that fathers would blow their earnings on *guaro* and drugs when their kids were hungry.

León was gentle.

Then his daughter fell ill. Her fever was so bad, her eyes were rolling into the back of her head, and her body shook with shivers. He rode his bicycle to El Progreso to buy medicine for her. It cost him the family's food budget for the month.

On the way home, he was robbed.

He handed over whatever money he had gladly; he didn't want any trouble. He knew of a guy who had been hacked to pieces in that same spot for resisting a holdup. He even gave them his bicycle. But when the gunmen asked for the pills, León wouldn't part with them. He couldn't. They were just pills, useless to the gunmen and lifesaving for his child. So one of the thugs took them—pried them from León's fingers. Then he just emptied the pills onto the ground and crushed them under his boots. Senselessly. For no other reason than to punish León for not obeying him immediately. Deep, visceral hatred filled León's heart.

Later that day, children in Villa Soleada were chasing each other around banana trees. Fathers were coming back from construction sites to take cold showers, and moms were sifting beans to remove pebbles. Jairo was humming a Christian song, watering the flowers in his front yard. He watched Fonzo and a few teenagers at the edges of the soccer field. Some of them were smoking pot, while others were taking turns cutting the grass with a machete. Jairo waved, and some of them nodded back.

"Lend us a ball, man!" yelled Fonzo.

"*Ufff*, I'm out of balls, brother," Jairo said, slapping himself on the forehead. "I'll have one by tomorrow!"

Fonzo gave him a thumbs-up, took a hit from his blunt, and lay down on the grass. Jairo continued watering his flowers. On the porch with him was Keimi, his ten-year-old daughter who enjoyed going to church as much as her father. Nina, his seven-year-old daughter, was helping him water the plants. The girls were his pride and joy.

Back at Colina de Uvas, a mob gathered in front of León's house. León paced, retelling the story of how he'd been mugged, of how they'd dumped the medicine for his daughter, who still lay in bed shivering. As the crowd grew, people took turns telling countless accounts of how they had been attacked that year. Not once had the police made an arrest. Their rage grew with each story.

León recognized the muggers, especially the tall one. He believed it was Toast Head from Villa Soleada. The community decided not to bother calling the police. It would be a waste of time. The men had had enough—there were quicker ways to find justice. They were off to Villa Soleada to kill Toast Head.

As the mob headed out with machetes and a thirst for revenge, Jairo was still on his porch, this time reading his Bible. On the field, the LMDVS guys were running laps and doing pushups. Jairo believed that all our outreach was perhaps starting to pay off. Despite their rebellious attitudes, the youth from LMDVS had been showing up to all the team events and tournaments. Many of them, having dropped out of school years before, had joined a scholarship program we'd started. In the program, teenagers from Villa Soleada took classes during the weekends (a common practice in Honduras, given the number of young people who had to work during the week to support their families). When someone from LMDVS asked for a job, we quickly hired them onto our construction team. Some people warned us that hiring men from LMDVS was dangerous. A few staff members were outright against the idea. But Jairo and I wanted to support these teenagers as much as we could, and keep a close eye on their lives. We believed that excluding them, which was proposed to us, would be counterproductive. And so, with great patience, our wonderful lead foreman Marco taught them the art of laying cinder blocks, plastering walls, installing rebar, and laying concrete slabs. Those who learned quickly became an integral part of our team. I shared Jairo's hopeful belief that one day Villa Soleada would be known for its graduates instead of its gangs.

Jairo later recounted what happened that evening. Toast Head had stopped by his house to shoot the breeze. Toast Head had moved to Villa Soleada a few months before to live with an aunt. He'd never told anyone *why* he moved, but it was rumored he'd fled from his hometown after stabbing a neighbor to death.

Now Toast Head leaned against the concrete electric post—which was about the only thing in the village taller than him—and asked Jairo to let him play in the upcoming tournament, even though he'd been missing practices. To prove his skills, Toast Head demonstrated a bicycle kick. Jairo laughed and said, okay. The two talked as the sun began to descend behind the soccer field.

Jairo glanced behind Toast Head. A group of men were gathering at the corner of the field, near the lemon trees. His cataracts made the silhouettes blurry, but he soon realized the men were neighbors from Colina de Uvas. He waved, but they did not wave back.

It was clear from their raised machetes that something was very wrong.

"Say your prayers, Toast Head!" yelled León. "You're dead!" The machete-wielding mob howled in unison, and ran towards Jairo's house.

"Go inside!" screamed Jairo at his two confused daughters. "Quick!" Toast Head ran into the house with them, and they slammed the metal door shut, double-locking it along with the windows. *BANG!* León and his men kicked at the door, causing the house to shake. They struck the metal with their machetes. Jairo screamed at his frightened daughters to get under the bed. Toast Head pulled out a revolver from his belt.

"Open the door, Jairo! And hand over Toast Head! We got nothin' against you and your family! But if you don't hand 'em over, we'll have some serious problems!" *BANG! BANG!* The house shook.

"Fellas! Let's talk this out!" shouted Jairo. "For the love of God! What's with this bad blood between the neighborhoods?"

"That son of a bitch has been muggin' us all month. He's dead!"

Aghast, Jairo stared at Toast Head.

"Those sons of bitches are lyin', man!" screamed Toast Head, his bloodshot eyes widening. "You know me, Jairo!" Jairo watched in horror as Toast Head cocked his revolver.

"Is there a problem here?" said a voice from behind the mob. It was a voice that gave people goosebumps.

The mob turned to see Equis, the head of LMDVS. He stood in front of a group of men from LMDVS and several of their burly fathers. Equis took an unhurried puff from his blunt.

"We're here to get Toast Head," said León. "We ain't got problems with you all. Stay outta this one." He whacked the door with his machete, but with less conviction than before.

"Stay *outta* this?" Equis laughed. León stopped his machete mid-air. "You're tellin' us what to do in *our* neighborhood now? On *our* home turf? You outta your mind, León?" León and his men went quiet. Jairo peeked out from a crack in his window.

"Fellas, are you hearin' this?" asked Equis, looking back at Egnacio, Fonzo, and his men. The standoff continued for a few moments as both groups stared at each other. The residents in Villa started to come out of their houses to see what the commotion was about, hissing at the outsiders. Before long, León and his men were surrounded by a mob much larger than theirs. The men from Colina de Uvas looked at each other nervously.

Equis, with superior numbers, broke the silence. "We ain't got problems with you, León. But if you don't get outta here, things might get outta hand."

León hurriedly explained what had happened to him.

"How do you know it was Toast Head," asked Equis, "if the guy who robbed you had a mask on?" León watched his men bring down their machetes and saw fear in their eyes. He did the same, reluctantly. "We're leavin' 'cos we don't want problems with you all, Equis! Tell Toast Head that if we see him again, he's dead!" But the entire time, he was looking at the ground, and not at Equis. As the LMDVS and the neighborhood stared them down, the outsiders stormed out. In Honduras, declaring war against a larger neighborhood was like signing a collective death sentence.

I arrived at Villa Soleada an hour later, and Jairo frantically explained the evening's near-catastrophe. "Why in the world is León declaring war on us?" I asked, shaking my head in despair. "He's on our soccer team, for crying out loud."

"After what he did today, I'm guessin' he's not playing with us anymore," said Jairo.

"So what do we do now?" I asked. "We have to douse this fire before people get killed."

"They think it's Toast Head. He's gonna have to leave the neighborhood if he doesn't wanna get killed."

I closed my eyes. People were already reluctant to send their kids to our bilingual school because of Villa Soleada's notoriety. War and bloodshed in the neighborhood would only make matters worse. Jairo and I sat in silence, unsure of our next steps. For a split second, I wondered if it was worth contacting the authorities. But I knew it wouldn't help. I decided to speak to Equis.

As I walked through the community, I passed Wilfredo and a band of fathers who were discussing the day's showdown. I heard the anger in their voices.

"Why do people always think it was someone from Villa anytime there's a robbery?"

"Maybe it was Toast Head, or maybe it wasn't! All we know is that we're always the scapegoat!"

On Equis's porch, I was greeted with fist bumps from a few LMDVS guys smoking pot. "We need to resolve this problem," I said to Equis. "What are you guys thinking?"

They looked at each other and raised their eyebrows. "We were about to ask *you* that!" said Egnacio, sparking nervous laughter from the group. "First off, Toast Head's gotta go," Equis said. "We're not sure if he robbed León or not, but he's causing us too many headaches. And we got nothin' against León and his men, but they can't be stormin' into our turf like that, armed and actin' like they run this place."

"They disgrace us like that in front of the neighborhood, and we're gonna let that slide?" Fonzo said.

"If we don't stand up for ourselves and confront the situation, what are the other neighborhoods goin' to think of us?" Egnacio added.

"Damn it! They'll think of us as fresh meat!" said someone else.

"Then maybe it's time to set an example," said Equis.

I could see the annoyance in Equis's face. His reputation—and of all the men in the community—was at stake. I clenched my teeth, knowing that in neighborhood warfare, retaliation meant a bullet was answered by ten bullets.

I walked back to Jairo's house, sensing impending doom. What good were a school, scholarships, and a soccer program if people ended up dead? "I have an idea!" Jairo said. "What if we buy León a new bicycle? We could prevent a potential bedlam with a hundred bucks."

His idea was brilliant. I gave him a fist bump, climbed into the pickup truck, and sped into town.

The following day, the men in Villa Soleada drank extra dark coffee and reminded their wives to lock the doors. Equis told the LMDVS to stay alert. If they saw any intruders, they should call for backup. Teenagers in the neighboring villages gossiped about the feud. Later that afternoon, I drove into Villa with a brand new yellow mountain bike. Jairo helped me hoist it onto the dirt. The LMDVS guys and several fathers offered to go with us to Colina de Uvas. Toast Head also insisted on going with us to prove his innocence, but the fathers told him to stay put. He agreed, and I breathed a sigh of relief.

The LMDVS guys were worried that the men from Colina de Uvas would interpret this gesture as a sign of weakness. They were reluctant about the plan, but Jairo reminded them about all the progress they had been making with the soccer team, the job training, and weekend school. The fathers backed up Jairo: we needed to give diplomacy a try before resorting to other measures. Nobody objected. It turned out, the LMDVS guys respected their fathers at times like this.

"Is it a good idea to take those machetes you've got there?" I asked the fathers.

"Just in case," said a lanky dad. "We promise not to use them unless we have to."

"You stay in the back," Jairo told me, as he directed the LMDVS guys and their fathers into a formation. "This is a problem between their neighborhood and ours," Equis said as he glanced at me. "If things take a turn for the worst today, you stay away. You got that?"

I nodded at Equis, trying not to look too scared. We walked towards the dirt road that separates the two communities. One by one, we crawled between barbed wire and slid down a small hill. We were in the shade of the palm jungle, right where León had gotten mugged. The LMDVS guys started to light a few blunts.

"Hey," Equis said suddenly, laughing his shrill laugh. "Look who's here."

It was León, walking back from work. The men gripped their machetes a little harder.

"What's up, León!" yelled Fonzo, grinning.

"That was quite a show yesterday, wasn't it?" Egnacio said. The two brothers smirked. León stopped dead. He slowly looked behind him at the empty, shaded road. I could only imagine what he was thinking. He was terrified, and his face showed it.

"Fellas!" León said, trembling like someone with hypothermia, "I thought all night about what I did...and realized it was all a big mistake! I shouldn't have come into your neighborhood like that! I was gonna come apologize later this evenin'!"

He took a step back. I thought he was going to make a run for it.

"Listen León," I said, "we felt bad, so we bought a bike for you. Here, take it."

"Wait, you did what?" He blinked a few times.

"We got you a bike, brother," said Jairo, "so you can go to work."

"What? I can't take this, fellas. My bike was old and in bad shape. This one's brand new."

"C'mon, take it!" yelled Equis. He was trying to be nice, but it came out unnecessarily harsh.

Jairo handed León the bike. "Let's go talk to your guys to straighten things out." We walked into Colina de Uvas together. The residents there saw us and gathered at the entrance. My heart raced.

"What's goin' on here?" yelled a man in a dark red T-shirt.

"We're here to mend our differences!" said Jairo. "We come in peace, brothers!"

"What are these bandits doin' in our neighborhood?" yelled a woman. A few kids who were running around in diapers threw rocks at us.

"If the thief was indeed from our neighborhood, we sincerely apologize," Jairo said to the crowd. "We wanted to show our support for León and gave him a new bicycle." He pointed at the yellow bicycle.

"That's diplomatic of you guys," said one of León's friends, stepping out of the throng, "but now you gotta promise to do somethin' about all the bandits in your neighborhood!"

"We're workin' on it. We have plans to—"

"You're actin' all crazy without any evidence!" yelled one of the LMDVS guys. "You don't know for sure it was somebody from our neighborhood!"

People started hissing and yelling from both sides. Men gripped their machetes tightly.

"Calm down, calm down!" yelled Jairo, waving his Bible. "Can both communities promise to try and resolve problems in the future through diplomacy, and not like yesterday?" The people of Colina de Uvas exchanged looks. Slowly, they calmed down.

"You'll see what we're capable of if you barge into our neighborhood like that again!" yelled Fonzo, who always had to have the last word and add unnecessary fuel to the fire.

"Oh yeah?" The sounds of unrest ramped up again. We had to get out of there.

"Hey," I said, as I turned to León, "I'm really sorry for what they did to you and to the medicine your daughter needed. Are we cool now?"

"Yeah, we're cool, man. Thanks for the bike…I really appreciate it." He looked me in the eyes and nodded, but he stared at the LMDVS guys with a reemerged defiance that he didn't have on the dirt path when he was alone.

We left, unscathed. "*That's* how we resolve problems!" said Jairo as he gave me a high five.

"They were lucky they didn't try to get clever on us!" said Equis, triumphantly.

"You should've seen León's face when he saw us on the dirt road!" yelled Fonzo. The others burst into laughter.

By giving León the bike, we'd proven that diplomacy worked. It was one more step towards the kind of Villa Soleada we wanted. Over the next few months, we kept adding to this foundation. We created more jobs in the community and grew our adolescent scholarship program. As Villa Soleada got slightly safer, the bilingual school improved and expanded. So did our waitlist of students. Eventually, so many families from all across the city wanted to enroll their children, we had to do a lottery to give away spots. We continued to move forward, holding onto the hope that peace was bound to follow.

BOOK 4

CHAPTER TWELVE

WHAT'S RIGHT ISN'T ALWAYS BLACK AND WHITE

"ROLL DOWN YOUR WINDOWS," INES SAID.

She was the program director for the Honduran government's agency for children and families. I followed her instruction as we drove slowly on the back roads of San Pedro Sula along the Chamelecón River. A shanty settlement sat on one side of the road. On the other side, two-story mansions with high-voltage security fences overlooked the cardboard houses. We took a sharp right turn and drove through a narrow road filled with potholes. "We're here," Ines said.

We had arrived at one of the state orphanages in San Pedro Sula. The perimeter walls were so high, we were engulfed by their shadow. As we waited at the gate, Ines told me about the agency and its programs. Between two to three hundred orphaned and vulnerable children were living in this facility.

"How did they end up here?" I asked.

Some of the children had lost their parents due to death, homicides, or gang violence. But the majority had at least one biological parent who was still alive. They had been separated from their families due to abuse, neglect, exploitation, or abandonment. Ines knew of harrowing cases where children had been tortured, tied up, beaten nearly to death, raped, prostituted, or left to starve by their parents. Some parents were too hooked on drugs or alcohol to parent. Others left their children behind, tried to cross the border, and disappeared. The agency did its best to keep families together, but many parents were unable to remedy their problems or suffered from mental health challenges.

The situation was a result of the systemic challenges in Honduras, like poverty, community instability, job insecurity, drug abuse, the widespread breakdown of the family, and the lack of mental health services and drug rehabilitation programs. Ines wished the agency could do more. But they had little funding, and even that had to first go through multiple layers of bureaucracy before the little money left trickled down to the children. It was apparent that the magnitude and complexity of the problems—both upstream and downstream—were simply too overwhelming for a small, underfunded agency to take on.

I asked if relatives took in children, a setup referred to as kinship care. She nodded, but explained that the traditional safety nets in Honduras, like the family support structure, were overwhelmed by the problem's scale. Furthermore, the process of tracking down relatives was a difficult one. Many Hondurans do not have addresses or cell phones, and the agency had to work with limited information, vehicles, caseworkers, and resources. When the agency found relatives, things sometimes worked out for the best. But relatives weren't always able or willing to help. And children who grew up with a relative could sometimes become second priority to biological children, ending up in abusive or forced labor situations. The complexity of the situation was dizzying.

"And foster care?"

The agency was running a small foster care program, but it hadn't been easy. Abused children needed stability and predictability to heal. But in foster care, they were often shuffled from one family to another. Furthermore, the agency struggled to find qualified foster parents, nor did they have the resources to adequately assess, train, match, and retain them. "It's practically impossible to monitor and provide ongoing support for foster children when the agency doesn't even have enough for gas money," said Ines.

"What about adoption, then?"

Adoption was extremely difficult, thanks to government policies. "I can probably count the number of kids who've recently been adopted with just the fingers on my two hands," she said.

"So then what options do these kids have?"

Very few. The agency usually waited for a privately-run children's home to call. But these homes had limited capacities, and strict criteria for who they were willing to take. Plus, the quality of care varied from place to place, just like in every other intervention.

Ines waved at the security guard who had arrived with an old shotgun slung over his shoulder. He nodded and slowly pushed open the gate. We walked on a concrete walkway alongside a stretch of unkempt grass, then entered a large, two-story building to emerge in a central courtyard with a broken water fountain.

"¡*Visita!* A visitor!" yelled a hoarse voice. I looked up at the second story. Rooms with iron bars surrounded the courtyard.

"¡*Visita!*" A set of fists banged on the iron bars. I couldn't tell which room the voice, echoing and bouncing on the four walls surrounding us, was coming from. Another child began to scream. Then another. "¡*Visita! ¡¡Visita!! ¡¡¡Visita!!!*" The lone voice turned into a chanting chorus. The children beat on the iron bars. My body vibrated. The walls rattled. I looked at Ines. She was on her cell phone, casually writing a text message. She put her phone in her pocket and walked over to a middle-aged woman carrying what looked like a hundred silver keys around her neck. They spoke briefly, and the lady with the keys walked upstairs. She unlocked a wooden door covered with scratches and scrapes. Like a river pouring out of a broken floodgate, children with tattered clothes, rashes, and unevenly shaved heads ran out to engulf us.

As a mob of children with plastic spoons in their pockets ran around us, I peered through the iron bars into an empty room. It had endless rows of metal bunk beds. There were gaping holes in the ceiling drywall. Wires and jumbled electric cables dangled from the holes. They were asking for a fire or electrocution to happen.

"The children created those holes," Ines explained, "as a way to crawl up through the ceiling and drop down into the kitchen to find food. Others find their way outside the building through the holes, climb over the perimeter walls, and run away." A cold chill ran down my spine as I imagined children risking their lives to jump off from twenty-feet high walls with barbed wire.

We walked against the current of kids and peered into a different room. "We house children with disabilities here," said Ines. I had heard that, in many low-income countries, children with disabilities were often sentenced to abandonment and life on the streets or in a state institution. I found out that it was true. A group of children with scars all over them were locked inside this dark room. Some of them were tied to their beds. Ines saw my startled face and explained that tying them down was the only way to prevent them from hurting themselves. I wanted to run into the bathroom and curl up in a corner.

We went outside. Hundreds of children were there, pushing, shoving, and punching each other. One boy picked up a metal pipe and started hitting the other kids with it. Another began throwing rocks at a group of girls. Those who were hit began to bleed and hobble away.

A mob gripped my backpack and grappled away my notebooks. The hat on my head vanished. An emaciated child dashed away with a box of crayons from my backpack and began eating the crayons. I wanted to close my eyes and pretend none of what I was witnessing was real.

Very few adults were in sight. "As you can see, we are way beyond capacity," said Ines quietly. "Children come in faster than we can find placements for them." A group of girls in tattered dresses surrounded her and took turns hugging her. The staff members, not the least bit bothered by the pandemonium, led the children toward a patch of grass in the back. The kids yelled into the air and tackled each other to the ground. They began chugging dirty tap water out of a spigot as if they had just arrived from a desert. A cluster of broken glass lay nearby. One girl picked up a piece and slipped it inside her jean pocket. Our eyes met and my heart sank. The expression in her eyes said a thousand words. It was one of sadness and total surrender. She looked at me for a few moments and walked away.

For whatever reason, a police truck drove in. A few officers got out and waved at the children. A mob of boys high-fived the officers. Then they began to grab at the officers' handguns. Others climbed onto the bed of the truck. One kid stole the car keys and snuck into the vehicle. The panicked officers tried to pull him away, but others slipped inside and touched the horn and all of the buttons. The kids on the truck bed began to scream and jump up and down. They had taken over the cop car.

Behind me, staff members were trying in vain to break up fistfights happening everywhere. I couldn't help but think of *Lord of the Flies*, the book about a group of boys that get stranded on an uninhabited island and their harrowing attempt to govern themselves. In one critical way, the children on the island end up better off than the children in the state orphanage. In *Lord of the Flies*, there is a mass rescue at the end. I sat on a concrete ledge and covered my face with my hands.

I turned to Ines and asked her what happened to the children as they aged. She took a deep breath and shook her head slowly. They tried to find placements for their children while they were young because very few people wanted to take in teenagers. "Once a child turns thirteen," she said, "they have to leave for the streets."

Girls who aged out of the orphanage were sent to another, more overcrowded state facility where gang members sometimes broke in to kidnap them. There used to be a state orphanage for older boys, but it was closed down when they found a boy bludgeoned to death. I was too afraid to ask what happened.

"Some of the teenage boys come back," continued Ines as she pointed her finger at the wall, "but end up on the other side of this wall at *El Carmen*." I'd heard about El Carmen—the largest juvenile detention center in the region. It housed young MS-13 and Mara 18 gang members, some of whom had committed murder. As I tried to swallow the reality that the state orphanage shared a wall with a prison, it hit me like a brick. I realized that they, too, had a pipeline here. But it wasn't the cradle-to-college pipeline we were attempting to create at Villa Soleada—it was the state-orphanage-to-state-prison pipeline.

As I walked around that afternoon, I held onto hope. One of the boys who had been bullying the others pulled out a small bag of cookies from his pocket. He shared the cookies with a few boys. I saw a girl, who had been screaming ragefully earlier, help a girl with physical disabilities walk. Another child who had been punching his peers moments before showed me a fruit tree that he watered every day. As I sat on a concrete ledge, a girl with short brown hair who looked about twelve walked up to me. She smiled and handed me a sheet of paper so dilapidated it looked like a used tissue. "*Mira*. Look," she said nervously. I couldn't recognize the letters at first. The sheet was full of stains and had been folded over too many times. I realized it was a list with several dozen vocabulary words. The girl told me that someone had given her the list long ago. For weeks, she had been studying the words, erasing them, and writing them again on the same sheet of paper. I realized that what I was holding in my hands was much more than a piece of paper. It was this little girl's only learning tool that was all hers—and her way of holding onto hope. I handed back the sheet and watched as she carefully folded it and put it back into her pocket as if it were a winning lottery ticket. She told me that she wanted to study at a university one day to become a nurse or a social worker. Somehow, despite her circumstances, she was brimming with optimism.

As I listened to her tell me about her dreams, I started to question myself for having felt so cynical earlier. She talked to me for quite some time, and when she finished, she shook my hand. She said goodbye, dodged a few rocks hurled her way, and left. I took a heavy breath and sat there quietly. I was planning to crawl into bed once I returned home to try and forget about the day. But that girl would likely be studying her vocabulary words later that night, and I wondered if there was a better way for me to move forward.

* * *

I walked through the state orphanage's courtyard and pulled out a soccer ball I had brought with me. "*Una pelota!* A ball!" yelled a boy. The others looked over and screamed with excitement. Together, we walked over to the dirt field at the back of the compound. We divided into two teams and began to play. The game quickly devolved into a free-for-all. The kids refused to pass the ball, and players on the same team started tackling each other. I thought of ending the game before someone got hurt. But one of the boys on my team passed me the ball. He sprinted a few yards into open space, using his lanky legs, and I passed it back. I moved into open space, giving him enough of an open angle. To my surprise, he saw what I did and passed the ball back.

We repeated the give-and-go passes throughout the game. Before the opponents could figure out what we were doing, we had won. "*Juegas como Andrés Iniesta.* You play like Andrés Iniesta," I said to the boy, speaking of the team captain of Barcelona Fútbol Club and the greatest passer in the world.

Little Iniesta gave me a high five, elated by the victory. I sat down on the grass, hoping for a quick rest, but the kids were bored. So I brought out paper and coloring pencils from the truck. The kids screamed, jumped up, and hugged each other as if they hadn't drawn in years. Little Iniesta told me his name: José.

"I want to draw characters from *Dragon Ball*," he said. "Maybe you can help me if you've heard of the anime."

I chuckled and nodded. Growing up, Dragon Ball had been my favorite anime. I drew out some characters, and the boys tried to copy them. The characters they drew looked like tomatoes with limbs, and none of them had the right number of fingers. Eventually, the boys gave up and left. José remained. His first attempts were terrible, but each successive drawing began to look better than the one before. "I didn't know drawing was so fun," he said. "This will be my new hobby." I smiled. It felt good to see someone discover a hidden talent.

As we drew together on the concrete porch, José asked about my family. I told him about my life, and he told me about his. "I started living on the streets because bad things happened at the house," he said. I didn't ask him what he meant by bad things. "Then I moved around from one group home to another. I didn't like how they treated me in the last one, so I ran away. But that turned out to be a bad decision. I got snatched up and thrown in here. Now I spend my days staring at a broken fan on the ceiling." He laughed a little to lighten the mood. His attempt made my heart ache. When we finished the last drawing, I gave José a box of coloring pencils to keep. His face brightened. He promised to keep practicing.

"Maybe one day I will get lucky," he said, "and end up somewhere where I can draw like this every day." I didn't know how to respond to something like that—and was frightened that such a modest request felt so out of reach for him. José loved soccer, and now drawing pictures, but rarely got to do such things. He had to stay in his room doing nothing most of the time. What's a childhood where you can't discover your interests or develop your unique talents? What's a childhood where you're just a number locked up inside a concrete room? What's a childhood without a home and family? As I watched José sort the coloring pencils in the box, I realized that his childhood was being taken away. A mixture of emotions crashed into me like a tsunami. José gave me a high five, thanked me one last time, and left.

I wondered what it would take to allow kids like José to grow up in a loving family. What could our organization do to help them regain their childhood? I wondered how much money we would need to start a program like that. I didn't know. But I told myself that we would do our research and find a way.

* * *

I began my research by visiting more than twenty children's homes across Honduras. I interviewed founders, staff members, children. I learned that there were many high-quality programs like Our Little Roses that helped orphaned and vulnerable children heal and break the cycle of poverty. The visits inspired me to consider opening a children's home at Villa Soleada.

One weekend, I took several parents from Villa Soleada to the state orphanage. I wanted them to be a part of the project. On the bus ride home, people expressed their conviction to help the children they had met that day. Wilfredo said he was grateful that his family had a home—he wanted to pay it forward by helping with any construction projects. Nita, a gregarious grandmother, expressed her excitement to help as a caretaker. When we returned to Villa Soleada, other community members rallied behind the idea. We were excited to move fast and get the kids out of the state orphanage as soon as possible.

However, our team found itself at a crossroads. Board and staff members asked if a children's home was truly the most effective intervention. I didn't have an answer, and agreed that we needed to consider alternatives, such as foster care, kinship care, and family reunification. Some cautioned me against opening a children's home, as they were said to be cost-prohibitive and falling out of favor.

I would later find out why children's homes were falling out of favor. In countries like Cambodia and Nepal, scam artists were trafficking children by keeping them in fake orphanages. These facilities were left in squalid conditions to arouse pity, and the sham organization pocketed any foreign donations. Media companies and celebrities began a movement to end this horrific practice. Conor Grennan's amazing book, *Little Princes: One Man's Promise to Bring Home the Lost Children of Nepal*, brought more attention to the issue.

But as the movement picked up steam, *all* children's homes were being described as the brutal orphanages in communist Romania or *Oliver Twist*. Some claimed that *all* children's homes—even well-run ones—were damaging to children. The sweeping generalizations confused me. The what-ifs paralyzed me. I felt there were good children's homes and bad ones across the world, and the same could be said of biological and foster parents. I wanted to find out if the critics' claims were true. After all, I didn't want to do something that would harm the children I intended to help.

My information from my site visits was purely anecdotal, so I began to dig through the research to examine what the empirical evidence said.

The research most commonly cited by the critics of children's homes was called the Bucharest Early Intervention Project, which studied children in orphanages in communist Romania.[21] These children faced horrendous, inhumane conditions. Children who lived through prolonged deprivation and adversity in these orphanages suffered from profound deficits in cognitive abilities, socio-emotional behaviors, brain structure, alterations in reward sensitivity and processing, and a greatly elevated incidence of psychiatric disorders and impairment. I was shocked to learn that neglect could alter the physical shape of the brain. The researchers compared outcomes of children who remained in the low-quality orphanages with children who were sent to a high-quality foster care program, and found that kids in high-quality foster care fared better. The study's results were frightening, but it said nothing about run-of-the-mill or high-quality children's homes. Comparing the outcomes of low-quality orphanages with outcomes of high-quality foster care was like comparing the athleticism of an out-of-shape amateur tennis player with a professional soccer player. Of course you would conclude that soccer players were more athletic than tennis players.

The other studies that shed a negative light on children's homes had severe limitations and flaws. For example, some had tiny sample sizes or made only short-term assessments. Furthermore, several researchers made it clear that their studies had a selection bias: children's homes often took in kids who foster families were unable or unwilling to take in—in other words, kids with the most severe cognitive and socio-emotional challenges.

Unable to find anything convincing, I wondered if conclusive data existed at all.

It turned out, I simply hadn't looked hard enough. A multi-year study on the long-term outcomes of children who had grown up in different children's homes in the US had already been published in two peer-reviewed journals.[22] Dr. Richard McKenzie, a professor of economics at the University of California, Irvine, and who himself grew up in a children's home in North Carolina, had carried out an extensive survey of more than 2,500 alumni from fifteen American children's homes. The research found that the children's home alumni outpaced their counterparts in the general population by wide margins in almost all social and economic measures, including educational attainment, employment rate, mental health, and positive attitude toward life. The alumni had a median income 10 to 60 percent higher than the general population in their age group; a 39 percent higher college graduation than the general population; and an incarceration rate one-third that of the general white population.[23] The results were so hard-hitting, I had to read them several times to make sure I wasn't misreading them.

When asked if they preferred to grow up in their orphanages or foster care, just over 92 percent of respondents preferred their children's homes, less than 2 percent preferred foster care, and 6 percent reported not knowing enough to say one way or the other.[24] Less than 3 percent had hostile memories of their children's home experiences.[25] University of Alabama historian David Beito replicated the study with several hundred alumni from another children's home, reaching pretty much the same conclusions.[26]

McKenzie stated that those with positive assessments attributed their success in life to the education and mentorship they received at their children's homes, as well as the work ethic, moral values, and camaraderie they developed there. McKenzie did not stop his research there. Not only did he want to know if good children's homes existed, which his study strongly indicated, but he also wanted to know if they could be run at low cost. They could. For one of the homes in the study, the cost of care (covering housing, recreation, supervision, basic amenities, education, and administration) per child in 1950 was less than $5,000 per year (in 1995 dollars). I noticed that the critics of children's homes didn't like to mention McKenzie's studies.

However, as McKenzie would state, the studies had clear limitations. The respondents were not drawn randomly from the national population of all former orphans. He admitted that children who had good experiences might be more likely to be on the alumni mailing lists and more likely to respond. Tracking down former residents of any given children's home and then surveying all or just a random sample of them was impossible. For me, the study had an even more significant limitation—it was done in the US, where conditions were vastly different from low-income countries like Honduras. The available data didn't give me enough answers. I was still confused.

But not for long. Unbeknownst to me, a study that did not have such limitations was already underway. At the time, the world's largest and most comprehensive research project on orphaned and separated children living in different low-income countries was being carried out. In 2009, researchers from Duke University shared their first-stage findings from the only longitudinal, multi-country observational study on children's homes. It used a two-stage random sampling survey methodology to follow a large cohort of orphaned and separated children.[27] It involved three thousand children, and was carried out in Cambodia, India, Ethiopia, Kenya, and Tanzania. About half of the sample group grew up in children's homes of varying size and quality, and the other half in "community" care (foster care or kinship care). The researchers expected children in group homes to measure poorly against their community care counterparts. But their assumptions were wrong.[28] The two groups showed the same scores in physical health, mental health, emotional and cognitive functioning, and physical growth. For some factors, children who grew up in group homes scored slightly better than their counterparts. The study found as much abuse and neglect in family settings as in institutions.[29] In addition, those in group homes experienced less exposure to sexual and physical abuse while in the homes (they experienced more before entering). The study concluded that children might be faring just as well in children's homes as in private homes because of better continuity, stability, and child-centric activities and education in children's homes. The Duke University study was more comprehensive, convincing, and relevant to our work in Honduras than anything I had seen. It lifted the confusion in my mind.

The researchers' subsequent study in 2014, with the same sample set, found that children in group homes had better physical health and emotional coping than those in family foster care.[30] According to the study's lead researcher, Kathryn Whetten, the findings were confirmed by a separate National Institute of Child Health and Development (NICHD)-funded study of three thousand children in Kenya, which found that children's human rights were less likely to be violated in group homes than in individual family settings. A third NICHD-funded study found similar results in China. Another study in Uganda showed that depression rates and anxiety were lower in children from group homes.[31]

Study after study showed that "all children's homes are harmful" was simply not true.

Deciding what's best for children without parental care should not be based on the type of building they live in, but instead on the care being given inside the building. That's what Dr. Kathryn Whetten, the lead researcher from the Duke study, believes. I agree. What the kids need, according to Whetten, is a stable, home-like environment with consistent long-term caregivers and steady sibling-like connections to other kids.[32] They don't do well if they're shuffled from place to place. My research taught me about child welfare, but it also taught me how people cherry-pick data to create propaganda and attack something.

* * *

Children's homes, like families, came in different sizes and forms. Once I had decided to set up a children's home, I needed a model to follow. I found it in SOS Children's Villages, an NGO that had been nominated for the Nobel Peace Prize.

SOS Children's Villages was founded by Hermann Gmeiner, who dedicated himself to providing for the war orphans created in the Second World War. In 1949, he created a family-centered childcare concept that was revolutionary. He built multiple homes near each other in what he called a children's village. In each home, a group of ten to twelve children lived with a housemother who became their primary caregiver. It was nothing like the overcrowded and impersonal orphanages of communist Romania or *Oliver Twist*. In the SOS Children's Villages, kids grew up with a mother, brothers, and sisters in a loving, family-like environment. Decades later, the *National Longitudinal Study of Adolescent Health* would reveal how important Gmeiner's concept is.[33] The study empirically identified the one factor—out of over a hundred variables—that was the most powerful in protecting children from negative outcomes: *a feeling of connectedness at home*. In the study, *connected* was defined as closeness to mother and/or father, perceived caring by mother and/or father, satisfaction with relationship with mother and/or father, and feeling understood, loved, wanted, and paid attention to by family members. When I first read about the study in Dr. Ed Hallowell's *The Childhood Roots of Adult Happiness: Five Steps to Help Kids Create and Sustain Lifelong Joy*,[34] it made me realize how much I took my parents for granted. I owed them so much for the sacrifices they made and the gratifying childhood they gave me.

Gmeiner starting with six hundred Austrian schillings (forty dollars) in his pocket but, through tireless work, he moved on to build 233 SOS Children's Villages in eighty-five countries over four decades. His accomplishments were of mythic proportions. After Gmeiner's death in 1986, SOS continued to grow, helping hundreds of thousands of children worldwide, including in seven cities in Honduras. Countless SOS alumni made it through college and ended the generational cycle of poverty and family dysfunction. SOS became the world's largest organization focused on supporting children without parental care and families at risk. When people ask me which one person in the world I would love to have lunch with, I often say Hermann Gmeiner.

I visited three separate SOS Children's Villages in Honduras. Then I drew up plans with Ines and the families from Villa Soleada to build a set of children's homes in the community. We decided the property would have a small farm, a playground, a soccer field, study rooms, an art room, and an exercise room. The houses would look as similar as possible to the rest of the houses in Villa Soleada. Each house would have a group of about ten children. There would be a Honduran housemother (and a housefather at the boys' home) who would commit to becoming a long-term caregiver and live with the children to provide a stable, supportive relationship. The kids would not be up for adoption (which in Honduras was nearly impossible to carry out legally) so that they find a sense of home at Villa Soleada and grow up in their own culture. The children and staff would interact like a big extended family. To integrate the children into the community, they would go to the same schools, soccer tournaments, and dances as the rest of the kids in the neighborhood. We would help each child find and develop their talents. Unlike most other childcare programs, including the US foster care system, we would not "age out" the kids. Instead, we would support them through college and beyond. I wanted the Villa Soleada Children's Home to be a place where children were given a chance to heal, thrive, and rebuild their futures.

We would trace each child's background, get documentation, and make sure they were placed with us through court orders. We would only accept children who were truly parentless or unable to grow up with their families. In his essays, Dr. Richard McKenzie writes that children without parental care need a menu of care options, as each child has varying needs. We decided to do exactly that. We would actively look for biological family members and give children the option of being placed with them if conditions were safe enough.

As planning and research went underway, Mission Honduras, led by Christof Wittwer, gave us a twenty-thousand-dollar donation to start the construction of the first house. Marco, now the director of construction for the organization, worked around the clock with Wilfredo and the fathers to build the home. They finished the living room, then the four bedrooms, then the kitchen. But we were devastated when the construction site was broken into, and our tools and supplies stolen. The fathers plowed forward, and I flew back to the US to speak at fundraising events—we needed to raise additional funds. As the first home went up, we began to build a second. The boys would live in one of the homes, and girls in the other.

Running our children's home using the SOS methodology was tricky, because we didn't know enough about their day-to-day operations to do so. Fortune brought me Elma, a young woman who had grown up at SOS Children's Village-Tela and was working there as a teacher. I asked her to run our project. She accepted, and began to train our team based on what she had learned at SOS.

As we moved forward, I needed to figure out how to finance the ongoing costs of running the project. Gmeiner had started a monthly giving campaign when he opened the first SOS Children's Village in Imst in the 1940s. Back then, without the help of the internet, Gmeiner and his staff went door-to-door each month to collect donations from their supporters. The effort was worth it. Within several years, thousands of people were supporting his organization.

We did something similar. Knowing that our supporters were mostly young and without much money, we asked them for $4 a month—the cost of one latte at the local coffee shop. We named the campaign One

Cup of Coffee. As soon as it launched, Mom signed up, and so did hundreds of others.

Elma and I spent hours working on the legal paperwork. We prepared countless documents for Ines, many of which required signatures from officials who lived in Tegucigalpa, four hours away. Meetings were often canceled without notice. More than one lawyer charged us for legal work and then disappeared. In every case, the people we contacted had something we needed, so we had to remind ourselves to be polite and likable, build rapport, and learn the rules of their games. It was excruciating.

Eventually, after months of work, our team turned in all the paperwork. Elma and I celebrated by going out for a smoothie. But the excitement was short-lived. "I'm so sorry, Shin," Ines said, "but the list of requirements I gave you was several years outdated." We needed to start the process all over again. I wanted to walk into the jungle to scream louder than the howler monkeys that lived there. Opening a children's home taught me about construction and fundraising, but it taught me even more about patience and navigating bureaucracy.

Nothing, however, prepared me for the phone call I would soon receive.

---- CHAPTER THIRTEEN ----

FAMILY IS WHERE LIFE BEGINS AND LOVE NEVER ENDS

THE CALL WAS FROM INES. SHE SOUNDED FRANTIC, HER voice trembling.

"Shin, we're in a state of emergency. We need you to open your children's home immediately."

I was confused. Ines had said she wanted to send us ten girls in a few weeks and boys several months later. We still needed to furnish the homes and buy supplies. We weren't ready to open.

"What's going on?" I asked.

"A fire broke out on the second floor of the state orphanage a few hours ago."

The live wires in the ceiling. Images of the prison fires I had heard about in Honduras flashed through my mind. In 2003, sixty-one prisoners were burned alive in a prison fire in La Ceiba. In 2004, another prison fire in San Pedro Sula killed 107 inmates. And Honduras would later witness the world's deadliest prison fire in the city of Comayagua, where 360 inmates would perish. I thought of José and felt the phone slipping out of my hand.

"Shin? Are you still there? Nobody was hurt. Everyone was eating lunch on the first floor when it happened." I closed my eyes and let out a deep breath of relief. "We evacuated the kids, though a bunch of them ran away during the process. The rest are staying at a temporary shelter. We don't have enough space or mattresses here."

"We're going to get things ready as fast as we can," I said.

"Shin, I need you to do something for me. A few organizations have come forward to take in some of the kids. But they mostly want girls and younger children. They find it difficult to accept children who struggle with severe behavior challenges. Would your organization be willing to take in kids I've had the most difficulty finding placements for? I have twelve boys, mostly in their teens. They are the ones who are left over."

Left over. The exact moment I heard those words, something heated up inside of my body. It was a visceral feeling I can't explain to this day. I told her that we would take all of the kids on her list. I didn't deliberate or mull over the decision endlessly like I sometimes did. As soon as I hung up the phone, our team got moving. We went shopping, bought soccer balls, and installed curtains. We finished everything that was supposed to get done in weeks in a matter of hours. When we finished the preparations, our entire staff got onto the bus and drove into San Pedro Sula. It was the morning before Thanksgiving Day.

In a run-down building with peeling green paint, we waited for the children. "These are the boys!" an officer said, as twelve boys shuffled into the room. Some of them recognized me and waved. The older boys maintained a hardened gaze. "I guess they picked me to go with you," said a voice I recognized. José. He was smiling, but he looked thinner and had bags under his eyes.

"You look like you haven't slept in ten years," I joked.

He laughed and gave me a high five and fist bump. "How are we supposed to get any sleep inside a warehouse?" he chuckled. "You should've seen us in the fire. It was like in the movies. We had to run upstairs through the fire and smoke to rescue the babies. I carried two of them down. One in each hand!"

The official motioned me over. "The twins there are Gerson and Pablo," she said, pointing to a corner of the dark room where two small boys, identical with shaved heads, were huddling together. "You'll find out why some people call them *Terremoto y Huracán*. Earthquake and Hurricane." The brothers were each holding a plastic bag with a pair of old sandals and T-shirts. "You take special care of them for me. They're the youngest ones in the group." The twins had a defiant look on their faces, but then they smiled and gave me a thumbs-up.

"And that one over there is Felipe," she said, pointing at a scrawny boy in a blue T-shirt. "We had planned to send him off with another NGO, but he hid in the back when they came to pick him up. We couldn't find him, so the NGO left with the other kids."

"Why was he hiding?" I asked.

"Apparently, he really wanted to go to Villa Soleada."

"We found 'em hiding behind a wall!" said José, as everyone laughed. Felipe smiled and shrugged. He was born in San Pedro Sula as one of many siblings. When his father was gunned down by gang members, Felipe took off for the streets. Eventually, he ended up at the state orphanage.

"That's Andrés," she said, pointing at an older boy with a thick build. "His mother disappeared trying to cross the border up north." Andrés ran away from home when he could no longer endure his dad's beatings. He got hit by a car while crossing a street, which explained why his teeth were crooked. After the beatings and the car accident, Andrés was never the same. He spoke with a stutter and suffered from constant headaches. "If you find Andrés' missing mother," said the official, "you might be able to reunite them." I thought of Andrés' mom searching for him in the desert, anxious and sick with worry.

"The oldest one is Kanelo." She pointed to the tallest kid in the room. He had a bandana tied across his slicked hair. I knew that thirteen-year-old Kanelo, who never lost a fistfight at the state orphanage, was considered the alpha top-dog of all the boys. If a kid wanted protection from another bully—and there were plenty of them—they bribed Kanelo with snacks. Kanelo's mom was dead, and his dad disappeared years before.

The official introduced the rest of the group. "Not all of them have birth certificates," she said, shrugging. "You'll need to investigate where they're from and how old they are." She handed me folders with some of their birth certificates. "Here, sign this."

I signed the sheet, and waited for more steps in the process.

"That's all," she said, shaking my hand. "Good luck."

* * *

The boys were all asleep when we arrived at Villa Soleada. Their new houseparents, Nita and Raffaelo, an old couple from Villa Soleada, greeted them with big hugs. The children walked into their new home and checked out their rooms. "This bed is mine!" yelled Kanelo as he jumped onto it. "I claim it!" José didn't seem to care which bed would be his. He was just thankful to have a new mattress.

Shortly after, I called over the boys from the village soccer team to join us for lunch. Chipmunks, the captain of the twelve-and-under youth team, showed up. He was so obsessed with soccer, I sometimes wondered if his brain was one giant soccer ball.

"I want all of them to join the team," he said, smiling from ear to ear.

Kanelo was sizing up the older boys from the team, including

Linaza, the tallest boy in the neighborhood. Kanelo puffed his chest out, but his eyes widened when they asked if he wanted to play marbles after lunch. He agreed enthusiastically. After we ate, Andrés took his plate of unfinished food and hid it underneath his bed. Another boy tucked tortillas into his pocket. Nita told them that they didn't have to do things like that because they would always have food from then on.

Gerson asked Chipmunks if there were any fruit trees in the community that he could climb. "More than you can count," answered Chipmunks. Gerson and Pablo hugged each other and cheered.

"What about the girls here?" asked Felipe. "Are they nice?" He raised his eyebrow to show his curiosity.

"Yeah, and Linaza has a sister we can introduce you to!" said Chipmunks. Everyone laughed and shoved Linaza. After lunch, the kids walked around the community with arms around each other's shoulders. I laughed at myself for worrying about the kids not getting along. The twins walked around saying hello to everyone, as if they were the new mayors in town.

I sat under a lemon tree that the community members had planted years before and watched the kids play soccer. I had imagined this moment many times over the years. "What's there to lose?" Ingrid had said back when the organization was one step away from shutting down. At that moment, I knew that giving the Honduran staff members leading roles in the organization was the best thing we could have done. Together, we created jobs in the community, got kids out of the state orphanage, and made a comeback. As I looked up at the light shining through the leaves, I wondered if the universe would reward us with a less tumultuous road ahead.

* * *

One of the first things we did was find out more about each child. The government had given us little background information, so we needed to do our own research. How had these children ended up with child services? Did they have biological family members who might be willing to take them in?

It turned out, Andrés did. After months of investigating, we located Andrés' mother who had gone missing after trying to cross the US border. In Honduras, family separation through migration is a major concern. (Sonia Nazario's Pulitzer Prize-winning book, *Enrique's Journey: The Story of a Boy's Dangerous Odyssey to Reunite with His Mother*, brings this concern vividly to life.)

In recent years, immigration has been in the headlines. According to a thirty-two-page 2017 report on migration by Doctors Without Borders, an estimated five hundred thousand people are forced to cross into Mexico every year.[35] The majority come from Honduras, El Salvador, and Guatemala, known as the Northern Triangle of Central America, one of the most violent regions in the world. Poverty, unemployment, and low wages leave people unable to provide for their families, forcing them to leave their homes in search of better opportunities. According to the World Bank, up to 55.4 percent of Honduras's population—and even more in rural areas—lives in poverty.[36]

Violence and corruption also force Hondurans to immigrate. Between 2006 and 2016, the Northern Triangle saw approximately 150,000 murders, which is considerably more civilian casualties than any other countries in the world, including those with armed conflicts or war (except for Syria). According to survey results in the Doctors Without Borders report, 57 percent of Honduran migrants reported that they never felt safe at home; 45.4 percent had lost a family member because of violence in the previous two years; and 75 percent had witnessed a murder or seen a corpse in the previous two years.[37]

The lack of justice in Honduras allows drug cartels to carry out crimes without fear of consequences, which perpetuates the country's violence and people's hopelessness. According to the Association for a More Just Society, the Honduran justice system has an impunity rate of 87 percent and a backlog of more than 180,000 murder cases, meaning that the majority of people who commit a crime will never be convicted in court.[38] According to Transparency International, in 2019, Honduras was the thirty-fourth most corrupt of 180 countries in the world.[39] According to Sonia Nazario, politicians in Honduras steal 30 to 40 percent of all government revenues.[40] Corruption weakens the country's institutions, which means that public hospitals lack running water or basic medicine, schools lack textbooks or roofs, and police have no gas or are easily bribed, furthering people's desperation.

The violence and desperation does not end when people leave their home countries. Migrants and refugees are preyed upon by criminal organizations as they enter Mexico. Many face beatings, abductions, robberies, torture, or sexual assaults during their journey. Sixty-eight percent reported being victims of violence during their transit toward the US, nearly one-third of the women surveyed had been sexually abused during their journey, and 60 percent of those treated by Doctors Without Borders for sexual violence had been raped.[41]

History shows that the US has fueled some of the carnage in Honduras. During a large part of the twentieth century, US banana companies exploited Hondurans. Backed by the US government, these companies helped put into place dictators that served US economic interests. It created a society marked with deep inequality. As a result, civil wars broke out in Central America in the seventies, and the US sent weapons, trained soldiers, and funneled millions of dollars into those wars. Hundreds of thousands of civilians were displaced, and many of them sought refuge in the US. The refugees, threatened by gangs in the US, formed their own. In the nineties, the US deported tens of thousands of gang members back to Central America. Today, gangs and cartels in Honduras are in a state of war as they battle to traffic drugs into the hands of US consumers. The people of Honduras, caught in the crossfire, are left with few options.

Organizations like the Association for a More Just Society believe that addressing poverty, violence, and corruption in Honduras will mean its people wouldn't have to immigrate. In an op-ed in the *Los Angeles Times*, Sonia Nazario discussed how to stem the immigration crisis at its root. In 2014, the US helped with criminal investigations and implemented pilot outreach centers in the toughest Honduran neighborhoods. Crime levels dropped, and two years later, the number of children at the US border was almost cut in half. According to Nazario, the cost to implement these programs is pocket change compared to the billions the US spends dealing with migrants and refugees. "We must deal directly with powerful forces pushing people out of their home countries and toward the US," she said. "If we do it right, we can use aid to reduce violence, poverty, corruption, and impunity and to bolster good governance. The money should go to vetted international aid and Honduran civil society groups instead of directly to the government."[42]

Andrés' mother had made it through Mexico and was living in Houston, Texas. Over the phone, she told us that he had a grandmother in El Progreso, not too far away from Villa Soleada. She would send money down each month to pay for Andrés' living expenses if he could live with his grandmother. When we told Andrés the news, he seemed excited. I told him that he was one of the lucky kids who had a biological family.

All of the boys tagged along to see him off to his grandmother's cinder block house. One after another, they hugged Andrés. He was sobbing by the time it was my turn to say goodbye. I could only imagine the mixture of emotions he must have felt. I would miss Andrés. He was a good-hearted kid who got along with everyone. He was easy to work with, was a focused student at our school, and trained hard during our daily soccer practices. He had thrived in the structured and disciplined lifestyle we had offered him. Over the months, he had grown taller, and his stuttering had become less noticeable. When he hugged me, I told him that he would be happier and better off with his biological family.

I was wrong. Andrés didn't get along with his grandmother. They constantly argued or went days without speaking to each other. He lost a sense of structure in his life and began to spend less time at home. He ended up with the wrong crowd in his neighborhood and dropped out of school. He even started to experiment with drugs and got hooked.

Knowing that his life had taken a turn for the worse, Andrés returned to Villa Soleada and begged us to take him back. I went for a short walk to think. Not knowing the criminals he had associated with or what his mother and grandmother wanted to do, I didn't know how to move forward. Before I could decide, Andrés ran away from his grandmother's home and disappeared. I found out that he had made a desperate attempt at crossing the border to find his mother in Houston.

Andrés' situation and many similar cases in the future would teach me that the debate between whether vulnerable children were better off with biological families, foster care, or children's homes was more complicated than any one-size-fits-all solution could claim. Family dysfunctions were complicated, including for me.

* * *

I was on my way to pick up Cosmo from the airport when the sky darkened. It was New Year's week. Back at Villa Soleada, families roasted pigs, danced bachata, and ate twelve grapes for good luck. Cosmo had called out of the blue to ask if she could visit. I said yes, thinking that maybe the resentment I held had died out. It was possibly time to make amends.

"I can't believe this truck's still going!" Cosmo said, as I tossed her luggage into the back of the Nissan Frontier. She had a few wrinkles around her eyes now. I wondered if she noticed a similar change in me. We exchanged small talk in the car, though it felt more forced than I wanted it to be. But I couldn't expect it to be like old times. After all, we hadn't spoken to each other in months. She updated me on her new life at New York University. It began to rain. I tried to roll up the window, but it was permanently off track and held together with duct tape. We got drenched, and I cursed myself for not having it fixed sooner.

That week with Cosmo was terse and awkward. On her last evening, we walked over for a family dinner at Villa Soleada Children's Home. Gerson was so excited, he kept overfilling the glasses and spilling water everywhere. Pablo threw rice and beans onto the plates, making as much noise as possible to get Cosmo to notice he was the most helpful of the bunch. Felipe handed out steamed vegetables and meat. He looked over his shoulder to make sure nobody was watching and quietly inched his vegetables onto José's plate. "Hey!" yelled Nita, the housemother. "You're eating double the broccoli because of that!" Felipe looked so stricken, we all laughed.

It was a beautiful evening. We held hands, bowed our heads, and José gave thanks. "Thank you for this meal, and thank you for giving us family. There are thousands of people outside these doors without food, without family. We promise to always be there for each other unconditionally. God bless."

Then we ate and reveled in the joy of being together.

"Cosmo, you should've seen when your brother tried to buy ice cream for this girl he had the hots for at the park! She ran away!"

...Riiip, riiip, hoooonk! Gerson jumped onto his chair and joyfully farted in Pablo's face. Cosmo fanned the air in front of her nose, laughing. "Shin used to do that to me all the time!"

"Cosmo, will you read us the books you brought? Please?"

The moon came out. The kids fell asleep in their chairs. We helped Nita and Raffaelo tuck in the little ones, and then we walked back to the guest house. The air was damp, the grass silver in the moonlight. Families of frogs, ducks, and rabbits appeared, then ran off under the light of the stars and moon. Not one cloud remained in the sky. We walked slowly, tired from all the laughter.

Cosmo stopped. "Hey, listen. The real reason I came down to Honduras this week was to make amends with you." She spoke softly but clearly, taking full ownership of the mistakes she had made before her departure. She apologized, and I knew it was sincere.

I should have done the same. I didn't.

"If you're ready, I want to put aside our past and move on together. What do you say?"

I was surprised by Cosmo. I wasn't expecting this. But what shocked me more was my own answer. I said yes, but it was so half-hearted anyone could tell I hadn't moved on. It was only then I realized how much resentment I still carried. I stood there in silence. I couldn't believe myself. I wish I had given her a firm yes to mend our relationship right then and there. Holding onto anger was like grasping a hot coal with the intent to harm someone else—it was immature and destructive. But I was still stuck in the past and unable to let go.

———— CHAPTER FOURTEEN ————

MOMENTS ARE MORE IMPORTANT THAN GOALS AND ACCOMPLISHMENTS

IT WAS PAST MIDNIGHT. MASKED MEN JUMPED OVER THE fence and crept into the back property of the Villa Soleada Children's Home.

Raffaelo, the housefather, heard a commotion from the pigpen. He and the security guard inched towards the noise—and were met with bullets. They took shelter behind a mango tree. The guard shot back until he was close to running out of shotgun shells. Security companies in Honduras made their employees pay for their own bullets, so our guard didn't have many. Luckily, the intruders jumped the fence and ran away.

When the sun came up, we found out our farm pigs had been mutilated. The mother pig was dead. "The throat's been slit with a machete," said Raffaelo. "The blood's still warm." He waved his flashlight at the fruit trees in the back to make sure nobody was hiding behind the shadows.

I tried to process what had happened. We had no idea why anyone would do something like this. All we knew was that violent break-ins in the area happened so frequently and indiscriminately that the families in Villa Soleada had to keep their windows shut during the hottest of summers. I hired an additional guard for the week. We were lucky: we could afford private security. Most Hondurans could not. George Orwell's words rang in my head: "Those who 'abjure' violence can do so only because others are committing violence on their behalf." As a child, I thought highly of pacifism. Spending time in Honduras made me realize that you sometimes had to use force to prevent further acts of violence.

Tired as I was, I had to be fresh. We were welcoming the first group of girls from the state orphanage that day. Their house stood completed just behind me; Yamilet was mopping the floors for the third time. She was to be the housemother of the girls' home. It was an easy decision for her, this woman who had been the first to pick up a machete to build Villa Soleada, and whose baby Dina was now studying in Villa Soleada Bilingual School—Yamilet would always dedicate her life to creating a better future for children.

"The rooms are ready," said Yalena as she checked out the bedrooms one last time. By then, Elma had resigned, stating that the boys were too much to handle. I had hired Yalena, whom I had worked with at DHC, as the new director of our children's home. Given her experience and background in psychology, she was exactly who we needed. "We better get going. The girls are waiting for us."

* * *

One by one, the girls stepped off the bus. First, Gloria. Then Nataly and Mirta. And lastly, Abigail.

The boys had their best outfits on and their hair gelled. Yamilet hugged each girl and showed them their new home. Gerson held the door open for the girls and gazed at me to make sure I noticed his gentlemanly manners. Pablo ran over to help with their small bags. As we set up a table in the front yard for lunch, Yamilet walked over with a plate with something I had never seen before. "Here, try this," she said and handed me what looked like a brown cube with hair. I bit into it as hot grease gushed out of my mouth. "It's fresh *chicharrón*—fried pork skin," she told me. The pig hair tickled my tongue. It was delicious.

"Thank you for your hard work," I said to the crowd in my prepared speech. "We looked forward to this day for years, and now we are here to celebrate together."

As everyone cheered, I waited for a sense of euphoria to take over. But for whatever reason, the joyful bliss I imagined never came. Instead, I felt like a boat lost at sea. A journey that helped me get up in the mornings had come to an end. I rarely enjoyed celebrations—no matter how many friends and family members were there—because I felt like they took time away from achieving the next goal. I kept this a secret, because I worried what people would think of me. But I knew I needed to figure out our next goal to regain a sense of direction.

I snapped out of my funk when someone slapped me on the shoulder. It was Ingrid. "The girls from the community want to play a game of soccer," she said. We opened up the mini soccer field and brought out a ball. The center of attention during the game was Abigail, a twelve-year-old who dreamt of becoming a nurse. She grew up begging on the streets while battling osteosarcoma, a type of bone cancer. About a year before, doctors had amputated her right leg to slow the cancer from spreading. But that did not stop Abigail from playing soccer. She moved around in her crutches and scored goals, fearless.

* * *

I was watching Abigail when Yamilet came over. "People are calling you," she said, "for a community-wide meeting."

"Right now? Can they wait a bit?"

"They said it was urgent."

I watched the girls' game for a few more moments, then headed towards the community soccer field, where a large crowd gathered. The sun beat down on me, and I felt weaker than I already was. The break-in was still on my mind—who were the culprits? The violence was starting to get out of hand. According to a rumor, several families planned to leave the community for good because they feared for their lives.

I noticed Wilfredo and his mother in the crowd and waved. They nodded, but turned away quickly. As I tried to figure out what was going on, I noticed a small group of men at the front. One of them was Tenaza.

Tenaza's drug problem had not gotten better. Over the years, he had continued to destroy several community projects while high. Weeks before, he was so drugged he jumped onto the truck I was driving and ripped off the side mirrors and the windshield wipers. When I calmly asked him to pay for the damages, I made the mistake of doing so in front of his wife—he said I would pay for that.

He wasn't the only one in the group at the front that the residents were afraid of. The LMDVS and their families were there too. They were upset at me that month. While refereeing a scrimmage during soccer practice, I had made several calls they thought cost them the game. And standing with them was someone who scared me more than Tenaza and all the neighborhood bullies combined: Royce, a disgruntled former employee who lived in the community. He wasn't a bad or violent person, but our organization had recently ended his job contract, which aggravated him. As soon as I saw him with his arms crossed, I realized what was about to happen. What I was walking into wasn't a meeting. It was a public persecution.

"This project is an elaborate ploy," Royce shouted. "Shin used our labor to build homes and now plans on selling them for profit!" The men in the front cheered. I glanced at the community members to see if they were shaking their heads like I was. Strangely, they weren't. They were all gazing at Royce.

"Think about it," he continued, "after months of promises, he still hasn't given us the land titles for our homes! He's purposely delaying the process!" The truth was far from it. We had already turned in all the paperwork to the government months before. But the bureaucracy in Honduras moved slowly. We called frequently to check in, but month after month, we were told to wait. I wiped the sweat on my forehead. "I can understand the frustration with the delay," I said. "But please allow me to expl—"

"Look at the wall he built around the school," interrupted Royce, pausing theatrically and making a sweeping gesture with his arms. "Can't you see he plans to take the school away from us?!"

I wanted to say that we had built the security wall because thieves repeatedly broke in, taking supplies that belonged to the children. Most schools in Honduras had walls with barbed wire. But Royce kept going. He didn't let me respond. The more I listened, the more confused I got. After all, why would anyone be upset for making it harder for thieves to break in? The LMDVS were smiling. At that very moment, I realized whoever broke in the night before wasn't trying to steal anything. They were showing us how vulnerable we were.

"Shin said he was going to start a company here in the community to create jobs. Years later, we're still waiting!" Royce had the gift of taking words out of context. Years before, I had told people that I wanted to create jobs to help them. I may not have started a physical company as they initially imagined, but we had created a nonprofit company that made it a priority to create jobs locally. By then, we were the largest employer in the area, employing at least one person in nearly half of the households in Villa Soleada. Ironically, Royce had been one of them until he was let go for what we thought were justified reasons (he disagreed). "Shin's changed. He used to play with the children. Now he beats them up!" The absurd fabrications went on for nearly an hour.

"*And*," Royce said, and this was his trump card. "He won't allow us to sell our homes even if we wanted to leave the community. He has us trapped here!" Royce was referring to a clause in the community's housing agreement. When we started the project, the municipal government asked us to include a clause in the land titles that would prevent families from selling their newly acquired homes. They had seen how housing projects in the area without such clauses turned out. People with substance addictions sold their homes to pay off debt, leaving their children on the streets. Gang members took over entire housing projects and forced residents to sell their homes. The clause protected families and ensured that children had roofs over their heads in the long run. The Hondurans called such a clause *El Patrimonio Familiar*—the family's legacy/birthright. The community had agreed to the clause unanimously.

When Royce requested the clause be removed, the LMDVS cheered. I had no idea what their plan was. But the blistering sun magnified my fatigue and the crowd's restlessness. I acquiesced. We decided to do away with El Patrimonio Familiar. Ultimately, Villa Soleada was their community.

Royce wrapped up his speech by urging everyone to stop supporting the school and SHH. I looked at Wilfredo, at his mother, and several others. I was hoping for someone to come to my defense. Everyone in the community knew me. We had worked together for years. We had celebrated birthdays. We had shared heartfelt conversations. Surely they weren't going to believe Royce's accusations.

But nobody stood up that day. Not one person. Royce had won. He knew it too—he stared me down with triumphant, red eyes. Something inside of me shriveled.

I walked away. The human ego is a fragile and scary thing, and I hadn't learned to work around it. The families were going to pull their children from the school and leave the community, and gang members were going to take over the neighborhood, as they had done in other housing projects.

* * *

I was wrong. On Monday morning, every single student showed up to school. Mothers were there too, volunteering. They were cleaning tables, collecting trash, and mopping the floor. I was afraid to look at them in the eyes, but they all waved and smiled. When I walked over to the office, I saw a line of parents I had never seen before. They were hoping to get their children on the enrollment waitlist. A group of staff members walked over and handed me letters of encouragement. "We believe in you," wrote someone. "Truth always wins," someone else scribbled.

Wilfredo came up to me later that day. He apologized, and I struggled to contain my feelings. He was sorry for what happened, and for not having said anything in the field. Most people in the community avoided confrontations. "We prefer to speak with our actions."

Then he shook my hand, and I had to tip my hat over my eyes. I thought back on all the moments and accomplishments I had shared with this community for nearly ten years. Together, we had built homes, schools, and libraries. But most importantly, we had built a foundation of trust so solid that our relationship could withstand the most inflammatory of accusations. It saved me.

* * *

We enrolled the girls at the Villa Soleada Bilingual School. After her first day of class, Abigail came home and hopped over with great excitement. "If I study hard, I can be more than a regular nurse," she said, "I can be a *bilingual* nurse." I gave her a Honduran high five. She talked about how she wanted to help other kids with cancer. Then she paused and said in a low voice, "I'm nearly thirteen." She was scared of turning thirteen, which was when kids were aged out of the state orphanage. Would she be asked to leave the children's home? I told her gently that we would support her through nursing school and beyond. She beamed.

I wished I smiled back. Instead, I looked away. There was something I needed to tell Abigail: her most recent CAT scan indicated that the cancer had returned and spread into both of her lungs. Her oncologist had told us that Abigail had close to a zero percent chance of surviving the year. We needed to prepare for the worst.

Yalena and I did what any parent would do—we decided to look for secondary and tertiary opinions. But we quickly faced a roadblock. While we were looking for options, the heads of the public health insurance program stole three hundred million from the Honduran healthcare system. As a result of such acts of blatant corruption, the hospitals lacked basic resources like running water and gauze. When the quality of medicines administered at the hospitals came into question, the Association for a More Just Society carried out an investigation. They found out that many medications were so substandard, diluted, or fake, they were no better than a placebo. Corrupt health officials were taking bribes from drug companies and suppliers to overpay for products that were shoddy or never arrived. According to Sonia Nazario, the corruption was so bad, the United Nations has had to oversee the purchase of most drugs in Honduras. Too many people in the country were dying as a result of bad medicines or a lack of available drugs.[43]

To make matters worse, it was all over the news that MS-13 had taken over parts of the hospital in San Pedro Sula. Armed gangsters held up patients, staff, and family members inside waiting rooms. Patients had to pay them off to get from one floor to the next. As gang members took over more floors, public hospital doctors went on strike. They hadn't been paid in months and refused to return to work until they received their salaries. After we tried all of the public hospitals, we visited a private hospital, called St. Jude Children's Hospital, and emailed friends in the medical field. As the days passed, Abigail's health deteriorated. Eventually, she had to quit school because it became too difficult for her to breathe.

One morning, Dr. Tania, a pediatric oncologist from a private hospital in San Pedro Sula, contacted us. She had just gotten off a call with oncologists from Harvard Medical School about Abigail's case. There was a new kind of treatment that could increase Abigail's survival rate from zero to forty percent. Yalena and I were ecstatic. Forty percent wasn't the most promising number, but it was infinitely better than zero. Dr. Tania warned us that the treatment wasn't cheap—it cost $25,000. When she saw our faces, she handed us a stack of academic journals about osteosarcoma. She told us to take our time to make an educated decision.

I spent hours reading the studies. They verified that the treatment was state-of-the-art and promising. I didn't know how we would find the money though. I wished I were a millionaire. I decided to go all out on my thirtieth birthday, which was coming up. I would ask friends to donate to Abigail's medical costs instead of buying me birthday gifts. I had no idea how people would respond, given that Abigail was a girl whom none of them knew. We lived in a world where children who begged on the streets, like Abigail, were shunned and cast away. I created an online fundraising page that explained the situation. I spent hours rewriting each sentence and posted a photo of the two of us pumping our fists into the air. As soon as I made the page public, Mom donated. Then Bob donated. Within hours, friends from all over the world jumped in to help. I couldn't believe it—in four days, our network had raised $39,000 for Abigail's treatment.

The day we took Abigail to the hospital, all of the kids from the children's home accompanied her. As she went into the doctor's room, our entire group formed a giant circle in the parking lot and recited a prayer. The chemotherapy was aggressive. It caused Abigail great pain. For the coming weeks, the staff members and I took turns staying at the hospital to comfort and cheer her on. We told her that the pain was temporary and that she would soon be back in school, studying to become a bilingual nurse. We told her to stay strong and keep fighting. Day after day, she endured the torturous process. She didn't mind losing weight. But when her hair fell out, Abigail was distraught. I joked with her that it was payback time for all the occasions she made fun of me for my shaved head. We both laughed. We bought her a wig. When I tried it on and winked at her, we laughed some more. I tried my best to lighten her mood.

The first round of treatment worked. The tumors on her lungs began to shrink. I told her that she was going to continue getting better. I told her that I was getting old and didn't want any other bilingual nurse but her to help me with my diapers. She laughed. As we welcomed her back home, I relaxed a little and went back to the office. There was much work to be done. By then, SHH had more than twenty Honduran employees, nearly thirty kids at the children's home, and over a hundred students at the bilingual school. The growth meant that our expenses had increased, and so had the hours it took each month to meet the budget.

Weeks later, when we looked at new CAT scans, I had to close my eyes. Abigail's tumors, instead of shrinking, had grown. They looked bigger than her lungs. Abigail could no longer breathe on her own. We found an oxygen machine and hired a nurse to stay with her at the children's home. The tumor pushed against her rib cage. It was so painful that she was unable to sleep or eat much. I couldn't believe it. She was getting better just weeks before. The pain continued to worsen. It was agonizing to see her suffer so much. The doctors gave us different kinds of painkillers. They worked for a while, but Abigail's mind started to become impaired. She began to mumble random thoughts.

"I'm scared of dying," she said to me one day. I didn't know how to respond. I was scared of death too. But as a healthy person, I got to pretend like death was in the far and distant future. Yamilet talked to Abigail about God and heaven, and that seemed to calm her down. Eventually, even the most potent painkillers stopped working. All Abigail could do was writhe in bed and gasp for air.

It took a great deal of effort just to get her into the car for her appointments. But I held onto hope. *People beat cancer all the time*, I told myself over and over. I deluded myself by making plans for all the fun things Abigail and I would do once she got better. I told myself that she would survive. The universe wouldn't allow a girl who had to grow up begging on the street and had never been to a movie theater or zoo to die like this. After all, I convinced myself, SHH exists so that kids from the streets and the state orphanage can have long, fulfilling lives.

When I get stressed over a problem I can't solve, I avoid the very things I should be doing. Though admittedly not the best tactic, it allows me to pretend like the problem will resolve itself or doesn't exist in the first place. That's exactly what I did with Abigail. I should have been spending more time with her, but instead, I spent longer hours at work, burying myself in endless meetings and my inbox.

Somehow, Abigail's health improved enough one week that she was able to speak and even walk a little. She said she'd always wanted to ride a horse, so Yalena seized the opportunity. She found a farm that allowed visitors to ride horses.

"Can you join us?" Yalena asked me.

"I can't," I said. "I have to work." I promised myself I'd go the next time.

The first time Abigail rode a horse was also her last. She passed away a few days after. The decision to not go to the farm is one I will regret for the rest of my life. Yalena made the necessary phone calls to organize a funeral service. She was just as exhausted and devastated as everyone else, but she kept herself together to be strong for the children. I wished I had her strength, but I was useless during the entire process. I felt paralyzed by shock and grief. As Abigail's casket was lowered into the ground, Wilfredo handed me a shovel to help him toss dirt into the hole. I watched Pablo and Gerson scatter dirt as they fought back tears. José grabbed a shovel and began to help. The others sat, weeping.

My tears mixed with sweat and dirt. Many emotions swirled in me, but one overwhelmed the rest: regret. *Why didn't I go with Abigail to ride that horse with her? Why had I buried myself in work? What email or phone call was more important? What meeting couldn't wait just a few days?* At the funeral, I realized how twisted my priorities were. For ten years, I had sacrificed family, relationships, friendships, and weekends so the organization could accomplish one milestone after another. I had been perpetually and obsessively in pursuit of "the next thing." But in the process, I had become a machine who spent more time at the office than with his family, friends, or kids at the children's home combined. I didn't want to admit it, but most of my personal relationships were in ruins or close to it. If there was anyone who I wanted to spend more time with, confess something to, apologize, or make amends with, I had to do it now. Not too long after Abigail's funeral, I picked up the phone and called Cosmo.

*　*　*

Early one morning, I got a call from William. He was our contractor for roofs; just the day before, he and his team had finished installing the roof to our new guesthouse. Now he called to tell me he had been robbed in the Alley. Five gunmen had jumped out with guns and machetes.

"They cut my brother," William said, his voice shaking. "Marcus said something and they hacked at him…"

William had rushed Marcus to the hospital, his clothes soaked with blood, praying his little brother would make it. By the grace of God, Marcus was okay but William—William had had enough.

"I know who was involved," he told me. "And I will take care of them."

"*Take care of them?*" His voice scared me.

"That's right. It's time we cleanse and free Villa Soleada. Enough is enough!"

In Honduras, it was too easy for anyone to hire a *sicario*, or a hitman, to kill someone. It only took a few hundred dollars, or sometimes, even less. When I hung up the phone, I realized what was happening in front of our eyes: a war was breaking out.

That afternoon, kids ran around the field with their paper kites. Next to them, the LMDVS guys and I were playing a small-sided soccer game. A white mini-bus was driving towards us, leaving a trail of smoke and dust behind it. William was on the bus.

I froze.

The door on the bus flung open, and a dozen men ran out carrying black cases. Time slowed. My heart raced. I closed my eyes, waiting to be sprayed by machine-gun bullets. Growing up in the peaceful suburbs of northern Virginia, I never imagined that I'd die from a stray bullet. Strangely, all I could hear were noises of celestial musical instruments. *I must already be up in the heavens*, I thought to myself. I was lucky—I must have died so quickly I didn't even feel pain.

But "heaven" also seemed to have the LMDVS guys—I could hear them talking—so I inched my eyes open. The men weren't carrying shotguns. They were carrying guitars, drums, and boxes of Bibles. A smiling William in a yellow dress shirt was waving enthusiastically.

"Shin, after some deep reflection," he said, "I realized what Villa Soleada needed wasn't more violence. What it needs is the gospel of God!" I laughed a nervous laugh and gave William a big hug. From that day on, William visited the community weekly to hold church gatherings and barbecues. William, the parents in the village, and our staff frequently met to discuss how to address the violence in the community. We agreed to do it through peaceful means and planned to expand the soccer program, job program, and William's church outreach.

The universe had other plans. One evening, Bravilio, a father from Villa Soleada who had had enough with the muggings, spotted the leader of the LMB, the notorious gang from the adjacent neighborhood, inside a billiard hall. Bravilio walked calmly inside, took out his machete, and chopped the gang member's head off. Bravilio walked away and never came back to the area. Shortly after, the rest of the LMB—who had stayed busy that year hijacking public buses—died in a massive shootout with the cops. Those who survived were sent to jail. Many of the LMDVS members shared a similar fate. Their problems started when they began to pick fights with rival gangs that were even more ruthless than they were. One LMDVS member was found hacked to death in his house. Another's dead body was found in the palm field with signs of torture. The cousin of one of the heads of LMDVS was shot and killed while riding his bicycle. The rival gangs didn't stop there. They began driving into Villa Soleada at random hours to hunt down the last of the LMDVS. Pressured, the LMDVS and their families began to sell their homes.

Over the years, MS-13, which controlled the south side of El Progreso, expanded its operation in the city. They set up a cell in our part of the city and gunned down one of the main dealers in the area to show that they had taken control of the territory. They were uninterested in petty crime and announced that they would kill anyone who stole or created problems in the neighborhood; given their devotion to drug dealing, the last thing they wanted was the police to show up.

One day, while I was taking the kids from the children's home to a neighborhood circus, MS-13 gang members approached me. They were carrying guns. "Chino," said the boss, "I have a question for you." Thinking he was going to ask for a war tax, I held my breath. But instead, he wanted to know if we had an open spot at the bilingual school for his eight-year-old son. He told me that I no longer had to worry about criminals breaking into the bilingual school.

Shortly after MS-13 arrived, the last of LMDVS gang members fled the community. Eventually, Royce left too. Tenaza was kidnapped, beaten nearly to death by a group of men, and decided to quiet down for a while. Just like that, the violence that had plagued Villa Soleada for years came to an end.

BOOK 5

CHAPTER FIFTEEN

TOUGH MOMENTS ARE OPPORTUNITIES FOR TRANSFORMATION

IT WAS 2017. DINA, ALONG WITH FIVE OTHER STUDENTS from the Villa Soleada Bilingual School, stepped off the bus. They were at Destiny Bilingual School, one of the most prestigious—and expensive—private schools in the city. Students from the twelve other bilingual schools in the region milled about the paved parking lot. Their cars were fancy; they flashed brand new iPhones. Dina, who used to be a baby the size of a papaya at Siete de Abril, was now a sixth grader at Villa Soleada—and the best speller in her classroom. Today, she was representing Villa Soleada at her first city-wide spelling bee competition.

Dina had been diagnosed with malaria only a few weeks earlier, so she was still weak. But today, her mother Yamilet made Dina's favorite breakfast—tortillas with melted cheese crumbs—and she had eaten a little. She'd practiced for this day for months. In addition to learning about fractions and reading books like *Tuck Everlasting*, Dina had studied a list of 1,200 new words in English.

"Bacon," said the official.

Dina took a deep breath. "B-A-C-O-N."

"Vacant," said the official in the next round. Then, in the next round, "compliment." Dina got both correct. She was inching closer to victory. If she won, she'd be the sixth-grade spelling bee champion of El Progreso, the fourth largest city in the country with over two hundred thousand residents. In many neighborhoods in Honduras it seemed that gang members outnumbered school graduates. Nearly 62 percent of adolescents from the poorest quintile are out of school.[44]

Dina's victory would give the entire Villa Soleada community hope and a glimpse of what was possible through sustained effort.

"Formless," the official said.

"F-O-R-M-L-E-S-S."

"That is correct!"

She'd won. Dina covered her face with her hands. She wanted to jump with elation but decided not to when she saw her opponent with his head down. She shook his hand. "Good match."

An hour later, as Yamilet sobbed in the crowd, Dina was awarded a first-place medal to take back to Villa Soleada.

* * *

A few weeks after the spelling bee, our organization received an extortion message demanding $4,000. I paced around the room, sat down, and reread the threatening message. We had never been targeted until now. "We'll send you a text message with further instructions on where to bring the cash," it read. Addresses of our employees, including mine, were written out. In Honduras, countless civilians, from fruit vendors to business owners, pay what is commonly known as *impuesto de guerra*—war tax—to the local gangs.

Sonia Nazario's research on extortion in Honduras showed that just in the capital city of Tegucigalpa, business owners pay an estimated twenty-three million each year in war tax.[45] Some lose 30 to 40 percent of what they make to extortion. Others have to pay off six different gangs just to stay alive. Of six hundred businesses in one neighborhood in the capital that were tracked, 150 closed because of the cost of extortion. Not paying means death. In the transportation industry alone, more than 1,500 Honduran workers have been murdered since 2010. Most were shot. Others were cuffed to their steering wheels and burned alive. To instill fear, the executions often happened in public and in broad daylight. According to Nazario, one thirty-four-year-old mother of two children decided to stop making payments to the 18th Street gang. She ran a small corner shop in her neighborhood. One day, an assassin showed up and shot her in the face. She stumbled towards her four-year-old daughter who was asleep, but died before reaching her.

I called a friend who owned a bus transportation company in town. "Pay," he said. "Pay, so you don't end up in a coffin. I've lost too many friends because of this. And no matter what happens, do not go to the authorities—*that's a sure death sentence.*" My heart rate increased as my friend continued. "Just negotiate the price down. They want money but don't want their targets to go bankrupt. They want to hemorrhage—not kill."

"You've paid it before?"

"I've been paying it for years!" I had no idea that behind his jovial demeanor, my friend had been dealing with something so terrifying. "These gangs know our addresses, daily schedules, and even the names of our children. My family and employees are still alive because I've never missed the bimonthly payment. That's why they call these payments *vacunas*—vaccines."

I thanked him and dialed a friend who owned a hotel.

"Don't pay," he said. "They're like sharks. They can smell weakness from a mile away. Once they get the first bite, they won't let go. When I got my first extortion message last year, I bought a shotgun and went straight to the authorities."

"You weren't scared of them finding out you went to the cops?"

"What do you think, man? Around my wife, I had to pretend I was all brave. But inside, I was so terrified I couldn't sleep for months, and my hair went completely grey."

"And what happened?"

"I slept with the shotgun under my bed each night. As a matter of fact, I still do. Thankfully, the calls stopped coming. They must've gone off looking for someone easier to prey on."

"What if it was all a sick prank?"

My friend said that it was possible. It wasn't unheard of for victims of extortion to find out that the perpetrator was a neighbor, colleague, or family member trying to ruin someone's life. "But you don't ignore something like this around here," he said. He warned me that the scariest thing about the threat was the mass paranoia it caused. His employees, not knowing if the threat was coming from somewhere far away or right next to them, had started to fear and doubt each other. I called more friends and found out that many of them had lived through similar experiences. Each person gave me a different opinion on how to respond. That night, I had to turn my cell phone off; each time it vibrated, fear and anxiety would course through my brain.

In the morning, I got in touch with the US State Department and a US military branch working in Honduras. An official from the military base advised me not to make the payment, and I agreed. He informed me that an investigation could only happen if I filed a formal crime report at the new anti-extortion unit of the Honduran police force. The thought of going to the local authorities reminded me of Hector, who was murdered shortly after reporting a crime.

In an op-ed in *The New York Times*, Sonia Nazario explains that the year before, 5,000 of the country's 13,500 officers and all forty of the highest-ranking officers were fired because they were suspected of being criminals, didn't pass a polygraph, or were incapable of doing their jobs. Of the 2,100 officers referred to the attorney general for prosecution, only one was convicted.[46]

I asked the official from the military base if it was true that the local police sometimes colluded with criminals. He confirmed that it certainly happened. But he reminded me that the anti-extortion unit was brand new and didn't have a bad track record. But how much of a track record could a newly formed unit possibly have?

I decided not to file the crime report, and instead go into hiding for as long as I could. For days, I kept looking over my shoulder, wondering if someone was spying on me. If all of this was some disgruntled person's twisted ploy to crush our spirits—which the authorities suspected—it was working. Several senior employees decided to quit the organization for fear of their lives.

I shut down the school temporarily—it was too risky. As I walked through the empty grounds, I noticed things that I usually didn't, like birds fluttering above me and the smell of the cut grass. I could even feel sweat evaporating off of my arms. My eyes focused on every shadow with unusual intensity. It was scary how heightened my senses were. The trivial worries that usually filled my mind were gone. I missed them because now my mind was filled with the doom of impending violence and random death. I felt like a hunted gazelle.

That evening, I organized a meeting with the families. I explained the threat and told them we would keep the school closed until the situation was resolved. Some shut their eyes and began to pray. Others shook their heads in anger and disgust. Everyone was trying to remain composed, but they were heartbroken. I saw a few of our students peeking in from the windows. They were clustered on the grass, petrified and worried.

"I say we get to them before they can get to us!" yelled a father wearing a wide-brimmed hat. "Who here says we hire some *sicarios*—hitmen?" Several parents yelled and nodded in agreement. "Just tell me how much to chip in!" said someone from across the room. I tried to stop a group of fathers from making actual plans to hire a sicario. People began to argue and shout as I lost control of the crowd. Then Jairo spoke up. "It's up to the organization to decide what to do from here. I have faith that the school will open again. But no matter what decision they make, we—the families from Villa Soleada—will protect the school with our lives!"

"So will we from Barrio de Amistad!" yelled someone. "And us from Primero de Enero!" shouted someone else. A few others yelled out the neighborhood they represented. The parents decided to form a patrol committee to protect the school and its staff. "We'll simply make it impossible for any of these criminals to get through!" said Jairo. The crowd cheered. I wanted to cry, but I held back my tears.

The younger kids at the children's home were getting ready for bed when I finished my meeting. It was late, but Yalena and I convened another meeting with the teenagers. We all shuffled into the study room. "Is what they're saying out there true?" asked José. He was now in high school, and his voice was deeper. Paintings he had finished at a private art studio in the city covered the walls of the room.

"Yes," I answered.

"What are they saying out there?" asked Pasifica. She had joined us as a little girl just weeks after we had inaugurated the girls home; now she, too, like José, was already in high school.

"They're going to close the home down, aren't they?" added Gerson.

His shoulders were slumped, and his eyes were red and watery. This was the first time that the twins were asked to join the meeting with the "older" kids. They were no longer little children. They were already getting ready for middle school, where they would learn algebra and read the same chapter books that their peers in the US would be reading.

"No," answered Yalena, "not a chance. But our family is under threat. We received an extortion message." The teenagers gasped. "We need your help keeping your eyes open for anything suspicious. You're now teenagers, and the little ones are looking to you for strength. We have to stand together and protect the family."

José assured us that the threat was undoubtedly a sick prank. He let out a nervous laugh, but nobody else was laughing.

"Based on what?" retorted Pasifica. "I'm sure that's exactly what all those bus drivers said! They dropped their guard, and now they're all in the graveyard!" She covered her face with her hands. She referred to the hundreds of workers in the transportation industry who had been publicly executed by extortionists in recent years.

After the meeting, José ran over to the small weight room we had. I could hear him doing his pushups and grunting louder than usual. Pasifica went into the house to check on the younger kids. Pablo, Gerson, and some of the younger children gathered outside under the lamp. They broke into pairs and walked around the perimeter of the property, flashlights and sticks in hand. Some of them had rocks in their pockets. Others were wearing armor made of cardboard.

"We've formed the Villa Soleada Children's Home patrol committee," Pablo told me, when I asked, "to protect the home and the little ones." He yelled a strange sound and swung the stick in the air, nearly hitting me in the head.

"The two of us," added Gerson, "have elected ourselves as the patrol leaders."

I watched the brothers sword fight each other with their sticks.

Eventually, they began to give out orders to the younger children, who ran off in their pajamas. Everyone rushed around the yard, screaming and banging whatever they could reach. It seemed there was no right answer. But, as I watched them, I knew that I was, without a doubt, the single most cowardly person on the earth. I was so scared of moving forward with the investigation, I had been planning on waiting for the extortionists to make the first move. I could have very well called it *the sitting duck strategy*. Meanwhile, the families from Villa Soleada, who had already risked their lives multiple times to protect the community, and even the kids from the children's home, were doing whatever was in their power to protect the organization. I felt embarrassed for having been so passive. Being proactive and putting the pressure on was the only way to not become the hunted. I decided to act.

* * *

Shortly after the extortion incident, Juan Orlando Hernandez won his second presidential term in Honduras in an election that was widely criticized as fraudulent. Before the election, President Hernandez's reputation in the country was already under significant question. The truth behind the 2018 presidential election would escape the people of Honduras. The Honduran Congress, faced with charges that up to sixty-five lawmakers had stolen $55 million in public funds, had made it difficult for anti-corruption prosecutions to happen.[47] In protest, tens of thousands of Hondurans took to the streets. Civil unrest broke out throughout Honduras as protestors burnt tires, blocked major highways, and clashed with police. More than thirty civilians were killed. Desperation followed as supermarkets and food pantries in the city began to run out of supplies. Street gangs and criminals took advantage of the instability. They waited at roadblocks and charged money for those wanting to walk through. We had recently reopened the bilingual school after the extortion incident; now we had to shut it down for the third time in seven years.

At the time, our organization was attempting to build eight public schools throughout northern Honduras. The nationwide turmoil made the process difficult and dangerous. When roads were blocked off, we had to turn around or were unable to purchase supplies. The highway leading to our project at Yolanda Melendez village school, where families relied on pineapple farming, was sealed off on most days. But the construction team was committed to meet the deadline. For too many years, children in Yolanda Melendez had received classes in a one-room schoolhouse with a damaged roof. During the protests, Wilfredo, Adriano, and several of our masons from Villa Soleada decided to stay and sleep in the community to finish the project.

On the final day of construction, I decided to join our masons to mix and pour concrete to build the floor. I wouldn't be much help, but building the floor, which took over forty people to do, reinforced our sense of camaraderie like nothing else. I enjoyed it—and so did the masons, who got to make fun of my clumsiness for the day. I got into the bus with a group of student volunteers from the US who were excited to meet the community. As the driver cranked up the radio, I looked out the window and wondered if there would be roadblocks along the way. It would be a major inconvenience, but at the same time, I understood why people were doing it. There wasn't much else they could do in a country where the oligarch held onto their power so tightly. By 2018, Honduras was one of the most unequal countries in Latin America.[48]

As we left Villa Soleada, I reflected on all the schools that our organization had built over the years…

CHAPTER SIXTEEN

YOU WILL NEVER KNOW YOUR LIMITS IF YOU DON'T TEST THEM

OUR ENDEAVOR TO BUILD SCHOOLS THROUGH HONDURAS started in 2008, with a chance meeting.

I was waiting in line at the municipal office to get some documents signed. A man walked out of the mayor's office and sat across from me. He looked distraught. I sometimes wonder if people think that I'm nosy, but that day, my curiosity got the best of me. I said *"perdóname*—excuse me," and asked him why he looked so upset.

He perked up, blinked a few times, and told me his life story and the history of his community. It turned out, he really wanted to talk to someone. He was the elected leader of the parents' association at Por Venir, a community not too far from Villa Soleada. For years, he had been begging the mayor to help build a school for his community. Every time, he waited in line for two hours at this office, only to be told to come back the following year. This year was no exception.

He confessed he dreaded having to deliver the same bad news to his community. So he was sitting there, delaying. As I listened, shared a few stories myself, and laughed with him, I began to wonder if there was something I could do to help. When I told him that I worked for an NGO, he became excited. He invited me to visit his community's school project. He waited for me to get my documents signed, and then we drove over to Por Venir.

"We're here," he said, as we parked in front of the community's makeshift schoolhouse. It looked like a dilapidated trailer house made of rotting wood, chicken wire, and sheets of rusted tin. The structure creaked and dust fell onto my head when I touched one of the wooden columns. Classes had to be canceled when it rained—which it often did—because water leaked through the holes in the tin roof. Two hundred students were crammed into the building, sharing just fifty desks. Teachers had attempted to drown out noise between the different grades by using pieces of rotting wood to separate the building into three sections. I now understood why the man waited in that same line, year after year.

That month, our organization won an online voting competition and were awarded enough money to build a three-classroom school at Por Venir. This was the first time I met Marco, the man I would later hire to become lead foreman of SHH during our restructuring, and who would become a cornerstone to our community. In 2008, he was a father with deep brown eyes who volunteered to help the construction for free because his son attended the school. During the planning process, I reread my weathered copy of *Leaving Microsoft to Change the World* with great excitement. The book, written by John Wood, a former executive at Microsoft, is a memoir of how he quit his corporate job to start Room to Read, an organization that has built schools and provided educational opportunities to children throughout the world. Cosmo and I had used Wood's book as a blueprint to carry out construction projects at Villa Soleada. We used it again to build the school at Por Venir. John believed in the importance of creating community buy-in by involving the community every step of the way. The process was known as "participatory development." John also asked partner communities to provide sweat equity—or contribution in the form of manual labor. Getting the community to feel a sense of ownership and responsibility for a project maximized its long-term success. Wood also encouraged organizations to create partnerships with local governments and businesses. We tried and it worked. We convinced the mayor of El Progreso to donate all of the sand we needed to mix concrete for all of our school projects in the city.

When Marco began the construction, he faced a problem Wood hadn't prepared us for—*so many parents showed up to volunteer, he had to turn many of them away.* I visited that first week and saw dozens of fathers, mothers, and grandparents digging trenches and carrying cinder blocks. As I watched the walls quickly go up, I wondered what John Wood must have said to himself while witnessing the first schools for Room to Read get built. Did he have any idea his organization would eventually be building thousands of schools and libraries throughout the globe to benefit millions of children? I hoped our efforts were contributing a grain of sand towards Wood's vision for more education in the world.

When the three-classroom school was completed, the teachers painted the walls yellow. One of them said that the color symbolizes joy, happiness, and energy. I wasn't sure if she made that up, but those were certainly the emotions I felt on inauguration day. At the ribbon cutting ceremony, Marco said something so far-fetched, it made the two of us laugh: "God willing, SHH will one day build schools like this for five or *ten* communities in Honduras!"

* * *

While the school at Por Venir was being built, I met with residents in Villa Soleada to figure out how we were going to address a major hole in our cradle to college pipeline: parental job security. Kids ate better at home, performed better at school, and grew up in more stable households when parents were employed. Given the illiteracy rate in the community and the depressed economy of the city, it was difficult for the residents to find jobs. The community members and I had brainstormed ideas to create jobs, like growing and selling fruit or building a clothing or shoe manufacturing business. But none of the proposed ideas aligned with the skills and assets the community already possessed.

Quickly, word got around in the region that our organization had built a school at Por Venir. Soon, parents and teachers from other communities told us they too needed schools. It seemed each community was willing to provide land and the four thousand to five thousand hours of unskilled labor needed to complete each project. But there was a problem—many of them lacked professional masons to provide skilled labor. The fathers in Villa Soleada said they could help build the schools. We hired Wilfredo, his brother Adriano, and a few others to see how things would go. It worked. *We had turned a problem into an opportunity.* Together with Marco—who by then was working for SHH as our head foreman—they built school after school, helping us streamline a construction process that we took from one community to the next. We hired every father in Villa Soleada who wanted to work with us as a mason. As we moved forward, the teenagers from the community, including many from LMDVS, began to join. They apprenticed under the fathers, and when they completed their training, they became part of the team. Together, we traveled from community to community with shovels, trowels, and hammers in hand. Building schools allowed us to address the country's education crisis and simultaneously bring job security to Villa Soleada.

At some point, we began to wonder exactly how many communities in Honduras lacked adequate school buildings. If we wanted to set a long-term goal and figure out how to get there, we needed to understand the scale of the challenge. Our staff traveled to Tegucigalpa and visited different branches of the Honduran Department of Education. Our staff normally wore sombreros and muddy boots to work; we laughed at how funny we looked in collared shirts. Our final visit was to PROHECO, a branch of the department that worked in the poorest and most rural communities in Honduras. There, an official showed us a chart with the answer we were looking for.

Of more than three thousand schools that PROHECO worked with, approximately one thousand of them lacked adequate school buildings. The office had been flooded with requests from partner communities to build school structures, but they simply lacked the funds. The official asked us to partner with PROHECO to build these structures. We agreed.

"How many can you do?" he asked.

I looked around and thought *about one hundred*. It felt like a far stretch, but I thought if we worked hard, we could do it. Then Marco raised his hand and said a number that took all of us by surprise: *"One thousand!"* He wasn't joking.

The construction of the school at Por Venir had impacted Marco's oldest son and the entire community to such an extent, he wanted to give that to as many communities as he could. "What would it take," asked Marco, "for us to provide children in our country universal access to an adequate school building like the one my son goes to?" At the time, each three-classroom school cost around $25,000 to build. I did the math. Without taking inflation into account, we would need to raise a minimum of $25 million to build one thousand schools. The goal was beyond our comfort zone and stretched what we thought was possible. For some reason, the goal—which was ten times larger than the original goal—gave me a rush of excitement I had never felt before. We decided to support Marco's inspiring vision.

The official from PROHECO thanked us. He shook our hands vigorously as if we had already built the one thousand schools. That troubled me. I suddenly began to worry that our decision was based on delusion and blind optimism. But it turned out that the bolder goal was exactly what we needed. To my surprise, the new goal fired up our supporters. Instead of raising funds to build one or two schools per year, they began to fund three, four schools, and sometimes more.

Marco and the team of masons from Villa Soleada poured their hearts and souls into the work. When we found out that a school nearby flooded when it rained, we built elevated classrooms. When we found out that kids in the village of Bella Aurora were studying inside a local pool hall bar because they didn't have a school building, the team rolled up their sleeves. We began by digging out boulders from the rocky plot of land that the community donated. When the boulders got too heavy, we called in the help of a bulldozer. When the boulders broke the blade of the bulldozer, we called in the help of an excavator. When we found out that Unidos Venceremos, a village without electricity or a reliable water source, was operating a school made up of mud, twigs, and a dirt floor, we helped build a school with a bathroom that had a roof water catchment system. We built a school for a group of children with special needs in the city of Potrerillos. We built a set of new classrooms for a vocational middle school that helped low-income students find jobs at the local textile factories. We built schools in marginalized communities hidden in the banana fields, up mountains, on hillsides, and inside sugarcane fields. Enrollment for some schools increased so much that we returned to build second school buildings in several communities. In 2016, we set an organizational record and completed ten school projects in one year.

* * *

As we built schools, we invited donors and volunteers from our student chapters to join our efforts in Honduras. Our youngest guests were in elementary school. Others were spending their retirement volunteering with us. Our supporters would come for a week and work alongside community members, as well as explore Honduras. They dug trenches, moved cinder blocks, and tied rebar to assist the masons who took on the skilled labor. They worked with community members, ate meals with them, and learned about their hopes and struggles. Through the shared experience, volunteers got an understanding of the physical and mental exertion community members were willing to pour into the school projects. They went home with a powerful sense of camaraderie. I was proud that volunteers could contribute to our cause and find the experience moving and rewarding.

I often received messages from volunteers who told me how life-changing their experiences were. For example, after volunteering with us, Colette Eustace, a student at Stony Brook University, switched her major from fashion design to international affairs, got a master's degree in international development, and found a job working for UNICEF. Anne Marie Boswell, who was the chapter president at Clemson University, forewent a career in corporate America and joined Teach for America. Matt Murray, who volunteered for us while at Virginia Tech, quit his corporate consulting job to work with us in Honduras for a year. After teaching English at our bilingual school, he returned to Richmond, Virginia. There, he got a master's degree in education and started a career in his new calling: teaching.

As the years went by, the number of volunteers who joined us increased. Given the fact that Honduras was the most violent country on earth (outside of war zones) in the early 2010s, the number of phone calls we received from concerned parents did too—but that didn't stop us. Soon, we were welcoming hundreds of volunteers each year. The revenue we brought in from volunteer fees helped us build more schools and hire more masons. At one point, our organization was bringing in nearly a million dollars per year. However, the number of resources and logistics it took to organize the experiences started to feel overwhelming. We struggled to figure out how to provide orientations, meals, housing, and transportation for hundreds of people in a place where there were constant road closures, civil unrest, natural disasters, blackouts, and security alerts. Eventually, our small team couldn't handle the demand. We began to make careless errors—like ordering the wrong amount of construction tools, showing up at the airport at the wrong time, and forgetting about allergies that volunteers had told us about. I slept so little I often forgot what day of the week it was. We needed more help.

We hired parents from Villa Soleada onto the staff. One group managed the guesthouse that we built near the bilingual school. Another cooked the meals. Others helped us purchase and prepare supplies—which we bought from family-owned businesses to boost the local economy. *What I previously thought was a crisis turned out to be an opportunity to create jobs.* To improve the experience, I read books on nonprofit organizations that created exceptional volunteer experiences—like BuildOn and Kaboom!—and companies that were known for their hospitality—like Starbucks, Zappos, Virgin, In-N-Out Burgers, and Union Square Hospitality Group. I put their ideas into practice. We listened to volunteers and gave out evaluation surveys. Through trial and error, we improved our meals, staff training, living arrangements, worksite efficiency, security measures, and even the music we played inside our buses. It worked. By 2015, our program was so popular and reputable that nearly one thousand volunteers were joining us in Honduras each year. We were organizing life-changing experiences, creating jobs, and raising more money for our school project than we ever imagined. All was good, I thought.

Then in 2015, I discovered a TEDx talk that shook me. It was called "What's Wrong with Volunteer Travel?" In the impassioned speech, Dina Papi-Thornton, who ran a volunteer travel organization in Cambodia, talked about the volunteer travel industry. Many programs, often run by corporate tour companies, lacked community engagement, cultural understanding, project evaluations, and sustainability. They were failing to benefit—and sometimes harming—the very communities they claimed to help. Papi went on to explain that volunteer programs often focused too much on serving and not enough on learning. Instead of learning being a byproduct of serving others, she believed learning from others needed to be the primary goal of service. She said, "Action without learning is ignorance. Learning without action is selfishness."

Papi's speech profoundly affected me. I shared it with my staff and held several meetings to discuss Papi's philosophy. As we examined our organization's volunteer program, we realized we were making embarrassing mistakes. Volunteers often wore sleeveless shirts and shorts at the worksite—which was outside of cultural norms in Honduras. We sometimes took short-term volunteers to the state orphanage to play with children who did not have stable primary caregivers—which had the potential of fueling attachment disorders. Our website had more photos and stories of our foreign volunteers than the local Hondurans who were doing the vast majority of the work—which was patronizing and a misrepresentation of the reality. And we were certainly emphasizing service more than learning. We were too focused on the volunteers' experience and not focused enough on the experiences of the local community members. Our lack of self-awareness and thoughtfulness was glaring.

To delve deeper, I read books like *Toxic Charity: How Churches and Charities Hurt Those They Help, And How to Reverse It*; *When Helping Hurts: Alleviating Poverty Without Hurting the Poor...and Yourself*; and later Dina Papi-Thornton's *Learning Service: The Essential Guide to*

Volunteering Abroad. I learned of horror stories where volunteers were asked to build projects that communities didn't actually need; build structures without the help of professional masons; or were placed in scam orphanages. I felt so disgusted and overwhelmed by what I learned. More than once, I considered shutting down our volunteer program. But deep down, I knew that not all programs were created equally. It was unfair to point out just the bad examples and demonize the entire industry.

I decided to find out if a volunteer travel program could have a positive impact on *both participants and local communities*. Not only did I want to find out, I wanted to prove it. Instead of putting an end to our program, I decided to mend it. I examined organizations like Habitat for Humanity and BuildOn that were running high-quality volunteer travel programs, and went to work. We created a strict dress code, stopped taking our volunteers to the state orphanage, improved our worksite training and safety protocols, organized workshops on the historical and cultural context of working in Honduras, and added more time for group reflections and critical discussions. We began to help volunteers think beyond their short visits and focus on ways they could help throughout the year. We trained them on movement building, fundraising, and event planning. It worked. Soon, our chapters began to raise more funds than ever before and spread awareness about our cause in creative ways. What they needed was the knowledge and skills that could help them create long-term, and in some cases, lifelong, impact.

Next, we needed to modify our website and marketing materials, but we didn't know how to move forward. There was no textbook to guide us. Then Dr. Shawn Humphrey, one of our Board members and an economics professor at the University of Mary Washington, shared with us something he was working on. It was called the *Sidekick Manifesto*. One paragraph read: "We are only visitors who do not share their history, who do not share their culture, who do not pay their taxes, who do not vote in their elections, who are only engaged for short durations of time, who have never ended our own poverty. In the story of poverty's end, we cannot be heroes. We are sidekicks." Shawn didn't think anyone else was going to read the Manifesto. It turned out, the Manifesto was exactly what the economic development community was craving. Upon its release, it went viral. Countless organizations who read it took the pledge to: *ride in the sidecar, be the constant understudy, step out of the spotlight, exercise narrative humility, and hang up their cape*. We did too. We modified our website and marketing materials based on the pledge.

* * *

As we built more schools, I wanted to know if what we were doing was *actually* working. I had read about so many well-intentioned development projects that ended up not achieving desired outcomes—and, in some cases, were left abandoned and unused. Even though we had been following John Wood's guideline on school builds, we didn't have the data to prove anything. We decided to find it. I read *Poor Economics: A Radical Rethinking of the Way to Fight Global Poverty* by Abhijit V. Banerjee and Esther Duflo and *More Than Good Intentions: Improving the Ways the World's Poor Borrow, Save, Farm, Learn, and Stay Healthy* by Dean Karlan and Jacob Appel, to learn about how randomized control trials (RCTs)—the kind of studies used in medical labs to see how effective an intervention or treatment is—could be used in poverty reduction projects. With great excitement, I called agencies that carried out such evaluation studies to see if they could collect some data for us. But the reality was hard to swallow. I found out that these evaluation agencies worked mostly with large organizations with massive budgets. Their lowest-tier studies cost tens of thousands of dollars to implement. We were small and strapped for cash. After a few days of shaking my head at the situation, I began to research our options. We found out that Acumen, an award-winning organization that provided development workshops online, had developed a lightweight impact measurement approach called Lean Data. Lean Data lets you collect feedback from clients and beneficiaries using informal but practical means. It was meant for small nonprofits and social enterprises that didn't have access to the time and budget required to run randomized control trials or other rigorous evaluation studies. Using the Lean Data method, we decided to collect the data ourselves.

We created a survey and visited the communities we had worked with. The data we collected suggested that, after the completion of a school project, school enrollment increased by 39.1 percent on average. The average number of classes canceled due to rain or inadequate protection from weather dropped from fourteen days per year (which in twelve years adds up to nearly an entire school year) to less than one day a year. The average number of teachers per school increased from 6.5 to 8.5, which meant we had created dozens of jobs. Ninety-seven percent of participants agreed that they were prouder of their school after the completion of the project; 94 percent of participants agreed that they believe more in women's capacity to contribute to projects; and 98 percent of teachers and directors agreed that the project helped them perform their jobs better.

However, the data was not enough to help our team overcome our overwhelming sense of inadequacy. We knew that our partner schools lacked access to basic tools like technology, textbooks, chapter books, and just about everything else. Upstream challenges in Honduras—like school desertion due to poverty, violence, and immigration—seemed to get worse and even accelerate over the years. Most discouragingly, systemic corruption made everything harder in the classrooms. For example, as Sonia Nazario would point out, an investigation uncovered that of eighty-five thousand teachers who received a salary in Honduras, only fifty-five thousand were real. The money spent on salaries for the "ghost teachers" went missing. So much money disappeared, real teachers often worked for months without pay. Teachers had so little power, all they could do was go on strike for weeks or months on end, which ultimately hurt the children the most; during some years, schools in Honduras opened just eighty-eight out of two hundred mandated days. Corruption largely explains why Honduras, the country that spent the greatest percentage of its budget on education in all of Latin America, had the worst test scores after Haiti in the continent.[49] Eventually, we had to confront a brutal reality—students and teachers needed more than just a building to succeed.

* * *

We looked at countless studies to find out what variables were affecting student achievement the most. We learned that the most important thing was teacher effectiveness. But at the time in Honduras, many teachers lacked degrees in education, especially in rural areas. Furthermore, ongoing professional development opportunities, which was an important part of a teacher's journey in high-income countries, was essentially nonexistent. To put it into perspective, 92 percent of teachers in urban areas and 98 percent of teachers from rural areas of Honduras failed a basic competency test administered by the Department of Education in 2019.[50]

In 2016, we started a teacher training program called Train for Change with leadership from Maxie Gluckman, the educator from San Diego who had helped revive our bilingual school when we shut it down during its first year of operation. Maxie put her expertise in curriculum design and teacher and leadership capacity development into practice. She and her team of Honduran educators set out to provide two hundred hours of professional development classes—with a focus on early literacy, lesson planning, and engaging students in critical thinking—to teachers who worked in our partner communities. As of the writing of this book, the program has reached 160 teachers in twenty-four schools. Teachers who went through the training were given opportunities to share their knowledge to other schools to scale Train for Change's efforts.

* * *

From 2008 to 2018, we spent ten years building as many schools as we could. Dina had won her spelling bee, we'd overcome an extortion threat, Honduras was back in the grips of civil unrest (thanks to the questionable election results), and I was on my way to mix concrete for Marta Yamilet Melendez community school.

When we arrived at the school, over twenty parents were already mixing concrete. They greeted us with handshakes and offered us sliced fruit. Soon after, the volunteers, including Alex, a Honduran-American who lived in Alaska, and his ten-year-old son AJ, put on their work gloves and joined the community members. As I watched nearly a hundred parents and volunteers working together in unison, I grabbed my water bottle and sat down to rest in a shaded area. Marco walked over. His face was covered with dirt and sweat.

As I shook his thick hand, I hoped that my hand felt harder and more calloused to him than it did ten years before when I met him. I watched Marco mix concrete at breakneck speed next to a group of young men. Marco had been eating a healthier, mostly plant-based diet that year. He was fifty-four years old at the time; he said that he wanted to maximize his odds of living long enough to build all the schools he set out to build. I closed my eyes and imagined what it would feel like to shake his hand on the groundbreaking day of the one-thousandth school project. I pictured an elderly Marco, with more wrinkles and grey hair, digging the earth next to his grown children and young grandchildren. Without a doubt, he'd still be showing us that he could work faster and harder than anyone else. I put on some sunblock and tied my work boots a bit tighter.

"*Tome agua*," said a familiar voice, "drink water." It was Pablo. He was tagging along for the day to help as a volunteer translator. Having studied for six years at the Villa Soleada Bilingual School, he was beginning to put his English skills to practice. He refilled my water bottle from a jug. He patted me on the shoulder, grabbed a shovel, and sprinted away like the wind. He joined Gerson, who was translating and making a group of volunteers laugh at his jokes. Over the years, the twins had joined me on countless school builds throughout the country. They were already in the seventh grade and able to mix concrete as fast as the adults. They were inseparable, like Wilfredo and Adriano. I shook my head at how quickly time had passed.

When AJ and a group of children poured the last bucket of concrete to finish the floor, the crowd erupted into jubilance. AJ, who was covered in mud, gave me a high five and dashed off to kick a soccer ball with the community kids. Alex walked over and told me how proud I must be. After all, Yolanda Melendez was the forty-first school construction project of the organization. By then, we had a staff of seventy employees—and 90 percent of them were Hondurans, including every single program director. We had successfully evolved into an organization powered by local leadership. I nodded at Alex, but I didn't tell him how I really felt.

* * *

I didn't tell Alex that beneath the outward successes, we were facing a pressing problem internally. We were raising hundreds of thousands of dollars through our one-time giving campaigns to build more schools—but we were running out of money to run the organization. For years, we relied on volunteer trip fees to cover much of the cost to run the bilingual school, children's home, and our overhead (which paid for things like salaries, benefits, insurance, staff training, office rent, utility bills, technology, fundraising, and marketing). Given the volatile nature of Honduras, the number of volunteers who joined us varied significantly from year to year. It made long-term planning—and sleeping peacefully at night—nearly impossible. Furthermore, as civil unrest and negative press coverage began to add to the violence, the number of volunteers willing to travel to Honduras decreased.

As the organization's size and the cost to run our programs grew, we managed to survive financially by cutting back on our already lean overhead. Each employee that was already doing two jobs began to do three. We invested less in things like team dinners, celebrations, and staff recognitions. We kept salaries as low as possible—as the CEO, my pay was just around minimum wage. We spent close to nothing on fundraising and marketing—for nearly a decade, I was the only staff member in charge of fundraising. In one way, I was proud; when I told prospective donors how low our overhead was, they praised me. But something inside of me said that we were headed down the wrong path. A TED talk given by Dan Pallotta, a humanitarian activist who worked in the nonprofit sector, revealed that what we were doing was, in fact, suicidal.

In his talk, "The Way We Think About Charity Is Dead Wrong," Pallotta condemns donors and charity assessment organizations for rewarding nonprofits based on how low they kept overhead, instead of the impact they created. The incentives they created forced nonprofits to shy away from investing in innovative fundraising initiatives, marketing campaigns, and staff members. As a result, nonprofits worked with staff members who were too overworked, underpaid, and burnt out. Correspondingly, they couldn't reach wider audiences, scale their programs, or reach their full potential—and the greatest challenges of the world remained unsolved. At the end of the talk, Pallotta urges nonprofits to challenge the status quo and invest *more* in their overhead expenses and their people—*not less*.

Pallotta's TED talk made me realize that I had taken the wrong approach to running the organization. Instead of strengthening the foundation underneath the skyscraper we were attempting to build, I had been drilling holes in it. By the time I nodded at Alex, our overhead budget was at a dangerous low. In a matter of months, or few years at most, our organization would cease to exist—with money still in the bank for school builds (legally, funds raised for a specified project could not be used for something else). What I had done with the organization was nothing to be proud of. It was my greatest source of shame.

CHAPTER SEVENTEEN

NO STRUGGLE IS INSURMOUNTABLE IF WE FACE IT TOGETHER

OVER MONTHS, WILFREDO HAD BEEN SLOWLY WITHDRAWing. No one knew what was wrong, but he had become distant from friends. He had even stopped coming to the soccer games, which was when I began to suspect something was really wrong. A fanatic soccer fan like him didn't miss games for light reasons.

Wilfredo's mom had told me that she was concerned about her son; it wasn't like Wilfredo to withdraw like this. Could I reach out to him? I had gladly agreed. "I'll take him out to dinner as soon as I can," I had said to her. "I promise."

That day at the Yolanda Melendez community school—as we all mixed concrete to build the floor—I watched Wilfredo. He was sitting alone to the side, not talking to anyone. I walked over and gave him a fist bump. We sat together quietly. A thought occurred to me: I had known Wilfredo for over a decade, but I didn't have a single photo of just the two of us. I shook my head at myself. I often forgot to take pictures with the people I spent the most time with. I lived as if the people I'm closest to would always be around. I called someone over and handed them my phone. Wilfredo and I stood next to each other, smiled, and lifted our thumbs as the photo of us was snapped. "959 more schools to go," said Wilfredo, as he nodded his stoic nod. As I walked away, I reminded myself to look at my calendar to see when I could take him out to dinner.

That evening at Villa Soleada, I sat at my table to write a plan to rehaul our outdated fundraising model. I had meant to do so for months. But like every other time I had tried, I couldn't focus. The idea of rehauling our fundraising model was exciting—but the actual process was not. It required thousands of tedious steps and uninterrupted concentration. It was all about delayed gratification and single-minded devotion. As soon as I opened up my laptop, worried staff members began to message me about a big riot that was said to happen that week. I knew I needed to stop multitasking and focus on the plan. But I kept messaging everyone back. It was exciting to respond to a natural disaster, disease outbreak, security threat, or civil unrest. It was instantly gratifying to help staff members or resolve a seemingly urgent problem. *It also gave me the perfect excuse to procrastinate on the things that mattered most.* I was too exhausted and distracted that evening. "I'll get it done tomorrow," I said to myself and closed my laptop. I went to bed, ignoring the fact that I was acting as if I would live forever.

A couple of days later, I was answering text messages at my favorite coffee shop when I got a call. "I have terrible news," said Jairo. "Wilfredo committed suicide this morning."

He began to weep. I looked at the other customers going about their lives as normal...pouring coffee, drinking, talking. I couldn't fathom it. Everything was different; Wilfredo was gone. Jairo kept repeating it. Wilfredo was gone. People looked at me, and then looked away immediately. I must have looked really pale and frightened.

When I hung up the phone, I stared at my coffee cup for a while. Then I got up and paced, because my heart was going to explode.

* * *

The entire Villa Soleada community gathered at a mountainside about a mile from Villa Soleada. It was hard to see Adriano trying so hard not to cry as he buried his brother. Wilfredo's mother hobbled over and hugged me. She was shaking and sobbing. I couldn't look her in the eyes. I had let her down, just as I had done with Abigail when she asked me to ride a horse with her. Wilfredo was the kind of guy who stood by my side during the scariest of times. Where was I as a friend when he finally needed me in return? How did I just watch from the side and not catch him when he was falling? Adriano closed his eyes and prayed intensely. Guilt and shame filled my body. Maybe Wilfredo's death could have been prevented had I taken him out to dinner.

I sat in the shade of a tree and put my head down. Wilfredo's death took me by surprise. Not too long before, he had told me about all the things he wanted to achieve—like saving up enough money to buy a new sofa for his home, seeing his children graduate, and building the one thousandth school together with his brother. Over the years, sixteen of my friends in Honduras had died—nine of them to murder, and the rest due to disease or accidents. All of their deaths were sudden. Without a doubt, each of them had goals that went unfulfilled. As I thought about the shortness of life, I thought about all of the things I still wanted to do. I wanted to be there for my friends, write a book, start a family, and most importantly, help the organization survive in the long run and reach its full potential. But as I reflected on my day-to-day activities, I didn't spend much time on the things that mattered most. In fact, I spent more time thinking about them than working on them.

I looked at the people standing around at the funeral. I wondered how many more decades or years each person had left. I wondered how many I had left.

* * *

After Wilfredo's funeral, I stopped acting as if I would live forever. I read a book called *The One Thing* by Gary Keller to figure out my life. It was exactly what I needed. In the beginning of the book, Keller asks: "What's the one thing I can do in my life that would mean the most to me and the world such that by doing it everything else will be easier or unnecessary?" I decided that overhauling our organization's fundraising model would be my one thing. Keller urged readers to write down a concrete plan and look for coaches and accountability partners. He explained that those who share progress on their goals with friends are 76 percent more likely to achieve them. I also learned that workers, on average, are interrupted every eleven minutes—and spend almost a third of their day recovering from those distractions. To make real progress, I needed to eliminate distractions, stop multitasking, and learn to say no. As soon as I closed the book, I went to work.

I met with the staff and drew up a plan to launch four new fundraising initiatives. The first of the ideas was to restructure our Board of Directors and redirect its energy towards fundraising and long-term planning. The second was to organize a summer fundraising gala. The third was to finish writing a memoir I had started years before. The fourth was to launch a new monthly giving campaign that would ask donors to give more than what we normally asked for.

Together, these initiatives would make up the four pillars for our organization's new fundraising model. When I looked at the finished drawing board, I realized how ambitious and aggressive the plan was. It was scary and energizing.

* * *

The first thing we set out to tackle was pillar one: our Board of Directors.

The first coach I looked for was Kunal Doshi, a friend who ran a growing organization called Brighter Children. After I shared my goals and challenges with him, he asked me how involved our Board of Directors was. I rubbed my face sheepishly. Our original Board members were smart, caring, and dedicated. However, back in the early years, I lacked the leadership skills, clarity in my vision for the future, and a way to help them understand the day-to-day realities of working in Honduras. As a result, disagreements and standstills filled our meetings. The situation was so counterproductive and negative, I downsized the Board. Our Board had been largely dormant since.

Kunal told me that it was challenging to build an effective Board— but he believed it needed to be my biggest priority. An engaged Board of Directors could help stabilize the organization and put it back on a path towards growth. For a Board to succeed, he said, members needed direction, specific responsibilities, and an accountability system.

I asked Jessa Coulter, a staff member who was so versatile she had her hands in practically every program, to help me restructure our Board. Having someone as organized and detail-oriented as Jessa lit a fire in the process. Together, we updated all of the necessary documents—something that had taken me months to figure out—in a matter of weeks. Having Jessa as an accountability partner was the best thing I did all year. We then wrote down a list of our twenty most dedicated and influential supporters. When it was time to invite them onto the Board, I became worried. The new responsibilities I would be asking them to fulfill were demanding. Many of them would think

I was asking too much of them and say no. But I remembered what Kunal had told me, and I decided to trust the process. He turned out to be right. The only invitees who declined the offer were two people who had scheduling conflicts with the meeting dates.

The night before our first meeting with the new members, I couldn't sleep. I tossed and turned, thinking about all of the painful disagreements during our original Board meetings. I feared I still didn't have the skills to rally the members toward the same vision. But the meeting went smoothly, and the new Board members appreciated having an organized set of responsibilities they would be accountable for. They internalized my most significant challenges and made it their priority to raise funds for our overhead. When I saw how eager they were to support the organization, I got so emotional I had to step out to the bathroom to recompose myself.

After the meeting, Alex Altman, one of the new Board members, came up with a virtual trivia event that we would replicate throughout the country. Several coordinated benefit parties, charity runs, and fundraising dinners. Others provided funding to strengthen our fundraising, marketing, and technology. The deficit in our overhead budget slowly shrank, and I realized I should have moved forward with the initiative years before. I was learning that most of the things I was afraid of were only in my head.

* * *

We moved on to tackling pillar two: how to increase funds through a summer fundraising gala.

With a bigger overhead budget, we were finally able to hire enough people who could help us with emails, incoming phone calls, donor relations, marketing, and videography. But we had no time to celebrate. Money to run our cradle-to-career programs in Villa Soleada, including the bilingual school, was running out. I offered Jessa, whose time had been freed up thanks to the new hires, a more prominent role in fundraising. With Jessa on board, we doubled the fundraising staff from one to two.

The two of us stayed up late studying the strategies used by Ubuntu Pathways and Pencils of Promise, two organizations we deeply admired. Both were taking risks to host large-scale fundraising galas that were expensive to organize. At first, Jessa didn't think we could pull off events like theirs. I wasn't sure either. The idea of investing thousands of dollars in upfront costs without any guarantees was terrifying.

But after many walking meetings together, we agreed that if we wanted to succeed, we needed to take risks. So we explored the idea of hosting an annual fundraising gala in Washington, DC—the city where we had the highest concentration of supporters. I told Jessa that if we could get enough supporters excited to join a planning committee, we would move forward. In the end, all we had to do was ask. So many Board members and local supporters were interested, we ended up with a planning committee much larger than we imagined.

But I had another worry. During our previous gala events, we had asked guests to donate towards specific building projects. It was easy to get people excited about a construction project because they were simple to explain and visualize. With the DC gala, we planned to ask guests to donate to a greater need: the day-to-day costs to operate the Villa Soleada Bilingual School. I was afraid that donors wouldn't be compelled to fund ongoing needs that were less exciting—like copy machine repairs and teacher salaries.

Still, we said we would take risks and so we forged ahead. We found a venue in Washington, DC, secured a catering company, tapped into our savings to pay the down payment for the event, and set a goal to raise $25,000. The committee created a meticulous plan and carried it out. However, it never occurred to us that we had made a serious mistake: we should have booked a bigger venue. We sold all 150 tickets and had to turn away dozens of people who wanted to attend the event. We ended up raising over $39,000. Given how afraid I was of launching the initiative, I couldn't believe it.

* * *

Pillar number three was to be the trickiest one yet, because to complete it, I had to overcome my personal fears.

Six years before, I had set out to write a memoir. I knew that a book could help our organization reach a wider audience and open up new doors, as it had for Room to Read, Pencils for Promise, Ubuntu Pathways, and countless nonprofits I admired from afar. In the beginning, I spent hours during the evenings writing, went on writing retreats, and excitedly told everyone that I was writing a book. But the process turned out to be harder than I expected. Most days, I caught myself staring at the screen or rewriting the same sentences repeatedly for hours on end. I felt like I was a first grader in ESL class all over again, unable to understand the words in front of me. As the years passed, my initial excitement and hope began to fade. Each time someone asked me how the writing was going, I would nod my head, fake a smile, and say "soon." But deep down, all I wanted to do was bang my head against a concrete wall. My inability to finish the book began to fill me with intense shame. I began to spend less and less time on it.

Then I met Tucker Max, a *New York Times* bestselling author and the founder of Scribe Media, a hybrid book publishing company. I saved up money and bought a flight to Austin, Texas, to attend one of his author workshops. I was starstruck when I shook his hand and immediately liked him—instead of wearing a suit and tie, he gave the workshop in a T-shirt and shorts. He said the outfit optimized his body temperature, which allowed him to focus wholeheartedly on providing value to the workshop attendees. I loved his pragmatism. One of the first things Tucker asked us to do was write down our fears as aspiring authors. I had never done anything like it. I nervously told Tucker that I was afraid that the book's quality wouldn't meet the expectations of family and friends. I was afraid I didn't have what it took to finish it. I was afraid that I would embarrass myself and get laughed at. I was afraid people would ostracize me. I was afraid that it would offend people. I was afraid of what the critics would say. I was afraid of public failure. I was afraid of ending up in court for revealing disturbing truths. It seemed I had a list much longer than anyone else at the event.

Tucker then asked us if the fears we had listed were realistic. I realized that some of my worries were improbable. Tucker also asked if any of us had a fear of succeeding. I didn't understand. Luckily, someone in the crowd asked what he meant. Tucker explained that many people didn't think they were worthy of achieving their goals, and as a result, sabotaged their efforts. As he talked about self-worth, shame, and feelings of inadequacy, I felt like he was speaking directly to me. Tucker, whom I had known for only two days, knew me better than my family did.

Next, Tucker made me ask myself tough questions: Is writing the book worth all of the effort? What is my plan to prevent each fear from happening or to reduce the impact if it happens? How will I use the energy from this fear to help me? If I don't write this book, what will happen? Even though the air conditioning in the room was on full strength, I began to sweat. At the end of the event, Tucker told me to stand up, and asked me whom I would be impacting if the organization reached a wider audience as a result of publishing the book. I thought about people in the field who would learn from my mistakes and avoid making them themselves. I then closed my eyes and thought about José and all the kids from the children's home. I thought about Dina and all the students at our bilingual school. I thought about Wilfredo and our staff. I thought about all of our supporters. I knew a well-written book had the potential of giving our story the publicity it deserved. Tucker waited for me to give him an answer—but I was so overwhelmed I lost my words.

Tucker noticed that I was struggling. He softened his voice and explained that fear was a good thing because it kept us safe. "I'm often afraid," he said. "It happens to all of us. But fear becomes a problem if it takes over and controls us." He assured me that my feelings were normal and even a good sign that I was digging into the hard stuff. Furthermore, he promised that his editing team would help prevent many of my fears from happening. He then taught me how to reframe my mind and turn fear into fuel, and anxiety into productivity.

"Your worst enemy isn't other people's judgment," he said. "It's your own judgment. You're the one who is stopping yourself." Tucker's truths hit me like lightning bolts. He explained that I had internalized the criticism and voices of other people and was playing them out in my head. He told me that I needed to read books about vulnerability and shame written by Brené Brown. It was time for me to put my story and knowledge into the world, get on the stage, and risk getting a bit of criticism. I wasn't sure if he was saying these things just to be nice—but I felt a fire light up inside me. For the following months, Tucker and his team stood alongside me every step of the way. They helped me understand my emotional wounds from my childhood. They made me realize that procrastination was how I ran away from my fears. Too often, I had failed to make an important phone call, make the ask, or work on the book. It wasn't that I was too busy—*I was too scared*. I carved out time to write, said no to a lot of other things, met weekly with my editor who kept me accountable for my progress, and went to work.

* * *

The last pillar we tackled was our most ambitious: our monthly giving program.

I got the idea from *Thirst*, a memoir about how Scott Harrison started Charity: Water. Charity: Water is an award-winning organization that provides clean water throughout the world. In its early years, Charity: Water relied mostly on one-time donations, just like us. Revenue fluctuated so much from month to month that, while Charity: Water was gaining tremendous recognition, they were struggling to pay rent and keep the lights on. Eventually, the organization moved away from its old fundraising model and focused its efforts on building up the organization's monthly giving and multi-year commitment programs. The pivot helped them become sustainable, grow, and reach more communities. Not only did *Thirst* validate many of my pain points and make me realize that other organizations struggled with the same challenges as us, it also gave me ideas on how to fix them.

My biggest takeaway from *Thirst* was as clear as water—if our organization was going to thrive, we too needed to expand our monthly giving program. At the time, several hundred student volunteers were giving four dollars per month through our One Cup of Coffee campaign. But it wasn't enough. What we lacked was a monthly giving plan for our older supporters—especially our student volunteer alumni—whom I believed had the ability to give more than four dollars each month. I was determined to follow Scott's footsteps.

After some brainstorming, I revisited an idea I had considered years before: starting a child sponsorship program. After all, many of the largest organizations in the world, like World Vision and Save the Children, promote child sponsorship programs. But after doing some research and small-scale experimentation, I found that child sponsorship programs were difficult to run. This is not to say they cannot be run successfully and create a positive impact. But it takes a lot of administrative staff and money to organize the letters, updates, and photos required to retain donors. Furthermore, given the fact that the children we worked with lived next to each other, I worried that a child sponsorship program could cause jealousy between the children and unintended conflicts within the community. Ultimately, I decided not to pursue a child sponsorship program.

I spent weeks trying to think of other ideas. But I was stuck. We needed to come up with something fast, as we were running out of money to keep the children's home and bilingual school going at Villa Soleada. Then one day, while I was out jogging in El Progreso, the idea came. It carried a punch but didn't have many of the complications associated with a child sponsorship program. I ran back to the house as fast as I could to write the two words down before I forgot: classroom sponsorships. We were going to ask donors to give thirty dollars per month (which would go into a general pot) and in exchange, they would receive monthly updates from a specific class (e.g., class of 2025) in the bilingual school. Donors would follow the progress of those students over the years—all the way until graduation day. The team liked the idea. But when they asked me why thirty dollars per month and not twenty-five or thirty-five, I felt embarrassed. I have to admit, I chose thirty dollars a month because it was what the other organizations used in their monthly giving programs.

I did some research and found out that the average American donated around 3 to 4 percent of their adjusted gross income each year to charities.[51] Another study showed that Millennials donated an annual average of $481 across 3.3 organizations.[52] Given the information, thirty dollars per month sounded reasonable. The amount was enough to make a huge impact for us but not so large that donors wouldn't be able to commit to it. My gut instincts told me to go for it. Given the fact that the school's logo was a tiger, we named the campaign Tigers Club.

I crunched some numbers. If we could get 380 supporters to join, we could cover our bare bones needs at Villa Soleada and stay afloat.

With one thousand, we could fund *all* of our needs at Villa Soleada and reach organizational sustainability. Tigers Club had the potential to be our biggest game-changer. Our team began to work on a logo, website, and donation platform. Our goal was to launch Tigers Club in six to nine months, sometime in the of fall of 2020. The seven thousand supporters who had visited us in Honduras were our most dedicated supporters and the most likely to sign up for Tigers Club. I knew most of them personally, as I had worked alongside and shared meals with nearly all of them. The plan was to call them one by one in what would become the biggest phone-a-thon in our organization's history. Although we planned on getting the help of volunteer callers, I wanted to make the majority of the phone calls myself. I believed that the odds of someone signing up would be much higher if I reached out to them personally. Somehow, the thought of making seven thousand phone calls didn't feel overwhelming. It fired me up.

However, we quickly faced a problem. Because the leading database systems, like Salesforce, were so expensive, we had been using different systems that were cheaper—and harder to keep organized. We discovered that contact information for our supporters was spread out across different websites and spreadsheets or was outright missing. It was a mess. For years, people had been telling me about the importance of having a solid database. I didn't really understand—until that time. If you don't have someone's phone number, you can't call them to get their support.

Our Board came through again. They provided funding to hire staff members to consolidate the data. Then Cassidy Webb, one of our new Board members, turned the data into an organized spreadsheet. She made it as easy as possible for me to start making the calls. But as soon as I looked at the spreadsheet, something happened. Suddenly, the idea of making the phone calls began to fill me with a level of anxiety like nothing I had ever experienced before. I shook my head and placed my closest friends and relatives—the very people who were most likely to join—at the top of the list. To make the process as easy as possible, I would call them first. But that had the opposite effect. Strangely, the thought of calling my closest people made my heart pound the loudest. Even though I had made hundreds of phone calls in my career, I was scared of making the first phone call for Tigers Club. My mind swirled. I was afraid that thirty dollars was way too much of an ask. I was afraid people would think that I was always asking for something. I was afraid that people didn't believe the organization was worthy of surviving. Or that the organization wasn't relevant in their eyes anymore. Or that I would break emotionally from all of the rejections.

As a result, I kept postponing the launch of Tigers Club. I kept going back and forth with the wording and design of the website. I kept telling the team that we needed to perfect the initiative "just a little bit more" before we were ready to launch it. "Just a little bit more" became an excuse for endless delays. As time passed, our reserves in the bank continued to deplete.

* * *

A kindergarten student from the Villa Soleada Bilingual School cut the blue ribbon with a scissor that was too big for her hands. The crowd of over three hundred people erupted into jubilance, hugging one another. I wiped the sweat off my forehead and snapped some photos. "Good morning, parents, teachers, students, and special guests," said Dina as she started her prepared speech. She looked up from her notes, stood tall, and smiled nervously. "We are ninth grade students who proudly represent the Villa Soleada Bilingual School."

At that very moment, we were inaugurating the newly finished, two-story high school building that the fathers in the community had been building for over a year. Our school opened in 2012 with less than fifty students and three grades. By 2020, we had 270 students, a preschool, kindergarten, elementary school, middle school, and high school. The crowd cheered as Dina continued to give her speech in near-perfect English.

I looked at Marco, who was standing proudly to the side and clapping. Somewhere in the crowd of students were his two children, Valentín and Georgina. Adriano was there with the rest of the masons. Without a doubt, he wished his brother, who had helped build every single building on the school grounds, was there. I did, too. I spotted Gerson and Pablo, who, as eighth graders, were the co-captains of the school soccer team. They were shushing their peers who were goofing off. Jessa, who had been involved with our work for over a decade, stood alongside a group of supporters who had flown in from California and New York to attend the event. Among the group were Ken and Lynn Hall, a couple from Sacramento who had given a large, one-time gift towards the construction. They were also the first family to commit to multi-year support for our operating funds. Their generosity, which came at a critical time, allowed us to strengthen the organization's infrastructure and create a website for Tigers Club. Bob, my mentor who had been there every step of the way, stood next to me. "I can't believe how grown up she is," he said. He, too, had met Dina back in Siete de Abril when she was a small papaya-sized baby. Fifteen years had passed.

Villa Soleada had started with a drawing from ten-year-old Camila that sparked a question: Is the cycle of generational poverty breakable in Honduras? When we started, we didn't have the answer. Over the years, the community members and our staff worked hard together, faced heartbreaks together, and moved forward together. We turned a swamp into a community. We identified and removed the barriers that had kept families trapped in the cycle of generational poverty. We learned through trial-and-error, improved our vision, made countless mistakes, and built up a cradle-to-college pipeline of programs. The early doubters didn't think our community and team would make it this far—we were just two years away from sending our first class of students, including Dina, to college. We were close to turning a community with a 0 percent graduation rate into a community filled with high school and college graduates. As far as I knew, Villa Soleada was on a path to becoming the most educated village per capita in all of Honduras. After more than a decade, we were seeing results that began to suggest that the cycle of generational poverty was, indeed, breakable in Honduras. As Dina ended the speech, I gave her a thumbs up and looked at everyone who was there. We had come this far because of our collective effort. As the crowd cheered, the finish line felt closer than ever.

None of us were prepared for what would happen next.

* * *

The same week of our inauguration, coronavirus disease (COVID-19) was declared a national emergency in Honduras—and throughout the world. Every school in the country, including ours, was ordered to shut down. We flew our volunteers and international staff home, stocked up on supplies, and created an emergency plan. Borders, airports, and even highways closed down. The Honduran government put into place a severe lockdown and arrested anyone who was found on the streets. Back in the US, our operations came to a halt. We had to cancel hundreds of fundraising events, including the second annual DC gala we had spent months preparing. We told dozens of student volunteers and donors who planned on visiting us in Honduras that year to cancel their trips. Overnight, we lost the majority of our revenue stream. I did the math and realized that, like many other nonprofits, we would run out of reserves in a matter of months. As I sat at my table, I clutched my face and began to shake.

Back at Villa Soleada, people remained home and closed the soccer field for the first time in its history. I walked through the school grounds. I couldn't believe how empty it felt. Just days before, hundreds of people were cheering and laughing right where I stood. As I looked up at the new high school building, which was empty—and would remain so for quite some time—I thought about the first time we abruptly closed the school down back in 2013 due to gang violence. In 2017 it was extortion. In 2018 it was civil unrest. In 2020, our fourth, it was a global pandemic. The first three times, I had held onto hope that the school would eventually reopen. This time, it felt different. I couldn't see a way out.

The evening was dark and humid when I gathered the teenagers from the Home for a family meeting. I explained to them what I understood about coronavirus. Some of them gasped in horror. Others went into a state of denial and made nervous jokes. I told them that we would be stocking up on food and implementing social distancing rules. I told them that for the coming months, some of their favorite mentors would be sleeping at the Home instead of commuting daily. It was an attempt to decrease the risk of the virus getting in. The kids looked at each other and smiled. Then I told them the bad news: the organization had lost almost all sources of its revenue. I didn't explain what that meant for our future. I knew the kids were old enough to understand—and it was simply too heartrending for me to say out loud that the Home and bilingual school may be shutting down permanently. Several kids closed their eyes and covered their faces with their hands. I clenched my teeth as I watched some of them crying that night.

Pablo, who by then was one of the best soccer players in Villa Soleada, covered his face with his long hair and shook his head repeatedly. Pasifica fidgeted, which she did when she was nervous. José sat there stoically, without saying much. Then Gerson, who looked restless, stood up. Growing up, he was always the rowdiest and most mischievous of the bunch. He was the kind of kid who would sneak out to go swim in the river when he was supposed to be doing homework. As the years went by, he began to help with chores without being asked, mediate conflicts, and speak up on behalf of the kids if something bothered them. By then, at age fifteen, like a twist in a movie that you never expect, many of the other teenagers saw him as the leader of the bunch.

Gerson said that this was a scary situation. His voice was shaking. "It feels like we're living inside a movie," he said. "I feel the same," I said and shook my head. A few others nodded. He then took a deep breath and reminded everyone that we had overcome extortion threats and other scary situations before. He slapped his bony chest and promised to step up by looking after the little ones. He nudged Hernan, one of our fifteen-year-old boys, who said he would help too. Others, encouraged by Gerson's sudden show of courage, said they would help the younger kids with their homework in the afternoons. Pasifica and José promised to organize art activities during the weekends. Pablo said he would help grow more fruits and vegetables at the garden in preparation for food shortages. When the messiest of the kids—including Gerson—promised that they would finally keep their rooms clean and sanitized, we all laughed. In that moment, as I witnessed the kids demonstrate how much they had grown, I was reminded that I needed to do the same.

"Dad, what is the plan?" asked Gerson. I closed my eyes and tried to remember when Gerson and Pablo began to call me Dad. It happened a few years before. When they started doing it, I told them that I wanted them to call their Honduran houseparents Dad and Mom. After all, I intended to make sure the kids were grounded in their local culture. But then the brothers told me that they should have the right to decide. They said that it didn't matter that I was of a different skin color. They told me they appreciated how I would go watch all of their soccer games. It was about who they felt best with, they said. I couldn't think of a good counterargument. I wasn't sure if I was worthy of the label, but I accepted.

I opened my eyes and cleared my throat. "The plan is, you all work with the staff to take care of the day-to-day activities. I'll make some phone calls to make sure that we can survive financially."

I left the meeting, knowing that if I waited any longer for the stars to align, everything we had spent a decade building would be taken away. Brené Brown's saying, "we cannot give our children what we don't have," became a literal truth.

That night, I reread Brené Brown's *Daring Greatly*, a book recommended by Tucker Max. Brené made me understand how my fears had evolved over the years. When I started the organization, I didn't let fear stop me—because back then, nobody knew who I was. Everyone, including myself, had low expectations for me. As the organization grew, and as I taught student volunteers how to face their own fears, I gained more recognition. According to Brené, because I hadn't learned how to handle the external validations and the pressure that came along with it, I began to convince myself that I was what I accomplished and how well I accomplished it. I became afraid of doing anything that had a possibility of failing and disappointing the tribe. I began to live less daringly and turned into a perfectionist. Brené made me realize why I didn't want to launch Tigers Club until the website was flawless—until the organization was perfect, until I was less fearful. She untangled why I had been acting as if I would rather have the organization die rather than pick up the phone. In my mind, if Tigers Club, something I had been working on for years, turned out a failure, *I was a failure*. I was living a damning example of how emotional self-preservation and selfishness hurt those around us. As I flipped through the book, I could hear Brené's voice urging me to believe that I was "worthy now, right this minute." With COVID-19, failure and fear were no longer options. *It was time to go all in.*

When the sun came up, I went for a run and got after it. Our operations team, now spread out between four countries and led by Amanda Fennell, wasted no time. They went straight to work on the logo, website, donation platform, video, and donor database for Tigers Club. We crafted an email that went through multiple iterations. The urgency of the situation unleashed an energy that we didn't know we had. What we thought would take six months, we completed in six days. Though the website wasn't fully ready, Amanda told me that we needed to launch. We were running out of money, fast.

The next day, we launched Tigers Club by emailing our fifteen thousand supporters. I sat at my table and took deep breaths. I picked up the phone to make the very first call for the phone-a-thon, and felt a rush of panic. My stomach began to constrict as I dialed the number. It didn't matter that I had called this person almost every day for the last ten years. It felt like I was walking up the classroom aisle to recite Robert Frost all over again. "Hello?" said the voice. The first person I called from that long list was my best friend in the world, Bob.

"I've been waiting for this call for years," he said as we both laughed. Bob signed up for Tigers Club right then and there. As soon as I hung up, I felt a rush of relief and amazement. I'd done it. It was terrifying yet exciting. I nodded, knowing that this was just the beginning, but also knowing that I never wanted to let fear make me miss out on my goals and opportunities ever again.

More than twenty people signed up within the first few hours. Cosmo signed up, as did others in the Fujiyama family. The numbers climbed. I thought people would complain that the website wasn't fully finished, but it turned out that making it public was actually a blessing in disguise. It allowed Imad Arain, our web developer, to get the feedback he needed to optimize the site. For the following days, I hunkered down at the children's home and made hundreds of calls while exercising on a portable step machine. Being in physical motion helped my mind stay in motion. The kids watched and giggled as I, sweating profusely, yelled into my headphones, clutched my face with each rejection, and rejoiced with each yes. They began to bring over coffee, snacks, and mangoes they picked from the trees.

The pandemic spread. Our tribe unleashed its potential. Right away, a team of volunteers signed up to help with phone calls. Our former English teachers from the bilingual school, led by Matt Murray, spread the word in different school districts across the US. Matt's mother, inspired by her son, asked her company to donate to our organization what they had planned to spend for her retirement party. Volunteer alumni from across the globe created personal fundraising pages and shared our campaign on social media. Others began to organize virtual fundraising events. One volunteer, Amanda Ellen, began to sell artwork and donated the proceeds. Another, Cody Bermudez, asked friends to sponsor his daily workouts. Morgan Willingham's second-grade daughter donated her allowance to the organization. Isa Woodward, a fourteen-year-old volunteer from New Jersey, donated birthday money to the organization. Jessa, Amanda, Cassidy, and the rest of the staff coordinated the different efforts, but they could hardly keep up.

As the weeks went by, and as the summer heat dialed up, my energy level began to decline. Then one day, Siobhan DiScala, a student alumnus who had volunteered with us while in high school, emailed me: "I worked countless hours at a deli for six bucks an hour to fund my first trip to Honduras. It changed my life. You taught me the power of having something to believe in. I know you all will pull through during this difficult time and come out stronger on the other side. I'm proudly a part of Tigers Club." Siobhan's message made me tear up big time. Another day, Mary Summers, the mother of a student volunteer, told me over the phone: "I know you have many calls to make. I know how hard that must be. Just keep going. Just keep going. Just keep going." Mary's words refilled my energy tank. Later, one of my friends, Steve Walters, texted me after hearing my voicemail: "Shin, sorry I missed your call, brother. I signed up for Tigers Club and will tell my parents and some friends about it." Shortly after, we caught up over the phone for two hours. Many supporters said they appreciated my call and thanked me for giving them something positive to focus on during the pandemic. Their encouragement was like rocket fuel. They made me feel like I could sprint up Pico Celaque, the tallest mountain in Honduras.

Within twelve weeks, I made over a thousand phone calls. I got rejected hundreds of times, and I have to admit, some of them were quite painful. Not too long before, I had thought I would crumble from all of the rejections. But I didn't. Each call made me a little less afraid. As Brené Brown had insisted, on the other side of fear was everything I needed. By the time I made the one-thousandth call, we had found four hundred sponsors for Tigers Club and raised an additional $160,000 for an emergency fund. We were almost halfway there towards our goal of finding the one thousand sponsors we needed to survive the pandemic. As I made phone calls, I worked on the book. After six years of chiseling away and thinking countless times that I didn't have what it took, I finished it.

As I moved forward with the calls at a grueling pace, I noticed the kids and I were spending too much time in front of screens. I decided to start a tradition where every Friday, the older kids and I would have a technology-free family dinner. We would get out Christmas lights and gather around a two-person grill to make hot dogs, hamburgers, or tacos. The small size of the grill and the rusty holes it had at the bottom meant that cooking food for a dozen people took a long time. But the slowness gave us an excuse to spend more time together. We would eat, share our thoughts, and celebrate another week of life together as a family.

Each of the kids seemed to have a different approach to these dinners. José would show up early and make it his job to light up the best possible fire. He would use the log cabin method, which became his pride and joy. The girls would get dressed up and fix their hair, even though nobody else would be present except us. It was a big deal for them. The boys, on the other hand, would basically come just for the food.

A few weeks into the tradition, we decided to make something that everyone asked for: pizza. At first, nobody believed me that you could grill pizza. They said we needed an oven. Yalena, who was staying over at the Home, looked at me and shook her head when I told her my idea. I told everyone not to worry—I kept it a secret that I researched a recipe on YouTube. I brought the grill out to the yard. The kids kneaded the dough. I revealed to them that all you had to do was cook one side of the dough and flip it before putting the ingredients on. When the first pizza came out perfectly, the kids looked at me as if I was the greatest chef from Naples.

We sat in a circle and ate pizza together. José, who had been one of the doubters, was nodding his head enthusiastically as he chowed down. By then, he had passed the national college entrance exam and was a freshman at Universidad Nacional Autónoma de Honduras, the state university. Before the pandemic, he would wake up at four each morning to take two buses to the campus in San Pedro Sula. He still hadn't declared his major, as he was hoping for a criminology department to open up. His deepest desire was to become a detective so he could bring justice to his country. We often worked out together using an old squat rack we had. We would flip through pages of Frederick Delavier's *Strength Training Anatomy* and try new exercises to see who could do more reps. Needless to say, José, who was twenty by then, beat me almost every time.

By the time Pablo came back from the bathroom, all of the slices in the first pizza were gone. He pretended to throw a fit and threw more charcoal into the grill as we all laughed. Pablo played for one of the top soccer academies in the city. He used to be unsure of himself and always angry. Through soccer, he built up his confidence, learned about work ethic, made friends, earned respect, and controlled his temper.

Hernan gave a bite of his pizza slice to Pablo. Hernan had moved in with us five years before, after he was found abused and tortured by family members. At the Home, he discovered a love for animals and enjoyed volunteering at the local animal shelter.

Pasifica, who never talked much but was always listening, began to flatten out the second pizza. By then, she was a senior at one of the best high schools in the city. I remembered taking her to San Pedro Sula the year before for her first half marathon, even though the idea of running in front of thousands of people terrified her. It was priceless to watch her cross the finish line and break out into a huge smile when she spotted me in the crowd. Pasifica's younger sister, Genara, got up to help. I remembered the very first week she went to the bilingual school as an eight-year-old. She was so terrified she refused to go unless I walked her all the way to her classroom. As an eighth grader, she was doing so well at the bilingual school that she often took classes with the ninth graders. She spent her weekends writing short stories, which often involved a protagonist who lost their memory and had to start life all over again. I loved reading her stories and watching her light up when I asked questions about her wild plot twists.

The two sisters asked me how much of the next pizza I wanted, and began making a lactose-free corner for me. That made me smile. Gerson began to dribble a soccer ball around the grill, nearly knocking it over. Yalena made him cut some onions and ham to calm him down. Gerson and I often spent hours together at a local coffee shop to discuss Jocko's *Way of the Warrior Kid* series, human psychology, and his dream of becoming an architect or engineer. Of all the kids, his growth surprised me the most.

As we laughed, shared feelings, and waited for the second pizza,

I looked at the kids and thought about how far they had come. Each came from unbelievably difficult situations where their livelihoods, education, and self-worth had been compromised. At Villa Soleada, they grew up in a caring, supportive environment filled with staff who reminded them daily that they mattered. The kids healed. They worked hard, made mistakes along the way, and kept trying. We stumbled forward together, hand in hand. It had been a privilege to walk alongside them on their journey and watch them blossom. The pandemic had filled our lives with horror, boredom, and isolation. But that Friday evening, as we sat around the old, two-person grill, we had each other, our dreams, and grilled pizza—something which just moments before, nobody thought was possible. As I bit into my cheeseless slice of pizza and gave a thumbs up to Pasifica and Genara, I hoped that these dinners were as meaningful to everyone there as they were to me.

* * *

A few weeks later, Eta, a Category 4 hurricane, wreaked havoc in Central America, affecting 1.7 million Hondurans and destroying entire neighborhoods. As I drove around the wreckage just days after to find missing students and staff members, news stations announced that Iota, a Category 5 hurricane, was headed our way. I couldn't believe it. Two hurricanes within two weeks of each other—in the midst of a global pandemic. I gripped the steering wheel tighter and thought of all the things that the Villa Soleada community had overcome over the years. Each challenge bonded us closer. Each tested our resolve. Each forced us to regroup and rebuild. Each taught us to stand up for each other and our community. We proved to ourselves that there was a way to confront the biggest, strongest, and most violent of obstacles. Though I had no idea if we were prepared for what was to come, I had learned that the one way to move forward was *together*.

EPILOGUE

AS OF THE DATE OF PUBLICATION OF THIS BOOK, ONE Thousand Schools, formerly known as Students Helping Honduras (SHH), has broken ground on sixty-six school projects, grown the Villa Soleada Bilingual School up to the eleventh grade, provided temporary refuge or a permanent home to more than sixty children at the Villa Soleada Children's Home, reunited more than ten children with their biological families, and has hosted more than six thousand international volunteers in Honduras. One Thousand Schools currently employs more than sixty local Hondurans in El Progreso. In the midst of Hurricane Iota, the Villa Soleada community—including the students from the bilingual school—and supporters came together to convert the bilingual school into an emergency shelter for more than one hundred displaced Hondurans. Here are ways you can support our work:

1. Make a one-time donation at onethousandschools.com/donate
2. Donate four dollars per month at onecupofcoffee.org
3. Join Tigers Club and sponsor a class at the Villa Soleada Bilingual

School for thirty dollars per month at onethousandschools.com/tigersclub
4. Join us for eight days in Honduras for a school build at onethousandschools.com/volunteer
5. Teach English at the Villa Soleada Bilingual School at onethousandschools.com/teach

TIMELINE

1. 2004: Shin's first trip to Honduras.
2. 2006: First campus walk-a-thon raises $140,000+.
3. 2007: Second campus walk-a-thon raises $288,000. Shin and Cosmo move down to Honduras, and construction of Villa Soleada begins.
4. 2009: Villa Soleada is built and residents move in. Shin is named a CNN Hero.
5. 2011: The Villa Soleada Boys' Home opens.
6. 2012: The Villa Soleada Bilingual School opens.
7. 2013: The Villa Soleada Girls' Home opens.
8. 2015: Students Helping Honduras (SHH) builds its twentieth school, a transitional home is built at the children's home, and Shin is invited to speak at the United Nations Headquarters.
9. 2016: The Villa Soleada Bilingual School opens a preschool.
10. 2018: SHH breaks ground on a high school building at Villa Soleada as well as its fiftieth school project in Honduras.
11. 2020: SHH hold their first middle school graduation ceremony at Villa Soleada, the high school building at the Villa Soleada Bilin-

gual School is finished, we survive a global pandemic, Tigers Club is launched, and the school is turned into a hurricane shelter for one hundred displaced Hondurans. José enters the state university, Universidad Nacional Autónama de Honduras.

12. 2021: Shin finishes this memoir, and Gerson and Pablo graduate from middle school.
13. 2023: Students Helping Honduras changes its name to One Thousand Schools.

ACKNOWLEDGMENTS

I WOULD LIKE TO THANK MOM, DAD, AND MY SIBLINGS Koko, Cosmo, and Gaku for putting up with me all these years. Working in Honduras has made me realize how lucky I was for growing up in a stable and supportive home. I would like to thank all of the teachers, mentors, and coaches who worked with me during my childhood despite the hard times I know I gave you.

I would also like to thank Bob Azzarito, the man who took me to Honduras. Thank you for standing alongside me since the first day of the journey, answering my phone calls at all hours of the day, and being my best friend. None of this would have been possible or as fun without you. I can't thank Henry Osburn enough for introducing me to El Progreso and putting his trust in me when I was a young college student. I look forward to eating more baleadas with you as we grow old together. I'd like to thank Doris Buffett for believing in me and giving us a chance when nobody knew who we were.

I honestly didn't think I had what it took to finish this book until I met the staff at Scribe Media. Thank you, Tucker Max, for believing in me and giving me a chance. You helped me understand who I was and set me up with Jessica Burdg, the best editor that an author could ever ask for. Jessica, thank you for being so patient with me, encouraging, and making me accountable for meeting deadlines. Thank you, Hal Clifford and Tashan Mehta, for adding the final touches to the manuscript, taking it to a whole new level.

Not everyone gets to go to an amazing university like the University of Mary Washington. I'd like to thank all the administrators, faculty, students, and alumni from my alma mater for supporting SHH from the very beginning.

The children and families I have had the honor to work with in Honduras continue to inspire me. Thank you for your friendship and the cups of coffee you have shared with me over the years. Thank you for being the inspiration behind this book. I would like to give a special thanks to those from Villa Soleada. We have overcome extraordinary challenges together. Thank you for all of your faith in the organization and in me.

There are so many people in the SHH family to thank, so to every person who has worked for us, volunteered for us, donated to us, attended our events, joined a chapter, sat on our board, created a fundraiser, or shared our message, THANK YOU.

ADDITIONAL READING

IN THE COURSE OF MY YEARS WORKING IN HONDURAS, THE following books have influenced me:

1. Abhijit V. Banerjee and Esther Duflo, *Poor Economics: A Radical Rethinking of the Way to Fight Global Poverty*
2. Rye Barcott, *It Happened on the Way to War: A Marine's Path to Peace*
3. Claire Bennett, Joseph Collins, Zahara Heckscher, and Dina Papi-Thornton, *Learning Service: The Essential Guide to Volunteering Abroad*
4. David Bornstein, *How to Change the World: Social Entrepreneurs and the Power of New Ideas*
5. Adam Braun, *The Promise of a Pencil: How an Ordinary Person Can Create Extraordinary Change*
6. Brené Brown, *Daring Greatly: How the Courage to Be Vulnerable Transforms the Way We Live, Love, Parent, and Lead*
7. Steve Corbett and Brian Fikkert, *When Helping Hurts: How to Alleviate Poverty Without Hurting the Poor...and Yourself*

8. Hernando De Soto, *The Mystery of Capital: Why Capitalism Triumphs in the West and Fails Everywhere Else*
9. William Easterly, *The White Man's Burden: Why the West's Efforts to Aid the Rest Have Done So Much Ill and So Little Good*
10. Conor Grennan, *Little Princes: One Man's Promise to Bring Home the Lost Children of Nepal*
11. Scott Harrison, *Thirst: A Story of Redemption, Compassion, and a Mission to Bring Clean Water to the World*
12. Gary A. Haugen and Valentín Boutros, *The Locust Effect: Why the End of Poverty Requires the End of Violence*
13. Doc Hendley, *Wine to Water: How One Man Saved Himself While Trying to Save the World*
14. Dean Karlan and Jacob Appel, *More Than Good Intentions: Improving the Ways the World's Poor Borrow, Save, Farm, Learn, and Stay Healthy*
15. Gary Keller and Jay Papasan, *The ONE Thing: The Surprisingly Simple Truth Behind Extraordinary Results*
16. Tracy Kidder, *Mountains Beyond Mountains: The Quest of Dr. Paul Farmer, a Man Who Would Cure the World*
17. Wendy Kopp, *One Day, All Children: The Unlikely Triumph of Teach for America and What I Learned Along the Way*
18. Nicholas D. Kristof and Sheryl WuDunn, *Half the Sky: Turning Oppression into Opportunity for Women Worldwide*
19. Jacob Lief, *I Am Because You Are: How the Spirit of Ubuntu Inspired an Unlikely Friendship and Transformed a Community*
20. Robert Lupton D., *Toxic Charity: How the Church Hurts Those They Help and How to Reverse It*
21. Jay Mathews, *Work Hard. Be Nice: How Two Inspired Teachers Created The Most Promising Schools in America*
22. Dambisa Moyo, *Dead Aid: Why Aid Is Not Working and How There Is a Better Way for Africa*

23. Nina Munk, *The Idealist: Jeffrey Sachs and the Quest to End Poverty*
24. Sonia Nazario, *Enrique's Journey: The Story of a Boy's Dangerous Odyssey to Reunite with His Mother*
25. Hansheinz Reinprecht, *The Hermann Gmeiner Book: The Story of the SOS-Children's Villages and Their Founder*
26. Jeffrey D. Sachs, *The End of Poverty: Economic Possibilities for Our Time*
27. James Tooley, *The Beautiful Tree: A Personal Journey into How the World's Poorest People Are Educating Themselves*
28. Paul Tough, *Whatever It Takes: Geoffrey Canada's Quest to Change Harlem and America*
29. Jim Ziolkowski, *Walk in Their Shoes: Can One Person Change the World?*

ABOUT THE AUTHOR

SHIN FUJIYAMA began volunteering in Honduras in 2004 when he was a college student. From his campus dorm room, he launched Students Helping Honduras (SHH), which would later be renamed One Thousand Schools, a nonprofit organization dedicated to fighting poverty and violence in Honduras. Shin is a graduate of the University of Mary Washington. For his work in Honduras, he was named a CNN Hero in 2009. He currently resides in Villa Soleada, Honduras.

NOTES

1. Sonia Nazario, "Someone is Always Trying to Kill You," *The New York Times*, April 5, 2019, https://www.nytimes.com/interactive/2019/04/05/opinion/honduras-women-murders.html.

2. Mireille Widmer and Irene Pavesi, "A Gendered Analysis of Violent Deaths (Research Note 63)," *Small Arms Survey,* November 2016, https://www.smallarmssurvey.org/resource/gendered-analysis-violent-deaths-research-note-63.

3. Canada: Immigration and Refugee Board of Canada, "Honduras: Update to HND32564.E of 15 October 1999 on Whether the Authorities Have Established the Regulations and Agencies Called for Under the Terms of the 1997 Law for the Prevention and Eradication of Domestic Violence Against Women (October 1999–December 2000)," Refworld.org, December 21, 2000, https://www.refworld.org/country,,IRBC,,HND,,3df4be3a20,0.html.

4. "Decapitan a una mujer y hallan otro cadáver a un kilómetro de distancia en Choloma," *La Prensa*, June 21, 2017, https://www.laprensa.hn/sucesos/decapitan-a-una-mujer-y-hallan-otro-cadaver-a-un-kilometro-de-BFLP1082003.

5. Thomas J. Scanlon et al., "Street Children in Latin America," *BMJ* 316, no. 7144 (1998): 1596–1600, https://www.ncbi.nlm.nih.gov/pmc/articles/PMC1113205/.

6. James D. Wright, Donald C. Kaminsky, and Martha Wittig, "Health and Social Conditions of Street Children in Honduras," *Archives of Pediatrics and Adolescent Medicine* 147, no. 3 (1993): 279, https://www.researchgate.net/publication/271264218_Health_and_Social_Conditions_of_Street_Children_in_Honduras.

7. Ibid.

8. Duncan Campbell, "Murdered with Impunity, the Street Children Who Live and Die like Vermin," *The Guardian*, May 29, 2003, https://www.theguardian.com/world/2003/may/29/duncancampbell.

9   Nicholas Kristof, "D.I.Y. Foreign-Aid Revolution," *The New York Times Magazine*, October 20, 2010, https://www.nytimes.com/2010/10/24/magazine/24volunteerism-t.html.

10 Hernando de Soto, *The Mystery of Capital: Why Capitalism Triumphs in the West and Fails Everywhere Else* (New York: Basic Books, 2000).

11 "Improving Health in Africa," The Water Project, accessed April 21, 2022, https://thewaterproject.org/why-water/health.

12 Alastair Ager et al., "Stress, Mental Health, and Burnout in National Humanitarian Aid Workers in Gulu, Northern Uganda," *Journal of Traumatic Stress* 25, no. 6 (2012): 713–720, https://pubmed.ncbi.nlm.nih.gov/23225036/.

13 Liza Jachens, "Humanitarian Aid Workers' Mental Health and Duty of Care," *Europe's Journal of Psychology* 15, no. 4 (2019): 650–655, https://ejop.psychopen.eu/index.php/ejop/article/view/2221/2221.html.

14 Fernando Yitzack Pavon, "Improving Educational Quality in Honduras: Building a Demand-Driven Education Market," *Princeton University Journal of Public & International Affairs* 19 (2008): 193–213, https://jpia.princeton.edu/sites/jpia/files/2008-11.pdf.

15 "Homicides in Honduras," ASJ-US.org, updated March 2020, https://www.asj-us.org/learn/honduras-homicides.

16 Sonia Nazario, "How the Most Dangerous Place on Earth Got Safer," *The New York Times*, August 11, 2016, https://www.nytimes.com/2016/08/14/opinion/sunday/how-the-most-dangerous-place-on-earth-got-a-little-bit-safer.html.

17 "Violence in Honduras," ASJ-US.org, updated April 2020, https://www.asj-us.org/learn/honduras-violence.

18 Kathleen Mullan Harris and J. Richard Udry, "National Longitudinal Study of Adolescent to Adult Health (Add Health), 1994–2018 [Public Use]," version 23, in *National Longitudinal Study of Adolescent to Adult Health (Add Health) Series*, Carolina Population Center, University of North Carolina-Chapel Hill, Inter-University Consortium for Political and Social Research, August 25, 2021, https://doi.org/10.3886/ICPSR21600.v23.

19 Gary A. Haugen and Victor Boutros, *The Locust Effect: Why the End of Poverty Requires the End of Violence* (New York: Oxford University Press, 2014), Location 16 of 7556, Kindle edition.

20 James Tooley, *The Beautiful Tree: A Personal Journey into How the World's Poorest People Are Educating Themselves* (Washington, DC: Cato Institute, 2009).

21 "About the Project," Bucharest Early Intervention Project, accessed on April 21, 2022, https://www.bucharestearlyinterventionproject.org/about-beip.

22 Richard B. McKenzie, "Orphanage Alumni: How They Have Done and How They Evaluate Their Experience," *Child and Youth Care Forum* 26 (1997): 87–111, https://doi.org/10.1007/BF02589359; Richard B. McKenzie, "The Impact of Orphanages on the Alumni's Lives and Assessments of Their Childhoods," *Children and Youth Services Review* 25, no. 9 (2003): 703–753, https://doi.org/10.1016/S0190-7409(03)00068-9.

23 Richard B. McKenzie, "The American Dream Is Alive and Well—among Orphanage Alumni!" National Center for Policy Analysis, issue brief no. 202, December 15, 2016, http://www.ncpathinktank.org/pdfs/ib202.pdf.

24 Richard B. McKenzie, "Orphanages: The Real Story," *The Public Interest* (1996): 100–104, https://www.nationalaffairs.com/storage/app/uploads/public/58e/1a4/e98/58e1a4e989d0d810254127.pdf.

25 Richard B. McKenzie, "The Best Thing About Orphanages," *The Wall Street Journal*, January 15, 2010, https://www.wsj.com/articles/SB10001424052748703510304574626080835477074.

26 Ibid.

27 Kathryn Whetten et al., "Three-Year Change in the Wellbeing of Orphaned and Separated Children in Institutional and Family-Based Care Settings in Five Low- and Middle-Income Countries," *PLOS ONE* 9, no. 8 (2014): e104872, https://doi.org/10.1371/journal.pone.0104872.

28 Katherine Harmon, "Orphanages Rival Foster Homes for Quality Child Care," *Scientific American*, December 17, 2009, https://www.scientificamerican.com/article/orphanages-rival-homes/.

29 Richard B. McKenzie, "Foster Care versus Modern Orphanages," National Center for Policy Analysis, issue brief no. 136, February 6, 2014, http://www.ncpathinktank.org/pub/ib136.

30 Dong Dong Li, Grace S. Chng, and Chi Meng Chu, "Comparing Long-Term Placement Outcomes of Residential and Family Foster Care: A Meta-Analysis," *Trauma, Violence, & Abuse* 20, no. 5 (2017): 653–664, August 31, 2017, https://doi.org/10.1177/1524838017726427.

31 McKenzie, "The Best Thing About Orphanages," *The Wall Street Journal*.

32 Jason Beaubien, "An Orphanage in Honduras Puts Love at the Top of its Priority List," NPR, August 9, 2018, https://www.npr.org/sections/goatsandsoda/2018/08/09/620285963/an-orphanage-that-doesnt-seem-like-an-orphanage.

33 Harris and Udry, "National Longitudinal Study of Adolescent to Adult Health," *National Longitudinal Study of Adolescent to Adult Health (Add Health) Series*.

34 Edward M. Hallowell, *The Childhood Roots of Adult Happiness: Five Steps to Help Kids Create and Sustain Lifelong Joy* (New York: Ballantine Books, 2003), 81–83.

35 Medicines Sans Frontieres, "Forced to Flee Central America's Northern Triangle: A Neglected Humanitarian Crisis," June 14, 2017, https://www.msf.org/sites/msf/files/msf_forced-to-flee-central-americas-northern-triangle_e.pdf.

36 "The World Bank in Honduras," The World Bank, accessed November 29, 2021, https://www.worldbank.org/en/country/honduras/overview#1.

37 Ibid.

38 "Honduras and Immigration," ASJ-US.org, accessed November 29, 2021, https://www.asj-us.org/learn/honduras-immigration/.

39 "Corruption Perceptions Index, 2019," Transparency International, accessed November 29, 2021, https://www.transparency.org/en/cpi/2019/index/hnd.

40 Sonia Nazario, "Pay or Die," *The New York Times*, July 26, 2019, https://www.nytimes.com/interactive/2019/07/25/opinion/honduras-corruption-ms-13.html.

41 Medicines Sans Frontieres, "Forced to Flee Central America's Northern Triangle: A Neglected Humanitarian Crisis."

42 Sonia Nazario, "Op-Ed: How to Secure the Border. Spoiler Alert: A Wall Won't Do it," *Los Angeles Times*, April 23, 2017, https://www.latimes.com/opinion/op-ed/la-oe-nazario-what-works-to-end-illegal-immigration-20170423-story.html.

43 Sonia Nazario, "Pay or Die."

44 Kemi Oyewole and Khaled Al-Abbadi, "EPDC Spotlight on Honduras," Education Policy and Data Center, 2012, https://www.epdc.org/node/5919.html.

45 Ibid.

46 Ibid.

47 Ibid.

48 The Editors, "Why Honduras Remains Latin America's Most Unequal Country," World Politics Review, January 6, 2017, https://www.worldpoliticsreview.com/trend-lines/20856/why-honduras-remains-latin-america-s-most-unequal-country.

49 Sonia Nazario, "Pay or Die."

50 "Cortés: Solo 175 de 2300 docentes aprobaron examen," *La Prensa*, November 24, 2019, https://www.pressreader.com/honduras/diario-la-prensa/20191124/282879437599833.

51 Financial Samurai, "The Average Percent of Income Donated to Charity Can Improve," Financial Samurai, October 29, 2021, https://www.financialsamurai.com/the-average-percent-of-income-donated-to-charity/.

52 "The Ultimate List of Charitable Giving Statistics for 2018," Nonprofits Source, accessed November 29, 2021, https://nonprofitssource.com/online-giving-statistics/.

www.ingramcontent.com/pod-product-compliance
Lightning Source LLC
Chambersburg PA
CBHW060516080526
44586CB00012B/502